Multiple Moderni¹
in Muslim Societies

Edited by Modjtaba Sadria

Aga Khan Award for Architecture

Preface

In over three decades, the Aga Khan Award for Architecture has premiated some one hundred exemplary architectural projects. This has been achieved through a meticulous process of identification and nomination of hundreds of schemes every triennial cycle, the on-site review and inspection of the most eligible and a final selection by an independent master jury. The Award recipients are communicated to the general public through publications and the media, contributing to the worldwide discourse on architecture and bringing to the surface issues that are often ignored by the so-called mainstream discourse.

In its search for exemplary projects, the Award strives for a better understanding of the context of our built environments and their inhabitants, to assure that nominated projects from different parts of the world, with diverse approaches, programmes and solutions to our spatial needs, are responding to the realities of their circumstances. This effort has taken the form of Award seminars on specific topics, field trips, the organisation of think tanks, as well as the meetings and discussions of the master juries and steering committees that constitute the Award's governing bodies. A crucial question facing the Award today is how to ensure that its concepts and processes remain relevant to the challenges of the 21st century.

One of the unique aspects of the Award is that in its activities it is not just concerned with architects and building professionals but considers architecture a social act and responsibility, thus engaging with and benefiting from the knowledge and expertise of practitioners of other disciplines, such as philosophers, historians, sociologists and artists, as well as government policy planners and decision makers. The Award has, in its turn, tried to act as a catalyst for these other disciplines, prodding them to consider architecture as an important element in the study of societies and the human environment.

During the Award's ninth cycle, Professor Modjtaba Sadria, as a member of the Award's steering committee, proposed a venture aimed at creating a repository of knowledge that the Award could draw upon as it faces new challenges of a rapidly evolving built environment. Professor Sadria suggested that the Award should organise a series of workshops that would "attempt to come to grips with the most significant issues dealing with the practice of architecture in Muslim societies". Under the title "Elements of Modernity in Contemporary Muslim Societies and their Relationship with Architecture", the workshops aim to grasp the ongoing process of "knowledge construction" that is shaping and re-shaping contemporary Muslim societies and their relationship with their built environments.

This publication is the outcome of the first workshop held in London in May 2007. Modjtaba Sadria's introduction lays out the thinking processes behind the workshop and explores the issue of plurality and modernities. Armando Salvatore and Masoud Kamali presented the two main papers during the workshop, which were followed by a presentation by Charles Jencks on 'Why Critical Modernism?' The discussions that followed during the four workshop sessions recorded in this book complement the presentations and constitute the arguments triggered by each presenter, the essence of workshop. After the workshop, a number of the participants submitted articles expressing their intellectual standpoints in relation to the issues discussed; these appear towards the end of the publication, immediately following the discussions.

A second workshop, to be held in Vancouver in 2009, will further explore the "Tangible Elements of Modernities", once again bringing together academics in the field of architecture and the social sciences in an interdisciplinary gathering, to attempt to come to a mutual understanding of these issues, and to relate them directly to the built environment and its inhabitants, with the hope that a better understanding of this dynamic relationship will give us the tools to create a better society.

Farrokh Derakhshani
Geneva, January 2009

Modernities: Re-posing the Issues

MODJTABA SADRIA

Discussions about modernity and Muslim societies, both from the perspective of the lived environment and the built environment, are rich, and many perspectives and approaches have been opened in the process of grasping, analysing and qualifying aspects of convergence, divergence, contradictions or harmony. It won't be an exaggeration to say, however, that we are far away from exhausting the debate. For many who are in a rush, due to the desire to satisfy social demands, their positioning in an ideological arrangement, the need to filter knowledge through mechanisms of policy making, or sometimes just by laziness, the attempt has been to close the discussion and to arrive at a position or stance and fix it as "the answer" to the issue. But, the survival and constant return of the debate on modernity in different Muslim societies is in itself the best witness that the debates have not been exhausted. To the general situation that we have had so far, related to how to see, to recognise or to observe the absence of modernity in Muslim societies, a new page has been opened with the concept of plurality of modernities. Fascinatingly enough, here too attempts are to bring up this new frame of analysis and the possibilities it offers in order to resettle the score of the games and reclose the discussions by a new affirmation, a new statement, this time derived from the plurality of modernity.

This is not the path that we chose for our encounter. Confronted with the alternative of taking a position and "solving" the issues of modernity in Muslim societies as it was posed, and the same issue as it has been posed now with the plurality of modernities, we could decide that the problem is solved and we have the answer to the problematic of modernity in Muslim societies. The other option is to pose the problem: if we consider this new frame of analysis that plurality of modernities offers, can we choose not to rush to solve the problem, but rather repose the question? Here we are not playing with words by creating the duality of posing a problem and solving a problem, they correspond to two different epistemological priorities, which are defined here.

Problem-Solving and its Problematisation

Problem-solving is a method which already has the aim of solving a problem technically, and according to an aim (Gotoh, 103). It likes to offer a fundamental solution to any problem (Hashimoto, 53). When identifying a solution, the method of problem-solving employs a

7

positivist approach. Knowledge is thought of as conventional and generalised in positivism; thus, the knowledge used to explain things has the same interpretation for all individuals. Hence, the problem that one is dealing with becomes a context-free object (Guba, 109).

In problem-solving, the way to problematise a problem is constitutive (that is, to give formal expression to it). Knowledge is used as an instrument to identify a solution, since positivists place emphasis on procedure. As Guba notes: "questions and/or hypotheses are stated in propositional form and subjected to empirical testing to verify them" (Guba, 109). So, problem-solving focuses on the solution, and how to reach or identify the solution, both with the premise that reality is apprehendable and driven by natural law. For this reason, problem-solving only intends to bring out a solution to a problem, but it does not necessarily focus either on the advancement of knowledge, nor on reaching a deeper understanding of why the problem exists to begin with. In other words, it attempts to adapt knowledge to reality; thus, the acquisition of concrete/useful/utilitarian knowledge becomes the core of any inquiry. In this sense, problem-solving is knowledge-acquisition because it uses knowledge as information to bring about a solution, but it does not add any new knowledge about the problem itself. In such an approach, a problem which occurs right now can be solved, but it cannot prevent the recurrence of the same kind of problem from happening again in the future.

When there is a law that is acknowledged by all individuals, then the diversity of human beings will be reduced (Wallerstein 1996; Etzkowitz 2005); this thought inherently criticises a positivist approach to problematisation in problem-solving.

A pragmatic/utilitarianism approach to knowledge stems from a hegemonic stance: the holders of truth need only apply what they know. Reality must be shaped, and reshaped, accordingly, and the minds of people, and of society, are also comprised in the "rim" in this reshaping enterprise (Etzkowitz 2005; Miyoshi 2000; Gibbons 1996). One purpose of problematisation in pragmatic/instrumentalist thought is to maintain an order of knowledge. It works as a function to maintain the singularity of a problem so that reduction of the actual and diverse meaning of the problem into a single consumable object is essential, so as to maintain the order of knowledge (Mackenzie 2005; Osbourne 2003).

As a result, the diversity of meaning of any problem, and the perception of possible relations to or with the problem, must necessarily be diminished.

Critics of the pragmatic/utilitarian approach to issues believe that an order of knowledge suppresses the imaginations of individuals and hides the actual process of ordering knowledge (Mackenzie, 112). Accordingly, individuals must be aware of specific problems from their own perspectives, and problematisation must come from their own specific and historical experiences; this shows the limits of knowledge and the possibilities for transforming it. Thus, it accepts a diversity of subjectivities related to the issue.

Another Understanding of Problematisation

Problematisation as a reaction to a pragmatic/instrumentalist approach reveals the importance of the order of knowledge and the singularity of any problem. The next stage of problematisation accepts subjectivity and a plurality of views. The term "problematisation" means "the endeavour to know how, and to what extent, it might be possible to think differently, instead of legitimating what is already known" (Healy, 51). Individuals understand any situation through a verification of facts (when, where, who, what, how, etc.), and believe that is why any such problem occurs (Nakahara, 6). Thus, problematisation suggests that individuals should liberate themselves from the given sense of any problem, because it does not believe in the premise of an apprehendable reality as suggested in a positivist approach, nor does it believe in keeping order of knowledge, as does a pragmatic/utilitarianist approach.

There are some conditions for problematisation. It must first collect information about regularities or information of the field (Bourdieu 2001b, 58). Then it needs both commitment to and detachment from the problem. Last, it needs to confront the existing understanding of the problem. These conditions help to reflect self cognition and world cognition; it is important to not accept things as-is (Gotoh, 89). Problem-posing is effective to confront the determinate and obvious situation. Problematisation is important for problem-posing in the sense that posing constitutes an object of thought.

Problem-Posing

Problem-posing, according to Paulo Freire, a theorist of education, is "posing of the problems of human beings in their relations with the world," so it aims to respond to the essence of consciousness (Freire, 7/13). For Bergson, the aim is to go beyond the seeming obviousness of most contemporary problems, using the method of intuition not to solve problems, but to dissolve them, in order to produce a new, more productive, sense for them (Osborne, 6 – 7). They both question existing conditions and seek to uncover problems subjectively. Foucault implies that the posing comes from ethics, which spring from the inside of individuals and stimulate possibilities of imagination. In the problem-posing method, individuals pose problems which treat power relations and posit that the arbitrary nature of things that have been treated with is the truth. Thus, it is provocative, and an object of problem-posing is a product of discursive formation and the authority of knowledge; the purpose of problem-posing is to liberate other possibilities in understanding both the sense, and possible outcomes, of the problem.

In problem-posing, knowledge is not merely describing reality. It is performative and diversifying, because it challenges the dominant understanding of reality which has attempted, and maybe even succeeded, in being considered "true".

The problem-posing method understands a problem as a challenge, and also understands that any challenge will create another challenge, which will then create a new understanding of the problem (Freire, 8/13). That is why, in problem-posing, individuals see things in a total or overall context with the relations of individuals in the world. Thus, problem-posing is knowledge construction. As Freire calls "a constant unveiling of reality" (Freire, 8/13), problem-posing doubts existing conditions and seeks to uncover the sense of existence of the problem, by opening the field of the problem to the plurality of subjectivity.

On Problem-Posing

The purpose of this part of my argument is to explain the problem-posing approach of knowledge production and its importance in providing possibilities for people concerned (thinkers, institutions, and society in general) to expand their perspectives on the senses, meanings, and possibilities for dealing with the problem that is posed, along with the impact of eventual decisions related to the problem.

Much time has passed since the social sciences withdrew from civil society. Among the results of this situation is the fact that the social sciences are mainly focused on ways of dealing with problems/issues to either serve interests or to maintain the status quo, or to allow more aggressive social actors to gain new shares in already-articulated interests converged within that status quo. "Pragmatism" thus becomes the core of most investigations and inquiries. The paramount aim of most proposals is to enlarge, deepen, and gain relative advantage within an already-set framework, a framework that, in fact, caused the emergence of the problem. Processes linked to this approach, that I will here call "problem-solving", are at present theoretically based on rational choice theory, or its derivatives; methodologically, they are in one way or another positivist; and they are institutional for policy makers, who look for the fastest possible answer to any issue. Commentators on this type of knowledge production ask for rapid, tangible, visible outcomes, often prior to elections times, or after human/natural disasters. Demonstrability of rapid, concrete outcomes is one of the main aspects of the consciousness of all the actors involved in a problem-solving approach to knowledge production. Most bureaucratic- and technocratic-funded research can be seen in this category. The fact that most research grants are channelled to these kinds of institutions, and that this is the kind of knowledge produced, have in the long term become a cause of the impoverishment of societies' ability to formulate their understanding of the issues with which they are dealing, with a minimum of intellectual autonomy.

Problem-avoiding approach

As a reaction to this situation, another road chosen by some contemporary researchers is to remove themselves from all social matters, to instead become the providers of a kind of knowledge that could called seeking the academic "truth", a transcendental "rim" that is out of, and above, society. The fundamental activity for what could be called the need for encyclopaedic knowledge (the quality of which practically determines any breakthrough in dealing with social issues), is taking distance from immediate social concerns.

The argument here is not to deny the capacities of these approaches, or the merits that they can have. Furthermore, though at first look they do seem so different, their common feature is their limitation. Each of them, problem-solving and problem-avoiding, has created a set of values and norms that singles out the validity of knowledge; the quest for knowledge comes from beyond their own horizons of investigation. Thus, in competition and in convergence, problem-solving and problem-avoiding confine the role of knowledge in dealing with contemporary social issues.

It is also important to mention that both problem-solving and problem-avoiding set the agenda for/of knowledge production from "above" society. Any insertion of social expectations from produced knowledge is limited to "significant" actors, those who are most visible and immediate, the holders of different capacities vis-à-vis the issue invoked.

The relation to a heterogeneous social context and pluralistic social concerns is often limited to a cosmetic presence. Society at large is reduced to the status of consumer as regards expected interaction with the produced knowledge. Thus, in either approach to knowledge production – problem-solving or problem-avoiding – the reified singular criterion of repressing a plurality of perspectives towards the issue that requires knowledge leads to instrumentalisation of knowledge, impoverishment of its quality, and disempowerment of society in general. Apathy towards the social aspects and the absence of creativity on the part of the producers of knowledge are the immediate twin implications of this situation.

In this context, the question becomes: Do we have any other options outside these two mainstream components of knowledge production? What are the issues related to excellence of architecture in the improvement of the lives of Muslim communities that an institution such as the Award tries to sense, understand, and grasp?

Considering that the Award does not intend to become a substitute for decision-making institutions in any Muslim society, or to challenge existing academic settings in this field in Muslim societies, what could be the possible relations to knowledge that will allow the Award to have relative autonomy in understanding the issues of architecture in contemporary Muslim societies? Is there any choice other than depending on, or the need of positioning towards, problem-solving and problem-avoiding?

I think that from an epistemological perspective, as well as institutional tasks that the Award has defined for itself, the problem-posing approach to knowledge construction can offer possibilities.

In my own understanding, the most important feature of a problem-posing approach is its capacity to expand the perspectives on the issues involved.

Some Features of a Problem-Posing Approach

The first feature of a problem-posing approach is to problematise the existing order of knowledge that has to construct "reality" and make it appear as something taken for granted. More specifically, a particular type of knowledge production could finally question the fact that our present understanding of things is considered to be taken for granted.

During recent years, the pre-eminence of problem-solving, with all its accompanying rational instrumentalism and positivism, has proven to be problematical. Other approaches, such as Marxism, constructivism or even pragmatic knowledge production, have tried, in one way or another, to re-problematise what has been taken for granted. Though any and all of these approaches have helped to understand the limitations of contemporary hegemonic modes of knowledge production, what I am suggesting, here, with a problem-posing approach, attempts to go further.

The second feature of problem-posing is that it takes the subjectivity and autonomy of individuals' intellects into account in the existing epistemic context and as important ingredients for knowledge construction. In other words, the criterion by/with which an intellectual problematises some aspect of the issue evoked is from his/her own perception, understanding of social priorities, and affinities. Institutional priorities and imperatives are subordinated to the perception – of the actor involved in knowledge construction – of social priorities, and even emergencies, as he/she understands them.

This is a Foucaultian sense of ethics, which is an attitude towards self, others, or even things. This ethic has a crucial role in a problem-posing approach. According to Foucault, a problem that is of concern to all people is not hidden, but appears by subjectively posing questions about certain existing conditions that are taken for granted. That is, a problem is not a hidden concrete issue, but instead emerges only after one subjectively poses questions to try to define the conditions as a "problem". In this process of problematisation, ethics works as a criterion for each individual. In other words, without ethics, an individual cannot problematise something that has been taken for granted.

This emphasis on ethics and, thus, the change of momentum of knowledge construction, casts requirements for change over almost the whole gamut of contemporary knowledge production. First of all, a problem-posing approach of knowledge construction changes the purpose of knowledge production. Pragmatic or Marxist approaches to knowledge production reached the most desirable (or most effective) knowledge. Knowledge construction as the outcome of problem-posing allows shared criteria to emerge and permits the judgement of what kind of knowledge is better than others. Without shared criteria, it would be impossible to judge. What quality of knowledge could help to understand the sense of the existence of a problem that is to be dealt with, what is the process of dealing with the problem, and what are the possible outcomes of the different solutions envisaged?

Ethics-based knowledge construction renders plurality of goal or criteria; so, for the person involved in knowledge construction, it would be impossible to judge what kind of knowledge is universally better than any other. Instead, the issues of knowledge construction – their priorities, contents, processes, desired outcomes, and eventual implications – become explicitly socially aware. This socially aware, epistemic context of knowledge construction empowers both the involved society and the active knowledge constructors.

The same can be said of the implications of ethical concerns towards self/other/things and allows researchers to distance themselves from truth-seeking and a comprehensive understanding of the world.

There are two further aspects to be mentioned: rising possibilities of mutually-enriching dialogical relations in the process of knowledge construction. When one problematises something that has been taken for granted, it becomes of prime importance to know the relationship between oneself and others concerning the involved knowledge. But to know one's own relation, one also has to position oneself within the network of human social and cultural relations involved both with the issue and the knowledge producers linked to or with it. In other words, each one can see phenomena from different perspectives, but they are interrelated and embedded within the social context in which the problem is posed.

Second, a problem-posing approach does not reject a problem-solving approach, as does pragmatic knowledge production. However, thanks to the plural ethical stance that problematises the order of knowledge in accordance with one's subjectivity and the need for a more comprehensive understanding of the issue, processes, and outcomes related to the issue, an enlargement of the horizon towards the problem, plural and comprehensive, becomes far more relevant than a problem-solving approach led by singular criteria. The purpose changes into one of uncovering and opening, rather than closing and eliminating.

The transformation of the purpose of knowledge production also changes the method of knowledge construction. Those involved in problem-posing have to venture outside their ivory towers towards social concerns.

This requires a change in one's relationship with the "other". In other words, the "other" ceases to exist in only an hierarchical relationship. Instead of binary oppositions, one could think of knowledge construction in terms of interrelationships and common histories.

The change of the purpose and method will lead to the transformation of the role of knowledge in society. In contemporary knowledge production, the role of knowledge has been to find "the answer", one that fits pre-set criteria; but when the criteria are pluralised, what is the role of knowledge? This is to give voice to local knowledge and subaltern stances, and to force decision makers, scholars, and ordinary people to grasp a holistic view of what is involved. This is to problematise the existing order of knowledge.

What has been our central interest during this encounter over these two days was to pose the problem: if there is a plurality of modernities, when one goes to different societies which one might consider as being one of these pluralities, what are the indicators that could be looked at as a tangible element for recognising modernity?

References

青山薫(2003)「親密「権」へのご招待」『親密圏のポリティクス』、pp.130-154

浅野智彦(1997)「構成主義から物語論へ」『東京学芸大学紀要3部門　社会科学』第48集、pp.153-162

岩崎浩(1999)「「余韻の残る授業」についての一考察」『上越数学教育研究』第14号、pp.21-28

上野千鶴子(1997)「記憶の政治学　国民・個人・わたし」『インパクション』103号, pp.154-174

大塚桂(1991)「コントの実証主義──基礎概念の検討──」『政経研究』第28巻第1号, pp.309-332

ギボンズ、ミカエル　「新しい「知識生産」：現代社会における科学と研究のダイナミクス」　『現代思想』24：6　1996 pp.265-279.

後藤彰(2003)「知識社会に関する分析」

コント, オーギュスト　霧生和夫訳(1974)

斎藤純一(1997)「表象の政治／現れの政治」『現代思想』vol.25, No.8, pp.158-177.

杉山あかし(1997)「差別のダブルバインドを解く」栗原彬編『講座　差別の社会学　第4巻　共生の方へ』東京：弘文堂, pp.55-69

竹内章郎(1994)「『弱さ』の受容文化・社会のために」佐藤和夫編『「近代」を問い直す』東京：大槻書店, pp.57-101

田崎英明「計算違い、あるいは平等について　──ランシエールとベルサーニ──」
http://www.alpha-net.ne.jp/users2/omth2/dampen/%E8%A8%88%E7%AE%97%E9%81%95%E3%81%84.html (2006/05/10)

半原芳子(2005)「地域の「対話的問題提起学習」の実証的研究」

橋本裕蔵(1997)「問題の発見」『社会科学入門』pp.50-58

ブルデュー, ピエール　桑田禮彰訳(1986a)「身体の社会的知覚」栗原彬編『叢書　社会と社会学3　身体の政治的技術』東京：新評論

　　　　　　　　　, 福井憲彦・山本哲士訳(1986b)「考えられるものと考えられないもの」『ACTES』No.1, pp.2-14

　　　　　　　　　, 田原音和監訳(1991)『社会学の社会学』東京：藤原書店

　　　　　　　　　, 石井英裕訳・改題(2001a)「インタヴュー　社会学と言語学」『環』Vol.4, pp.274-284

　　　　　　　　　, 加藤晴久訳・改題(2001b)「大学的知とは何か」『別冊環②』pp.57-74

フレイザー, ナンシー　仲正昌樹監訳(2003)『中断された正義　「ポスト社会主義的」条件をめぐる批判的省察』東京：御茶の水書房

松葉祥一(2003)「『分け前なき者の分け前』を求めて」三浦信孝編『来るべき＜民主主義＞　―反グローバリズムの政治哲学―』東京：藤原書店, pp.143-156

山口毅(1998)「社会問題研究の一課題——構築主義社会問題論における存在論的グリマンダリング批判以降——」『東京大学大学院教育学研究科紀要』第38巻、pp. 229-236

山本啓(1980)『ハーバマスの社会科学論』東京：勁草書房

ランシエール，ジャック　松葉祥一・大森秀臣・藤江成夫訳(2005)『不和あるいは了解なき了解——政治の哲学は可能か』東京：インスクリプト

파울로 프레이리, 남경태역(2002): 『페다고지』, 그린비 (Paulo Freire, Pedagogy of the Oppressed, translated by NAM GyongTe(2002), Greenbee).

Agger, Ben. *Critical Social Theories: An Introduction*. Boulder: Westview Press, 1998.

Bachelard, Gaston. *Atarachii kagaku teki seishin*. Tokyo: Chikuma shobou, 2002.

Baert, Patrick (2003) Pragmatism versus Sociological Hermeneutics. *Critical Theory: Diverse Objects, Diverse Subjects*, Vol. 22, pp. 349-365.

Bourdieu, Pierre (1992) "Thinking About Limits" Theory, Culture & Society Vol. 9, pp. 37-49.

Bourdieu, Pierre and Loic J. D. Wacquant (1992) "The Purpose of Reflexive Sociology" in Bourdieu, Pierre and Loic J. D. Wacquant *An Invitation to Reflexive Sociology* Cambridge: Polity.

Bryant, Christopher G. A (1975) "Polsitivism Reconsidered" *Sociological Review*, Vol. 23,, No. 2, pp. 397-412.

Constantinos Christou, etc (2005): *An Empirical Taxonomy of Problem Posing Processes*, ZDM. Vol. 37(3).

Delanda, Manuel, "Deleuze and the Open-Ended Becoming of the World", www.diss.sense.uni-konstanz.de/virtualitaet/delanda.htm (in *a Lecture on the Conference: Chaos/Control: Complexity*, 1998) (09/05/2006).

Deacon, Roger "Theory as Practice: Foucault's Concept of Problematization". *Telos*. No. 118 (Winter 2000), pp. 127-142.

Delanty, Gerald (1997) *Social Science: Beyond Constructivism and Realism*. Buckingham: Open University Press.

Dew, John "TRIZ: A Creative Breeze for Quality Professionals". *Quality Progress*. 39 (1) (January 2006), pp. 44-51.

Etzkowitz, Henry, "Bridging Knowledge to Commercialization: the American Way", www.acreo.se/upload/Publications/Proceedings/OE02/abstract-etzkowitz.pdf, (12/10/2005).

Formalisation of Problem Posing and Problem Solving. *Cybernetics and Systems Analysis*. Vol. 31. No. 3 (1995), pp. 428-433.

Foucault, Michel (1984) "Polemics, Politics, and Problematization: An Interview with Michel Foucault" in Rabinow, Paul (ed) The *Foucault Reader* New York: Pantheon Books

Foucault, Michel (1996) Subject and Power: Translated by Yamada Tetsuro in Hurbert

Foucault, Michel (1997) *Essential Foucault: Selections from Essential Works of Foucault, 1954-1984. Vol 1*. New York: The New Press. Eds Paul Rabinow and Nikolas Rose. Trans. by Lydia Davis. Polemics, Politics and Problematizations. Retrieved May 15, 2006, from http://foucault.info/foucault/interview.html.

Foucualt, Michel. *Discipline and Punish: The Birth of the Prison*. New York: Vintage Books, 1977.

Foucualt, Michel. "Polemics, Politics, and Problemizations: An Interview with Michel Foucault". *In The Foucault Reader*. Rabinow, Paul eds, pp. 381-390. New York: Pantheon Books, 1984.

Freire, Paulo (1970) *Pedagogy of the Oppressed*. New York: Continuum. Ch. 2. Retrieved May 11, 2006, from http://www.marxists.org/subject/education/freire/pedagogy/index.htm

Glassner, Barry (2000) "Where Meaning Get Constructed" *Contemporary Sociology*, Vol. 29, No. 4, pp. 590-594.

Gonzales, Nancy A. "A Blueprint for Problem Posing". *School Science and Mathematics*. 98 (8) (December 1998), pp. 448-456.

Gonzales, Nancy A. "Problem Posing: A Neglected Component in Mathematics Courses for Prospective Elementary and Middle School Teachers." *School Science and Mathematics*. 94 (2) (February 1994), pp. 78-84.

Gramsci, Antonio. Selections from the Prison Notebooks. London: Lawrence and Wichart, 1971.

Guba, Egon G & Yvonna S. Lincoln (1994) "Competing Paradigms in Qualitative Research" in Denizin Norman K and Yvonna S. Lincoln (eds) Handbook of Qualitative Research, London: Sage Publications.

Healy, Paul "A 'Limit Attitude': Foucault, Autonomy, Critique", History of Human Sciences, 14:1, 2001, pp. 49-68.

Habermas, Jürgen (1985) Theorie des kommunikativen Handelns. Translated by Kawakami Rinitsu (1981).

Hall, Stuart (1992) "Encode/decode" in Hall Stiart, Dorothy Hobson, Andrew Lowe and Pail Willis (eds) Culture, Media, Language. London: Routledge, pp. 128-137.

Hara, Emi and Nakagawa Nobuhiro (2000) Kouchikushugi-No-Shakaigaku (Constructivist Sociology). Kyoto: Sekaisiousha.

Healy, Paul (2001) "A 'limit attitude': Foucault, autonomy, critique" History of the Human Sciences, Vol. 14, No. 1, pp. 49-68.

Horita, M., Enoto, T., & Iwahashi, N. (2003, October). Tagenteki giron kouzou no kashika shuhou: Shakai gijutsu to shite no seisakuronngi shien. Shakaigijutukenkyuu ronbunshuu, Vol. 1, pp. 67-76.

Horkheimer, Max, and Theodor W. Adomo. Dialectic of Enlightenment. New York: The Seabury Press, 1972.

Imada, Takatoshi et al. (2001) Fukuzatsukei-Wo-Kangaeru: Jikososhikisei-Toha-Nanika-II (Thinking about Complexity: What is Autopoetics).

Kenichiro Meo "Kenkyu-Keikau-Sho no Kangaekata" Diamond-Sha. 1993.

Koval, V. N., A. V. Palagin, and Z. I. Rabinovich. "Issues of Methodology and L. Dreyfus and Paul Rabinow. Michel Foucault: Beyond Structuralism and Hermeneutics (1983), pp. 287-307.

Ledwith, Margaret "Community Work as Critical Pedagogy: Re-envisioning Freire and Gramsci." Community Development Journal, Vol. 36. No. 3 (July 2001), pp. 171-182.

Luhmann, Niklas. (1984) Theorie Der Gesellschaft Oder Sozialtechnologie (1971). Translated by Sato Yoshikazu.

Lukacs, Georg. History and Class Consciousness: Studies in Marxist Dialectics. London: Merlin Press, 1971.

Mackenzie, Adrian, "Is the Actual World All That Must Be Explained? the Science and Cultural Theory: Review Essay of Manuel Delanda, Intensive Science, Virtual Philosophy (2002) and Isabelle Stengers, The Invention of Modern Science (2000)", Journal for Cultural Research, 9:1, 2005, pp. 101-116.

Miyoshi, Masao, "The University and the 'Global' Economy: The Cases of the United States and Japan", The South Atlantic Quarterly, 99:4, (Fall, 2000), pp. 669-696.

Marcuse, Herbert. One Dimensional Man: Studies in the Ideology of Advanced Industrial Society. Boston: Beacon Press, 1964.

Motion, Judy (2005). Participative public relations: Power to the people or legitimacy for government discourse? Public Relations Review, 31, 505–512. Retrieved May 15, 2006, from http://wms-soros.mngt.waikato. ac.nz/NR/rdonlyres/e5i4yi74ood7njecjyrhymwii376jzx46ntise6yyas2ef26pkgfoelwgxffghxtxldluqijjcnpbg/ ParticipativePublicRelations2006.pdf.

Nikitina, Svetlana (2002). Three strategies for Interdisciplinary teaching: contextualizing, conceptualizing, and problem-solving. Interdisciplinary Studies Project Project Zero, Harvard Graduate School of Education. pp. 1-34. Retrieved May 11, 2006, from http://www.pz.harvard.edu/interdisciplinary/pdf/SvetlanaStrategies.pdf.

Nishihara, Kazuhisa et al. (2004) Kuritiqu-To-Shiteno-Shakaigaku: Gendai-Wo-Hihanteki-Ni-Miru-Me (Sociology as a Critical Study in Contemporary Soceity).

Osbome, Thomas "What Is a Problem?", History of the Human Sciences, 16:4, 2003, pp. 1-17.

Osbome, Thomas (2003) "What is a problem?", History of the Human Sciences, pp. 1-18.

Paulo Freire Institute, www.paulofreire.org

Sadria, Modjtaba "Shogakusei ni mo wakaru kokusai kankeiron nyuumon: Funso wo manabazushite kokusai kankeiron wo kanarunakare. In *Shogakusei ni mo wakaru daigaku no gakumonn*. Chuo daigaku sogoseisaku gakubu eds, pp. 87-114. Tokyo: Geishin shuppansha, 1996.

Sewart, John J. (1978) "Critical Theory and the Critique of Conservative Method" *American Sociologist*, Vol. 13, No. 1, pp. 15-22.

Shima, Hiroaki (2003, October) Consulting ni hitsuyou na mondai kaiketsu houhouron, pp. 42-46. Retrieved May 11, 2006, from http://www.shimax-lta.jp/genkou02.pdf.

Silver, Edward A. (1997) "Fostering Creativity through Instruction Rich in Mathematical Problem Solving and Problem Posing".

Wallerstein, Immanuel, *Historical Capitalism with Capitalist Civilisation*, Verso, London and New York, 1996 (1983).

From Civilisations to Multiple Modernities:
The Issue of the Public Sphere

Civilisational Legacies

There can hardly be anything odd about raising the issue of modernity with regard to Islam. "In the sixteenth century of our era, a visitor from Mars might well have supposed that the human world was on the verge of becoming Muslim" (Hodgson, 1993: 97). This quote from the historian Marshall G.S. Hodgson conveys the sense that at the dawn of the modern era Islam represented the most vital civilisation in the world. Bernard Lewis's question "What went wrong?" can't be completely dismissed, but it should be re-phrased. More interesting might be to ask if there is something of the then hegemonic, Islamic proto-modernity enshrined in the power and culture of the three flourishing empires, the Ottoman, the Safavid, and the Mughal, which survived Western Europe's turning of the balance and assumption of its hegemony? Would it be then possible, in light of this early modern configuration of Muslim power, to reiterate the motive of a blockage of political and economic development brought about by an all-encompassing doctrine of divine authority that withheld a full legitimisation of political power and so prevented a truly modern state formation?

To answer this question requires dealing with the issue of tangible aspects of modernity within the framework of multiple modernities. This endeavour might start by tackling a basic question that is at the origin of the trajectory that led many scholars (predominantly political/historical sociologists like Shmuel N. Eisenstadt and Johann P. Arnason) to rupture the idea, still popular in the early 1970s, of a unique grand trajectory of political modernisation and to envisage instead multiple alleys.[1] They asked, "To what extent are the paths to and patterns of modernity dependent on civilisational legacies, how significant are, in this regard, the differences between major civilisational complexes, and what kinds of connection can we make between the internal pluralism of modernity and the civilisational pluralism of its prehistory" (Arnason, 2003: 13).

In a field where the notion of civilisation has been mainly associated with the Huntingtonian "clash" (to which only later theoreticians of a "dialogue of civilisations" have tried to reply) this bid for "civilisations" might appear at first glance to lead away from an opening of the concept of modernity. Yet it marked the beginning of a long trajectory that would make modernity not

---

[1]   Curiously, the conceptual starting point of their theorising was not "modernity," but "civilisation".

only more open and plural, but also more adherent to an increasingly complexifying world, and thus more "tangible." Far from reiterating culturalist biases, this notion of civilisation was intended to spell out the interaction of cultural variables and material power structures.

This notion was dealt with in a series of conferences mainly sponsored by the U.S. interdisciplinary journal *Daedalus,* in Jerusalem and Italy in the 1970s and then in Germany in the 1980s. An effort was made to delineate a plurality of tangible aspects of the interaction of power and culture in correspondence with specific characteristics of the social and political history of various world regions. Civilisation was intended not as a marker of cultural monoliths determined by predominantly ideal constellations, sustained by Weberian-type cultural elites or *Kulturträger,* but as a framework articulating structures and institutions linking power to culture, based on a material and economic basis of prosperity and expansion (cf. the work of Johann Arnason: 2003). This complex, plural and dynamic understanding of civilisation was deemed necessary in order to reconstruct a conceptual framework which would then allow for the definition of the commonalities and differences that exist among the variety of paths to modernity world-wide. This approach also attempted to specify the shifting weight of cultural factors in the pluralisation of those paths vis-à-vis factors related to the accumulation, contestation and distribution of power and wealth.

In order to understand this approach one should spell out its basic conceptual investment. Social movement and institutional innovation are key dimensions of change that are neither structural nor cultural. They are facilitated by an initial differentiation in the body of society between the rulers and the formulators of the normative fundaments of the cosmological *and* the socio-political orders. In several "axial civilisations" crystallising from the middle of the 1st century BCE onwards there emerged across Eurasia rulers devoid of fundamental sacral legitimation, and therefore bound to respect the normative and ethical codes formulated by clerics. Moreover, the order itself of society itself was subject to ongoing contestation by whatever faction or counter-elite could effectively contest the dominant interpretation of the normative fundaments of the socio-political order. Movement and innovation originated from this perpetual challenge, launched by "heterodox" groups towards the correct norm, the *orthe doxa* constructed by the cultural elites who were in control of the largely autonomous institutions which were deputed as producers of valid knowledge. In the Western part of Eurasia both biblical prophets and Greek philosophers played the role of challengers and innovators. How many discourses do we hear about the twin heritage of the "West", namely Greek philosophy and Hebrew prophecy? And yet this is the civilisational legacy of the West at large and therefore also of the Islamic civilisation.

Of foremost interest here is not merely the hermeneutical construction of civilisations as specific cultural traditions and the civilisational polemics that go with that construction, but the tangible, even structural, dimensions of the transformation of civilisations into the cradles of a plural morphology of modernity. While it cannot be denied that a differentiation of state power and religious authority was integral to the development of Islamic civilisation, traditions, and centres of power, it is important to take note of both the capacity for amalgamation and the continuity of Islam as a "community of discourse" (John Voll) or a "discursive tradition" (Talal

Asad). Islamic civilisation retained this capacity from a glorious epoch of political expansion and cultural florescence through to an era of subordination and resistance to the encroaching West. In particular, the synthesis of Hebrew prophecy and Greek science-*cum*-philosophy brought about by Islamic civilisation demonstrated both its outlook and the possibilities for further development, differentiation, and hybridisation with other civilising traditions.

The starting point for comparison and evaluation should be the dynamics of movement and innovation and the limits intrinsic to those dynamics, in particular the tension between the autonomy of the self-transformative, largely autonomous, elites and the autonomy of the power structures generated through heterodox challenges. Who remembers the much criticised, neo-Khaldunian cycle of rise and collapse of political formations by Ernest Gellner? No doubt the formation of the three big Islamic empires of early modernity, Ottoman, Safavid and Mughal, signaled the crossing of a threshold in the perpetuation of this cycle, where the ruling elites (largely drawn, in all three cases, from heterodox or semi-heterodox movements) were capable, if only to a certain degree, of strengthening their autonomy, to the detriment of the autonomy of the "ulama".

A different story unfolded in Central and Western Europe. In those regions, the previous unstable balance between spiritual and temporal powers were to be upset, not so much by the ideological elements of the Protestant Reformation per se, but rather by the enhancement of the elements of conflictuality triggered by thus far marginal, heterodox groups into a systematic attempt to colonise and alter the centres of the political power. The result was a long period of Wars of Religion, culminating in the Peace of Westphalia in the middle of the 17th century, which sanctioned the power of the ruler to control the public articulation of religion in his political domain (*cuius regio eius religio*) and so suffocate religious unrest.

Western uniqueness was neither the result of specific civilisational components, which were largely shared with the Islamic world, nor of distinctive institutional configurations.[2] It was the product of the acceleration, and mutation, of the "axial" dynamics of challenge to the socio-political order through heterodox elites to alter the balance for ever. The solution was a *tabula rasa* of the previous sources of legitimacy and the legitimisation of a new source of power, the modern state, which in due time would be characterised as a nation-state.

Religious radicalism

One key dimension of the analysis of multiple modernities is therefore the tendency of a society to form organised movements that challenge the normative orders. The first big antinomian movement in modern Western history was a radical religious movement, the Puritan revolution led by Oliver Cromwell. Therefore the most tangible trigger of modernity's explosion was, in its English prototype, a type of religious radicalism explicitly aimed at taking

---

[2] Such as the feudal system, urban municipal autonomies, and the heightened competition between the pope and the emperor that corroded both institutions' long term viability as autonomous powers.

over the political centre. This seems to contradict the present discourse concerning moderate vs. radical Islam, but it is a firm point in the comparative analysis of multiple modernities.

A counterpart to this apparent contradiction, that the main agent of political modernisation (the first "great revolution" in Western history) was carried out by a radical religious movement, is the basic limit of the secularity models incorporated in Western nation-states as a result of a complex and even contradictory historical process. Such secular states were everywhere (including in France) based on a dynamic control of the religious field through the state, but not on a renunciation by the state to use religious values, in direct or indirect form, as cohesive elements of the majority cultures and as legitimisation formulae of the constitutional frameworks. This is the case of the frequent invocation of the sacred "dignity of the person" by Western secular politicians as a value well-rooted in Christianity.

We see then how Western modernity appears to be built on a double civilisational foundation, one that allows for particularly vehement antinomian tendencies requiring the autonomy and innovative capacity of protest movements and their capacity to penetrate the political centres, often at a price of awful violence and destruction, and another that configures modernity itself, issued of the Western hegemony over the global system yet without adjectives, i.e. modernity *per se*, as a progressive civilisation *sui generis*. The strength of Western modernity lies in its capacity to merge civilisation in the plural, rooted in the world of religious and cultural traditions, and in the singular, coinciding with a now global modernity, yet originally rooted in the power and the autonomy of the modern state.

Non-Western modernities, including Islamic ones, can only be articulated through folding their identities back on their own civilisational legacies, a movement that at first glance may appears regressive, but in fact has much progressive potential. Take, for example, the Arab intellectual discourse on *turath* that erupted in the late 1960s which coped with the hegemonic force and the singular meaning of modernity as such a civilisation *sui generis*, Western in origin yet universal in scope. It is this type of modernity that can articulate a universal civilising process in the sense elucidated by Norbert Elias, which aspires to build impersonal and efficient institutions (bureaucracies) and representative systems (democracies). The innovative capacity of non-Western modernities seems to be particularly impaired at this highly formalised institutional level. They seem to be left on the receiving side of civilisation.

At the level of less formalised structures of cooperation, regulation, and solidarity the case is different. Within civil societies and public spheres the degree of originality and innovation allowed within non-Western modernities is substantially higher. The cultural programmes of distinctive civilisational origin can still operate with some degree of autonomy and nurture specific configurations of civil society, social movements and the public sphere even where, such as several cases in the contemporary Islamic world, the issue of state reform in the name of participation, efficiency and transparence seems to be stalemated, caught between the danger of foreign (read Western) intrusion and the perpetuation of endogenous autocracies. To the extent that the regulative capacities of territorial nation-states is starting to lose the power, or the aura of power, it once possessed, the alternative modernities found at this sub-institutional level deserve attention.

Yet this step can only be performed by avoiding viewing such alternative modernities, and their tangible factors, through the exclusive lenses of civilisation in the singular, Western modernity, and via the social science discourse that goes with it. Nurtured by radicalism, including religious radicalism, first exalted and then sedated, made invisible or latent in the progressive constitutional designs and sharp distinctions between the private and the public spheres of Western societies, this type of modernity cannot nowadays furnish categories of analysis and comparison that deal fairly with radical and/or religious challenges to established authority at the level of civil society, social movements, and the public sphere.

The concept of the public sphere shares with the idea of "communicative action" the notion of acting, arguing, and deliberating in ways that are legitimated through a rational pursuit of collective interest. The difference between the functionalism of capitalism and state bureaucracy and the function of the public sphere as a "third sphere" of society (Somers, 1995) is put in relief by a critical perspective supported by protest movements. Accordingly, the quintessential character of modernity as a self-propelling system is at its highest at the "movement" level, which is the least feasible to be reduced to a bounded sphere. In the present world political conjuncture, movement has not only a transnational radius but also a transnational legitimacy. Its political efficacy is nonetheless fragile.

While the "public sphere" as the final product of a series of developments (as an arena or "sphere") is largely modern, European, Western, and "Westphalian", the normative character of its communicative function, the underlying idea of social connectivity and the public use of reason and argument are not necessarily so.

The transnational Islamic public

A transnational Islamic public is perhaps the most visible and powerful instantiation of an exit strategy from the Westphalian frame into a simultaneously sub-nationally and trans-nationally based type of "sphere" that satisfies some key presuppositions of Habermas' communicative action, without fitting into the bounded character of a national citizenry. The paradox dissolves if we analyse the reasons for this development on three levels: the existence of a strong tradition within Islam defining the *what* of this public sphere, i.e. a conception of the common good to be made public; the *post*-postcolonial collapse of confidence in the emancipatory potential of Third World approximations of Westphalian, national developmental states, along with a recrudescence of themes of anti-imperialist struggles for justice and dignity; the world economic dimension of globalisation that on the one hand elicits Islamic responses, and on the other favours an exit from the exclusivity of the Westphalian frame.

These three levels are quite tightly intertwined in the actual world political constellations. An Islamic public sphere or "public Islam" is based on the traditional notion of *maslaha* (of the common good or public interest), both a jurisprudential and theological concept (Masud, 1995 (1977), Hoexter/Eisenstadt/Levtzion, 2002, Salvatore, 2007). The notion of *maslaha* is increasingly invoked for supporting a critique of delegitimised postcolonial regimes, operating under the aegis of international agencies overseeing programmes of "structural adjustment." Such a critical discourse reflects Muslim reformist views of traditional notions denoting justice and a participative commitment to community welfare like *maslaha*. This discourse calls for the implementation of standards of justice and participation both beyond and beneath the national level. It therefore fits a diluted Westphalian framework of postcolonial nationalism and the transnational, at times aggressively universal, idea of a global Islamic community, or *ummah*, which can be made sense of in the framework of plural civilisational legacies.

There is no "fiscal" basis to this discourse of *maslaha* outside of the national frameworks of taxation and redistribution, but one should not underestimate the efficacy of networks of solidarity and mutual financial help on specific issues, ranging from catastrophe relief through education to support for national liberation movements or boycotted governments committed to those Islamic tenets (see Salvatore/LeVine, 2005). Islamic socio-political movements and networks provide at the same time the intelligentsia and infrastructure for a transnational Islamic public. Their reference to a multi-levelled community (local, national, and transnational) is frequently supported by claims to justice, participation and, increasingly, democracy. Legal implementation does not coincide in this sphere with the administrative apparatus of a territorial state, yet the proliferation of meta-legal orientation and advice through the vehicle of advisory legal opinions (*fatwas*), or even more informal methods, in the press, electronic media and especially on the internet, provide a normative climate for the Islamic sphere. The model does not exclude the capture of residually contestable territorial, administrative spaces. At stake is the redefinition of Islamic normativity, or *shari'a*, the understanding of which has become more contested than ever. Some of the transnational Islamic public, such as European Muslims, build the vanguard of this contestation and redefinition. This process remains focused on the *what*, while it avoids an open determination of the *who*, i.e. of how membership is defined, how membership rights are accessed, and how authority over members is determined. It is a transnational public that exalts the movement dimension to the detriment of institutional crystallisation.

One should not forget that the Westphalian momentum has been in the Islamic civilisational world substantially weaker than in Europe, because it manifested itself most acutely only at the colonial and post-colonial stages. The three great early modern, pre-colonial Islamic empires never crossed a Westphalian threshold of autonomisation of political power and sovereignty, since they were never shaken by such an intensive wave of religious unrest and radicalism as was Europe. The political and cultural elites that took over after the end of colonialism were often incapable of incorporating wider masses in their blueprints of development, social justice, national dignity, and especially of democratic participation. At the same time, the development of a "public Islam," even when stemming from battles at the state-national level, was always nurtured by transnational solidarity and local activism. Both streams of engagement gained part of their strength from subsequent waves of Western-led economic globalisation, which enfeebled the states and thereby favoured the transnational flow of communication and finance.

The transnational congeniality of the Islamic sphere precedes West-centred globalisation. Since the Middle Ages Islamic civilisation has been the closest to a global transcivilisational ecumene with a political economy based as much on commerce as on a wide non-profit sector. The growing sense of a global Islamic, markedly post-Westphalian, public sphere builds on those historical experiences, yet transforms them profoundly. Neither is this sphere restricted to the influence of elites. Traditionally, transnational fluxes were not limited to big traders and elite scholars, but also open to lesser scholars, Sufis, and pilgrims. Nowadays socio-political movements with a strong Islamic orientation benefit from transnational publicity even if their chief goal is to gain power at a central state level. Yet as long as they are not capable or not allowed to do that (not least, for lack of a functioning central state to take over), they can resort to sub-national communes and transnational networks, no doubt with mixed results, dependent as they are on wider conflicts involving those global powers that govern the exit from a Westphalian framework. Yet affectedness and publicity, identity and communication, tend to overlap in this transnational Islamic public, both in the dimensions of cohesion and unity and on the fault lines, like that between Sunni and Shia.

"Public Islam" draws on a premodern, precolonial, pre-Westphalian civilisational background and is nurtured by post-Westphalian transformations marked by the singular Eliasian civilising process. The fact that the functioning of this transnational public sphere cannot completely bypass a national framework reflects both its potential strength and its structural vulnerability, not least vis-à-vis inimical global powers holding both the political weapons and the financial instruments to circumscribe its influence. Structurally, such a transnational public with a high level of affectedness faces global financial and political-military powers with a low level of transnational accountability. While the normative legitimacy of a transnational Islamic public can be measured at a level comparable to the politically expansive radius of Habermas's "communicative action" (through solidarity, publicity and mobilisation), an assessment of its tangible dimensions and political efficacy remains issue-dependent due to the multiplicity, informality and vulnerability of funding patterns, legal supervision and political mobilisation.

References

Amason, J. (2003) *Civilisations in Dispute, Historical Questions and Theoretical Traditions,* Leiden and Boston: Brill.

Calhoun, C. (1992) "Introduction", in Calhoun, C. (ed), *Habermas and the Public Sphere,* Cambridge, MA: MIT Press.

Hoexter, M., Eisenstadt S. N., Levtzion, N. (eds) (2002), *The Public Sphere in Muslim Societies,* Albany, NY: SUNY Press.

Habermas, J. (1984 [1981]) *The Theory of Communicative Action,* Vol. I, *Reason and the Rationalization of Society,* trans. Thomas McCarthy, Boston: Beacon Press.

Habermas, J. (1987 [1981]), *The Theory of Communicative Action*, Vol. II, *Lifeworld and System: A Critique of Functionalist Reason*, trans. Thomas McCarthy, Boston: Beacon Press.

Habermas, J. (1989 [1962]) *The Structural Transformation of the Public Sphere*, trans. Thomas Burger, Cambridge: Polity Press.

Habermas, J. (1990) "Vorwort zur Neuauflage", *Strukturwandel der Öffentlichkeit*, Frankfurt: Suhrkamp.

Habermas, J. (1992) "Further Reflections on the Public Sphere", in Calhoun, C. (ed), *Habermas and the Public Sphere*, Cambridge, MA: MIT Press.

Habermas, J. (1996 [1992]) *Between Facts and Norms: Contributions to a Discourse Theory of Law and Democracy*, Cambridge, MA: MIT Press.

Hodgson, Marshall G. S. (1993) *Rethinking World History*, Cambridge: Cambridge University Press.

Koselleck, R. (1988 [1959]) *Critique and Crisis, Enlightenment and the Pathogenesis of Modern Society*, Oxford: Berg.

Masud, M. K. (1995 [1977]) *Shatibi's Philosophy of Islamic Law*, Kuala Lumpur: Islamic Book Trust.

Salvatore, A., and LeVine, M. (eds) (2005) *Religion, Social Practice, and Contested Hegemony*, New York: Palgrave Macmillan.

Salvatore, A. (2007) *The Public Sphere: Liberal Modernity, Catholicism, Islam*, New York: Palgrave Macmillan.

Somers, M. R (1995) "What's Political or Cultural about Political Culture and the Public Sphere? Toward an Historical Sociology of Concept Formation", *Sociological Theory*, 13: 113-144.

Discussion

Asef Bayat

Knowing Armando, I think this paper for him is very clear. I do not know if I am able to express his views correctly or not, but I think the fundamental question he is asking is whether or not there is such a thing as "Islamic modernity" as a part of the problematic of multiple modernities.

Armando does not agree with those who argue that, because there are divine authorities in Islamic societies, these divine authorities prevent the formation of a modern state [and that therefore] one cannot speak of Islamic modernity. He actually looks at the issue of modernity from a different perspective; he introduces the notion of civilisation. Because civilisation, culture being a significant element in it, allows differences and at the same time allows the retention of certain core elements of whatever he understands as modernity. On this basis he rejects, as many others have done, the equation of modern life and society with secularism. He says that, even in the West, modernity was triggered by Puritan religious movements. He seems to suggest that perhaps Islamic movements in the Muslim world might play such a role.

I think it is important to look at the consequences of modernity for religion. We should not forget that modernity does, in many ways, weaken religion but also that there are times when modernity actually reproduces the religion. So it is crucial to look at it as a contingent phenomenon.

On this basis he suggests that if the public sphere, as scholars like Habermas insist, is a central part of modern life, Muslim societies [must] also have it. Islamic modernity is possible for Muslim societies, on the one hand, by sticking to their legacies and, on the other hand, by coping with the hegemonic modernity that we have in the West.

What remains unclear is what those core elements of modernity/modernities are. What are the tangible elements of modernities? What are these core elements that make sense of modernity? Sometimes he refers to movements and innovations. I am not really sure, movement and innovation toward what? This is very important because if we are to attempt to understand and identify these core elements, we might come to the conclusion that there are no such things as multiple modernities. There could be one modernity with different forms. For example, sometimes it is suggested that in Paris there were cafés as a public sphere, but in Muslim societies there were, are, public baths, therefore Islamic modernity is different from French [modernity]. I do not understand this because we can consider these variations as different forms. It is essential, therefore, to come up with these core elements.

At the cost of being very crude, I want to stick to the traditional understanding of what modern is. From this viewpoint modern is complexity and organisation, and the resolution of this complexity in social and economic life. So as societies become more complex, they develop division of labour, industries, cities, division of occupation and so on and so forth, which means rationalisation, and at the core of rationalisation is the notion of reason. Science very much relates to this. In fact, even the modern state can be understood in these terms. After all, the modern state is supposed to be a bureaucratic and rational state. In all of this it seems that individuals play a significant part. At the same time, it seems to me that these processes, if one looks at them contingently, can produce individuals. For example, the development of the modern city does create modern urban individuals and undermine communities, but as I will discuss later, it might also regenerate communities-distanciated or imagined communities. In the way I understand modernity, reason and the individual are the central players. This looks like a very crude Western/universal modernity.

I agree with Armando that secularisation is not one of the inevitable consequences of modernity, although it sometimes accompanies modernisation and secular life and secularism can be a consequence of modernity. At the same time, modernity can regenerate religiosity because of the cost of modernity. Uncertainty and other products and costs of modern life can pave the way for the reproduction of religion.

The last point I want to make is that I think it is important to realise that these processes might affect certain groups more than others. In other words, these processes do not affect the entire population of a particular society because people have different capacities and abilities to be modern. Not everyone can afford to be modern. Modernity has economic, intellectual and social costs and one needs to have the economic, intellectual and social capacity to be modern. I am taking all this from my urban studies in poor neighbourhoods. I came to the conclusion that a lot of poor people do want to become modern and benefit from modern life [such as] technology, being an individual and autonomous, etc. but cannot afford to be so. They simply cannot afford to go through the discipline of modern life, discipline of time, discipline of space, discipline of contract, and so on and so forth. Because they cannot afford to become modern, they resort to traditional modes of reciprocity, negotiation, self-help activities and so on.

Charles Jencks

I think in discussing such a big subject you have to be a little bit technological about defining terms, especially when you are talking about modernity and the modern... because of the cognate terms in the sense that modernisation, modernity and modernism, the three inwards, come as a loose package, if not highly interrelated. We know that this has been a discussion for many years.

The word modern [was first used] in the third and fourth centuries as a positive polemical Christian word designed to outflank the pagan Roman hegemonic modern world. In Rome there were one million people; you cannot be more modern than to have a million people in a city. Modernis, meant to be more modern than the modern, was, if you like, the polemical usage of modernism. It is important to decide how to talk about this.

I think historians generally accept that the modern world and modernity started much earlier than Armando said; that is to say way before Oliver Cromwell and Westphalia. The consensus is that the modern world, modernisation and the modern global economy, [originated] somewhere around Florence. For instance, when Paul Kennedy talks about the modern world as the modern state, the greatest creation of the modern world, he suggests that it started somewhere in the early Renaissance. Of course it was not a big thundercloud coming into existence all of a sudden; it starts in the economic sphere with modernisation. Other economists remind us that in the West it took something like 800 or 900 years for people to understand the notion of the modern economy, as Adam Smith understood it. On the contrary, in Dubai, for instance, they have leapfrogged, leapfrogged and leapfrogged. They understand the modern economy better than Abu Dhabi, which is [now] trying to catch up.

I bring that up because I think modernisation is still an engine of modernity or the modern – I am now using the modern and modernity interchangeably as distinct [from] modernisation and modernism. I am not a Marxist but I do think that the economy and modernisation is the driving force here, and it is an earlier force than Oliver Cromwell. However, I accept the part of this paper that [asserts that] its relations to religion are key. I agree with Asef (Bayat) and Armando (Salvatore) that it is not just secularisation. The religious relationships are interesting. I remember Farrokh (Derakhshani) talking about fundamentalism as a form of modernism. As sociologists suggest, it is a very important form of modernism. Particularly, when modernisation fails, fundamentalism is a [form of] modernism to deal with that. What I am making a plea for is a sharpening of words. I am not suggesting we use modernism 1, 2, 3, but I do think that until we get to know each other, we should clarify our views of these words because I think they are really multiplicitous.

Jeremy Melvin

I found the paper fascinating. I think that it has many points of interest, an awful lot of which, I have to confess, are beyond anything I feel competent to comment on in any serious way. But there are some things I want to discuss and take further. I thought I would start by saying something about the issue of modernity... I spend a part of my time at the Royal Academy of Arts in London working on the Architecture Programme. The first exhibition there, in 2000, was an attempt to recreate the Paris exhibition of 1900, exactly one hundred years earlier. It was a selection of works made that year and I think about 60% to 70% of the works in the Paris exhibition were brought to London a hundred years later. This stimulated us in the Architecture Programme to think about the implied definitions of modern, modernism and modernity that arose as a result of these different works which were mostly, not entirely, made within Europe, from Russia to Portugal, and from Finland to the south of Italy.

Seven years on, we are still trying to do it. We have not gone very far. I think that confirms that it is an extraordinarily difficult project. Since Professor Salvatore's paper was very much about political constitutions, I thought it might help if I raised issues about architecture so that we can see where they fit and where they do not fit. I think we should start with discussing the relationship between modernity and the physical environment, which I would consider to be the business of architecture. It can be mainly rural, it can be mainly urban, we could be talking about specific buildings or boots or any other specific physical environment. During the [reading of the] paper I was thinking about the Western model of the political state, and immediately to my head came the city of Karlsruhe in Germany, a semi-circle, with radial streets going off it, in which the radial streets focus on the prince's palace. That seems to me to be an extraordinarily strong and very literal depiction of a political idea in the physical environment. So I think it does happen, but it is very rare, and difficult to replicate. I think we all [would] feel uncomfortable living in Karlsruhe where everything is focused on the palace. But it obviously shows how political structure can be reinforced in a physical structure. This was a political sense attempting to be unified. It was suggesting that there is one way and that all other ways, by definition, are wrong. However, when we deal with issues of the modern, modernism and modernity and the multiple implications they have, it becomes even more complicated.

I think if we look at the other end, the condition of buildings, I think it is very important to remember that buildings have at least two very important strands to them. One is that buildings and the built environments do certain things or allow certain activities and functions. Sometimes only by implication, they open possibilities. Sometimes they create opportunities. Sometimes what they do is very little or strong. It may be an educational building, a medical building or a building without an actual physical function; but I think this is always an important underlying element of what architecture is.

There is another really important element in architecture and that is that buildings represent and embody ideas and beliefs. Sometimes the ideas and beliefs that are raised by a particular building and the activities it houses are not quite co-terminal. Sometimes tensions arise between those [ideas and beliefs]. One could think that this is a rather crude depiction, but a building designed in the European classical tradition in the manner of a country house might contain a hospital, as sometimes happened in the early nineteenth century. It does not necessarily mean it cannot work but it opens a tension and sometimes it opens the possibility of imaginative space that could be a really interesting thing. The tension, in these cases, is between what is implied and alluded to in the architecture and what is going on in the interior. An interesting feature of European modernism in the middle of the twentieth century was that you could have an absolutely perfect relationship between the above mentioned elements, one that fits exactly between the representational qualities... and the functional qualities of the building.

As well as doing things and allowing things to happen, and representing ideas, buildings represent investment. In certain societies, it might just be the investment of the time of the people who build it, but increasingly it is an investment of money. Moreover, buildings can be made from components that come from all parts of the world. The money and the economic system that is behind it, and I am not speaking as a communist, is a trans-national entity. It cannot be totally controlled by political power. It has its own existence and does not neatly follow political policies. Professor Charles Jencks suggested earlier that if we look at the notion of the modern state, at least in the European context, we have to go back to the early Renaissance. I think it is absolutely right that the big expansion of trade in Europe was one the issues that gave rise to a modern state based on trade from which taxes could be raised. Of course, without taxes the modern state would find it very difficult to exist.

The next point I want to raise goes back to my point about buildings doing and representing things. I think it is very important that the commercial empire of the Medici family predated Machiavelli who did not come on to the scene as political theorist until the early 16th century. It was Machiavelli who gave one the earliest and clearest definitions of the political state, which the 19th century cultural historian, Jacob Burckhardt, characterised as the 'state as a work of art' – not that it was about painting and sculpture but that every element of the state was thought about and reasoned and was not the product of tradition, not art as in fine art or high art. It was the Medicis who developed the idea of the palace type; the building type that predates the idea of the state. This may not be always right, but it shows that the building type, both functional and representational, is extremely important.

As Professor Bayat mentioned earlier, the idea of the French café might have an analogue in the Islamic bath. But I think if we are looking at what is happening now, we could also extend this into things like airports which clearly have a character, for all sorts of reasons, that have traditional cultural references, hotels and, of course, what is going on in Dubai, which I have not visited but have noticed that [there are] very strange buildings going up there.

If we are to look at the relationship between the physical form and social form there are a number of points that we should pay attention to, particularly when dealing with the notion of multiplicities of modernity. One of the issues is the expression, exercise or display of power, I do not mean power in the coercive or negative way, I mean the [form] of organisation of the state; how states are organised and how social relations are developed within them. This is a really important issue and I am afraid I do not have the conceptual framework to put any flesh onto this, but I think it is to do with the role of the media. I think the media has developed into a mechanism for the expression of power.

Just to give a rather simplistic anecdote about this, many years ago a distinguished journalist called Martin Jacks gave a talk at the Royal Institute of British Architects. He was asked to say, from his point of view, what were the most important issues in contemporary society. One of the three he came up with was the ending of deference. He was obviously talking in the British context: the idea that when the Queen or any [other] member of the royal family walks into the room we no longer feel that we have to bow. I think this is wrong and slightly misses the point. It is not the end of deference; it is the transfer of deference. The mechanism which has allowed us to transfer our deference from queens, kings, emperors, etc. to pop stars, sport stars, and people who appear on reality television programmes is to do with the role of media. A lot of this, not all of it, is driven by commercial [concerns], there has to be some commercial system behind it. I think the implications this raises for architecture are very difficult to recognise and any comments I make about this will be very naïve.

The other issue is something that comes before in the West but is not limited to the West, the role of affluence and the features of architecture in an affluent society. According to John Kenneth Galbraith in *The Affluent Society*, the affluent society is one where there is no meaningful distinction between luxury and necessity. I think this is extremely important because once we break the link between necessity and luxury, we are into a completely different idea of what physical space, be it inside, outside, public or private, really is. I think architecture, particularly much of the thinking that goes into the multiple ideas of modern architecture, has had great difficulty with the idea of affluence because, at least in the past 200 years or so, much of Western architectural theory has been predicated on the idea that you make a building with the minimum amount of physical mass needed to make it stand up or with the minimum amount of space in the exactly correct shaping to perform a particular function. This is trying to make an artificial distinction between what is necessary and what is luxury, [a distinction] which Galbraith... would deny.

Just to recap, these are the main points I raised: the idea of what a building does, the role of the building type, the relationship between the social form and the physical form, the importance of the media, and the issue of affluence and [its effect on] the notion of multiple modernities. The final point I would like to raise is about education, something that I am also involved with. What are the mechanisms by which ideas are transmitted? Can we work on a field of knowledge here? I think how education works with this is extremely important.

Farid Panjwani

Thank you very much for this opportunity to share some thoughts with you. I got the paper last evening and struggled for long hours to decipher it. I found it very rich and full of ideas that would take hours to discuss. It was very informative and insightful, as well. I will divide my comments into two parts. First, I will try to extend some of the ideas that are in the paper and give some further thoughts on them. Then there are some questions that I have, which I will table and perhaps in the further discussions we will take them on. I will also give reasons for why I have those questions.

Let me start with the first part, which has to do with the extension of some of the ideas that are in the paper. I will start with the very first sentence in the paper which [concerns] a very nice comment from Marshall Hodgson: "In the sixteenth century of our era, a visitor from Mars might well have supposed that the human world was on the verge of becoming Muslim". I think this is not only true in 16th century but also 17th century. At least in the first part of the 17th century this would be very much true. In fact, as far as England is concerned, and I am referring here to the work of Nabil Matar, there was a fear among people that Christians were converting very quickly to Islam. There was actually a term for that: "turning Turk". In the late 16th and early 17th centuries many plays were written that captured and reflected that fear. For example, we have plays like Renegado, Tragedy of Suleiman, and A Christian Turned Turk, written in the early 17th century.

Not only this, but, as you know, coffee was introduced in this period. It was called the "Mohammedan berry" and it generated a lot of discussion in the English society. There was a fear that it was an Ottoman conspiracy to convert the English to Mohammedanism by the "Mohammedan berry". Although I have not looked at it, I wonder whether there are parallels between this reaction and some of the reactions that were there in the Muslim world when tea was introduced. It would be very interesting to look at that.

Closer to our concern, I refer to Professor Salvatore's remark that the bringing together of the synthesis of Hebrew prophecy and Greek science opened up many possibilities. And in the 17th century when the new mode of scientific thinking was emerging in the West, this synthesis and mode of thinking continued to have relevance in Europe and particularly the works of Averroes and *Hayy ibn Yaqdhan* of Ibn Tufail became very widely read particularly because they were talking about divinity through your own reason. So in their attempt to reconcile the scientific mechanistic world and a religious worldview... they found the writings of Muslim philosophers very interesting. At least one author claimed that John Locke's interest in human understanding, after which he wrote his Essay [*An Essay Concerning Human Understanding*, 1690], started off when he read the translation of *Hayy ibn Yaqdhan*.

The second point which I would like to make is regarding Professor Salvatore's comments about the positive potential of the religiously inspired social action, protest and radicalism. I think in this regard, the work here does not seem to have a theoretical base; it is very empirical in its approach. I would suggest that one looks at the works of German philosopher, Ernst Bloch. He was a twentieth century philosopher who, working within the Marxist tradition, reinterpreted Marx's notion of ideology. He argued that ideologies, including religious ideologies, have pejorative as well as positive elements. He [describes] ideologies as Janus-faced; they have both mystifying and utopian elements. I think because religions have... these [elements] they are, in some contexts, in tension with modern developments and in some other contexts they seem to work with it. This social protest and radicalism perhaps emanates from the utopian possibilities in religion and that allows it to be a social critique. I think looking at this kind of work may help us go further in this direction.

Let me now quickly move on to the second part of my comments which are questions. I will start by echoing Professor Bayat's comments and some of the hesitancies he had in accepting the very notion of multiple modernities. It seems to me that the paper, as well as the workshop, accepts the notion of multiple modernities quite unproblematically. Many people are writing about it, but I seem to find myself still hesitant to uncritically accept it, and I hope we have the occasion to debate this. I believe that the stress on historical and contemporary diversity that underpins the notion of multiple modernities and its critique of the hegemonic singular notion of modernity is correct. But I wonder whether it is correct in terms of the significance it gives to this diversity and differences. I wonder if on the one hand the notion of a singular modernity might be underplaying diversity and the notion of multiple modernities might be overplaying diversity.

In some sense, it becomes an empirical question and there I think our evidence is quite equivocal and ambiguous. I think we find in certain studies that there are many deep-seated cultural differences. But then there are also studies that show attitudinal commonalities across the world, so I think the critique of the conventional singular modernity can be accepted, but whether we can then jump to the notion of multiple modernities is not [for me] yet resolved. A few weeks ago I read an article from Volker Schmidt who has proposed the notion of "varieties of modernity" instead of multiple modernities. Also, there is the possibility that one can see modernity itself having various aspects, intellectual, social, political and material and technical aspects. It might be possible that in some parts of the world, certain aspects of modernity have developed while others have not, and that is where the differences can be explained. I hope that we can keep the possibility of alternative ways of moving forward after the critique of conventional modernity opens.

I also find that the paper does not clearly tell us what modernity is and what the definitions of alternative modernities are. Already terms like proto-modernity and early modernity are used for empires like Ottomans, Moghuls and Safavids. I feel that these empires themselves were complex and... able to have autonomy vis-à-vis the Ulema. This kind of internal diversity has to be addressed. Finally, it seems to me that at least the elective affinities, if not the deep connections that has been made between Habermas's notion of communicative action and the Muslim practice of *maslaha* needs to be questioned and challenged. I think it is a good and brave attempt to see this as a possible tangible element of multiple modernities but I am not sure if it works and I think it may be a little bit over-stretched for several reasons.

First I think the Habermasian notion of communicative action has certain pre-requisites. Although the paper mentions it, I could not find them listed. In the words of Habermas himself, one of these pre-requisites is that this action is oriented towards achieving, sustaining and reviving consensus; consensus that rests on the inter-subjective recognition of criticisable validity of claims. I am not sure if *maslaha*, still operating in the theological framework of Islam, allows these kinds of open possibilities. Moreover, we know that *maslaha* was one of minor sources of law in the classical paper. It has become major precisely because other sources of *Usul al-Fiqh* are not providing the responses that are required.

I refer to Professor Jencks's discussion of the emergence of the notion of modernity. Here I have a quote from Habermas that says, "The word modern in its Latin form "modernus" was used for the first time in the late 5th Century in order to distinguish the present, which had become officially Christian, from the Roman and Pagan past. The term "modern" appeared and reappeared exactly during those periods in Europe when the consciousness of a new epoch formed itself through a renewed relationship to the ancients, whenever antiquity was considered a model to be recovered through some kind of imitation. The spell the classics of the ancient world cast upon later times was first dissolved by the ideas of the French Enlightenment. Specifically, the idea of being modern by looking back to the ancients changed to the belief, inspired by the modern science, in the infinite progress of knowledge and the infinite advance towards social and moral betterment." I think this gives us some tangible element of what to look for in non-Western contexts if we want to look for modernity; if we accept this idea of modernity as a future-looking phenomenon. In this context *maslaha* roots itself in the past and it is forward looking. Because of these reasons I am not convinced by his argument, although I acknowledge that it is a brave attempt.

Masoud Kamali

I will start by saying that Professor Salvatore's paper has many points that are interesting and at the same time very problematic. As Professor Bayat mentioned, one should ask, What is modern? If there are modern institutions or societies, what do we mean by modern? The answer depends on the multiplicity of theoretical traditions in the West, if we have to call it the West. I am sceptical of the notions like "West", "Muslim World", and Weber and the Weberian tradition of uniqueness of the West and a single modernity. I think discussing ancient and medieval civilisations and the exact time the word modern was first used is not interesting today. What is interesting today is to say that we have one modernity which is the Western modernity. Professor Salvatore, for example, is really saying that we do not have Protestantism in Islam and Islam is not used for legitimisation of modern change.

Another problem which he discusses but is not historically true is that he relates modernity to democracy. Historically they have had nothing to do with each other. Turner has shown very clearly that modernity has nothing to do with democracy. According to him, Fascism, Communism, Nazism and liberalism are all modern and the last three are not democratic. Just to take another example, China is modern without being democratic. Nazism was also very modern, efficient and cost-effective.

I also was not convinced by his arguments regarding the public sphere and the Muslim world. I believe that the public sphere has a long tradition in the Muslim world. I am sorry to use the term "Muslim world" since we know Shia and Sunni in Islam are very different. Secularism in Shia [Islam] happened much earlier, during the Safavids, starting with the first king. In 1501, the Safavid king said, "I am the shadow of God on earth". After 100 years, however, Shah Abbas said, I have nothing to do with God or religion, I am a secular man.

My other problem with this paper was with its discussion of Enlightenment. It seems that we are still using the term Enlightenment with a totally positive meaning in mind and thinking that it is all to do with rationality and positive change. We need to also look at the euro-centrism of the Enlightenment. Even those who accept instrumental rationality as the core of modernity criticise it as one of the four kinds of rationality. Enlightenment, for example, [is also related] to racism and colonialism. I think that different people with different cultures, histories and traditions can have their own [form of] Enlightenment.

Regarding the issue of secularism, I think we cannot call any single institution modern. If we do this, we are making the same mistake of people like Anthony Giddens. According to him, a modern country has four different institutional arrangements: surveillance and control, capitalism, market economy and militarism. One can see that many of these existed in the Muslim world long before [they came into] existence in Europe. The professional army, for instance, was first achieved in the Ottoman Empire. Freedom of religion was also first seen in the Ottoman Empire, as part of the Islamic law, and so on and so forth. I am not going to go into details; I just wanted to open up the discussion.

When we are talking about multiple modernities, what is it that we are discussing? Can we think of modernity as explained by people like Jürgen Habermas and Ulrich Beck? For example, they suggest that we have Anglo-Saxon, liberal modernity, Swedish modernity, etc. You can compare Sweden with Iran. For instance, in Sweden all the journals and TV channels are owned by parties, unions are part of the government, and [there is] no civil society. One could see a similar situation in Iran. So comparison of different parts of the world can be done through the theory of multiple modernities without being trapped in the problematic discussion of a single modernity and the tradition of uniqueness of the West and debates over when modernity starts.

The whole discussion about multiple modernities was started by Shmuel Eisenstadt in a gathering at Uppsala University in 1996. Eisenstadt, one of the most renowned theorists of multiple modernities, defended the possibility of having different kinds of modernities which are not completely different; they are rather different arrangements of modernity. For example the American Supreme Court might have the same function as Iranian religious courts and Council of Guardians. So these different institutions can be compared as two parts of different modernities.

Abdou Filali-Ansary

Professor Armando Salvatore has opened a number of big boxes all full of questions. I think he suggests a number of things that need to be discussed and studied in depth. Building on what has been said until now, I would like to express some fears.

I use the word fear because this paper [proposes] a link between modern civil society and public sphere and what Hodgson regards as the major feature of classical Muslim societies, the fact that there was an open space across vast geographic areas in which it was possible to have an open market of ideas, goods and populations. In these countries, polities had marginal roles; the political was limited to a minimum and politicians were those who maintained the order and defended their territory. Society had managed to gain and build some autonomy and to create a market in which communication between its components was possible. This may be a rough description of Hodgson's claim. What I understand from this paper is that Armando wants to link this to what is happening now around us, the impression that the modern media and the internet is allowing some forces in the Muslim world to express themselves and try to discuss the political issues using religious language and to bring again something that was described as playing politics on the field of religion.

In the two cases, we do have the impression of an open space of some kind of exchanges taking place across limits that are created by geography, languages and cultures. I fear that this kind of comparison may bring from the window something we are trying to push from the door. It may bring... some form of essentialism. He thinks that the fact that Muslims are here and there and that they are facing or rejecting the nation-state is one form of modernity. He also suggests that a kind of modernity might have preceded the nation-state, and it is Islam. I am afraid of this continuity.

My second fear is that these kind of connections and these broad categories may lead us to see not the tangible elements of modernity in Muslim contexts and the varieties of Muslim contexts. [At least two tangible aspects may be pointed to:] One is before the colonial wave with some major changes that mainly began in the Ottoman Empire. These changes that began in the 18th and 19th century signalled transformations and changes along the lines that we see today as being some form of modernisation. The other is the reaction after the integration of Muslim societies in the world economy and the rest of the world through colonisation.

What is happening is not only passive reception or submission, and there are so many tangible elements of modernity that are most relevant to our discussion here about architecture, because in the built environment there is so much to look at and consider as tangible elements of modernity. The population boom of Muslim countries, for example, puts pressure on the environment and generates reactions. Maybe the AKAA should bring us at some point to ask questions about which of these reactions could be seen as positive sides, something that would lead us to open ways of facing the challenges of nowadays. So I am afraid that Armando would take us away from looking at what has happened at some point in the 18th century and what is happening now in the 20th and 21st century.

My third fear is that it may distract us from looking at the idea of modernity itself. Modernity has been the subject of a continuous discussion since a few decades ago. Of course, we can time the origins of the word to very long in the past, but the idea of modernity has been the focus of so much debate in the past few decades. Modernity has been a concept of a variable shape, and variations of its shape have been the outcome of discussions that have been taking place. So we want at the same time to reach out to the diversity of expressions, but also to try to understand what makes these forms of expressions so diverse and also have something in common at their core. I think here that we want to look at tangible elements of modernity and we have the opportunity to push this debate forward, to bring to it perspectives from Muslim contexts; to open some positive avenues and not keep turning around the specifity of Muslim societies and making apologatives like "we were modern before modernity" and "we were open before openness".

Stefan Weber

I followed your thoughts and fears and I am very happy that you stressed them. I had a certain unease with the paper that I will try to summarise in four parts. When we are talking about society, we have to also look at social strata. If you have the theory of communicative action, you should also look at different elements of Muslim societies who follow different discourses, which Abdou mentioned in his fear number one.

Second, in the paper and our discussion, we need to distinguish and to be very critical about three points: The first one is terminology. We have to be certain what we are talking about. The second one is how we define things and how other elements define if this is happening or not. If we are talking about modern times, the modern, and modernity, I would propose to think about modernity not as something that has to do with urbanisation, industrialisation, etc., but since in our discussion we are thinking about cultures, it is better to discuss which ways of group interaction we have among different cultures. For example, in the 19ᵗʰ century, we have new ways of transportation and communication under the mention of interaction. And when it comes to this interaction, I have certainly very much unease to talk about civilisations, because civilisations as an entity which is very clearly defined and understood has nothing to do with modernity in the 19ᵗʰ century and today.

Today we are not living in the age of different cultures and civilisations as entities that stand against each other, but in a multi-layered set of societies that are very hard to distinguish form one anther. If we are talking about modernity, I think we should first look at interaction and not dismiss moments in history that these interactions had fruitful moments. [There are] certain moments in history when different elements match and create something new, an example of which is the 1906 constitutional revolution in Iran. Today talking about modernity and cultures is much more difficult and distinguishing what is what is harder because we are more or less living in the big bowl of a big soup and there are different meeting points of different strata of societies.

Masoud Kamali

I think I have to make it clear that the theory of multiple modernities does not imply that we have thousands of kinds of modernities that have nothing to do with each other. This is not the case and nobody has ever discussed the theory of multiple modernities in this way. This theory is a reaction to post-modernism and constructive to nothing. Multiple modernities theory is a kind of understanding of the differences in modernities [that] at the same time recognises the commonalities of these different modernities. This theory is a critique of the euro-centrist understanding of modernity, the Weberian uniqueness of modernity, a modernity which started in the West and, as Giddens suggests, is our destiny. The theory of multiple modernities opens up new avenues for exploring the world that we are living in. What I have said is the only task of this theory and the only thing that it can help us to do.

Deniz Kandiyoti

I was wondering what this collectivity, the workshop being hosted jointly by ISMC and AKAA, was up to. I am surprised at this abstract discussion to help AKAA in concerns relating to the built environment, and I think this is the problem I am having with the paper and the way the whole discussion is going. I do not think you can really approach a concrete discussion of modernity and contemporary world via such incredibly formalistic and abstract categories. You have got to be able to minimally recognise some kind of empirical reference or empirical content to these categories. Let us take for inspection just something out of the air, the concept of trans-national Islam that appears in this paper. What is it about? Is this a Petro-Islam propagated by the Gulf States? Are you thinking about the whole package of finance, ideas, and indeed built environment consequences? Or are we referring to the various apparatuses of the cold war that have been set up in various countries propagating different kinds of Islam like madrasas in Pakistan with consequences in Afghanistan? What is this trans-national Islam? We do not know. So here is an empty category, and it is only when you start filling those categories up, the filling of these categories is heavy with consequences.

This also brings me to the question of modernity itself. I think I no longer find the concept of modernity particularly useful. I will try to explain why. It is because it produces what I call a multi-disciplinary cacophony in the sense that different people in different disciplines mean quite different things by it, and we have got to recognise these differences. The people I love to listen to most are my architect colleagues, because they are able to talk about genre and form and at least we know what we are dealing with. There is a moment; there is a genre, there are things that, whether you are in Russia or Brazil, you can identify as tangible products, forms, and sensibilities that you can call modern. But when we get to social sciences, things become a lot more complicated. So let me try to unpack two tangible manifestations, one has to do with society and the other with politics.

First, let us look at society. When you look at the sociology of modernisation, you realise that we are stuck in the notion of prototype and the result of prototype is that everything else has to become either non-modern or alternative to modernity. The concept of alternative modernities has explicit within it the inescapable and the notion of a prototype or multiple modernities. Where does this notion of prototype originate? I would say it originates very simply in the quite justifiable effort of generations of sociologists trying to find indicators of modernity, and actually these are quite sensible. They are talking about societies where most people are literate rather than not literate, where most people live in urban areas rather than villages, where family sizes are not out of control, where a demographic transition has taken place. We know about these things very well. Of course, there can be a complete disjuncture and you can have certain facets of modernity without the others.

When we get to politics it gets even more complicated; hence we are having a difficulty with democracy. One of the most illuminating things I have read on this is by a Soviet historian called Stephen Kotkin looking at what he calls the inter-war conjuncture where he looks at what political modernity has meant, which he sees as the phenomenon of statecraft in between the World Wars. And this is the advent of mass society which suddenly has citizenries to deal with rather than subjects. There are also mobilisational states. Whether this is the Soviet system, or Nazism and so on, it is a very different conception of the relationship between states and citizens, and there is a kind of mobilisation element. This has huge consequences for the built environment, because this is when the state starts representing self in certain specific ways. Now it can take the rock forms like desert states like Turkmenistan with 5 million people in it and absolute monuments to the ruler, but also roads lined by super-modern 5-star hotels that are perfectly empty.

So we have to take on board the question of images of modernity and the contractions of modernity now circulating globally. Hence, we have to unpack the societal, the political and different manifestations. By the time we have done that, I am not sure what mileage we get out of the concept of multiple modernities, because it seems to me that the market is absolutely key.

Let me just finish my comments by saying that the defects of the concept of modernity became evident to me when I started working in Soviet Central Asia, which many authors take as the epitome of the high modernist project: planned economy, state intervention, forced modernisation, alphabetisation, electrification, and so forth. The extraordinary discovery that I made was that this heavy state progress of modernisation had resulted in a freezing in time of societies in the regions I was looking at, what you might call arrested development. The command economy had frozen the relations of these rural areas, which had become unfrozen very rapidly in Turkey. We must not forget the key word: capitalism. Here you have a modern state project resulting in a very rigid stratification whereby the urban areas are European, Russian, Ukrainan etc., and rural areas are indigenous with no migration, no mobility, and very low urbanisation rates and at certain periods de-urbanisation. People having such difficulties living in urban areas that they go back to the rural areas. When you look at this example you think, why talk about modernity? Maybe we should find some other language to express these concrete phenomena.

Charles Jencks

If you get rid of modernity, you re-invent it, just like multiple capitalisms and non-capitalisms. We have to think of these three areas: modernisation and, of course, its driving force, capitalism, the market economy, and the global economy. I agree that it is problematic, but as John Gray, a philosopher at LSE in London who has written on multiple capitalisms, says, a great failure of theories about these things today is that they assume the victory of one of the multiple capitalisms where there is no indication any more than multiple ecologies, multiple global warmings, etc. Global warming has many differential consequences in different parts of the world, and so forth.

I want to go back to the Turkish coffee issue, that Turkish coffee, and I think [this] is a wonderful fear, will convert you. I love the idea that you convert people through coffee. I think tea and opium can have the same effect. What is so important about opium and tea in running the world economy and the Eastern economies? The great thing is that money is inter-convertible. It makes the universe seem small. If money is driving the global economy, it is the ultimate opium because it is convertible. You can convert any currency into any other easily.

I was recently in Dubai and looked at Sheikh Makhtoum's capitalism, what one can call Sheikhi capitalism. He is building the seven most modern buildings, the four largest malls, and the largest islands in the world. If you look at his economy and the way Sheikh Makhtoum's capitalism has been working, you will see that through luck, position, hard work and determination, he has managed to have never had a recession since the 1930s. This is the only economy that has more or less grown since 1945 through a series of leapfrog capital injections led by him or his family and a whole lot of accidents. It is, after all, on the route to Hong Kong, it is a port city, and they use architecture, media and celebrities very well. You can see, in a funny way, that there is a universality to his economy. And this is why he is frightening Abu Dhabi into action, to strike back.

I say this to stress that the notion of economy, capitalism and modernisation do have a universalising effect and are universal, in the sense that money is universal. Umberto Eco says that the great thing about money is that x=y and then y=x. The only thing we all accept without questioning is money as a universal standard. Money is one way that we can compare multiple modalities. Therefore, I agree with Deniz (Kandiyoti). Let us be particular and tangible and look at the economy and then connect it to other things.

Modjtaba Sadria

As a host, I guess I have to stand in for the colleague whose ideas are dear to me, and as you know, for understandable reasons could not join us here today. Those of you who know him, know that he has been deeply involved in the concept of the public sphere in Muslim societies. To my knowledge, he is still working on it. He has been arguing in favour of specificities in the formation of the public sphere in the Muslim societies, and in this paper he is continuing the same argument. I think what he brings to us here, which we have not discussed before, are the questions, What is Muslim modernity as a contemporary phenomenon? By which criteria have westerners thought that the rest of the world is not modern? He is bringing to us what is at the core of the Western experience of modernity, and arguing that we have had important anti-modernity forces in the West that are in fact, part of its modernity. This is for us a fundamental argument.

Armando is suggesting that when we became modern, in our modernity, there were radical anti-modernities. In other words, anti-modernities are fantastic components of our experience of modernity. I think if we exclude this fundamental point, this paper would be one of his weakest papers so far. I would attract your attention to this core element of his argument. He is not the only one who thinks this way. I myself buy this argument and will try to push it further in my paper that will be delivered tomorrow afternoon.

Ashish Nandy asks why religion is again rising in the world? What is this power of religion? Why [do] we have a "Muslim Problem" in every Western society? This story did not start from 9/11 in New York, or 7/7 in London, it goes back to at least the second half of the 20th century [since when the] West has been talking about Islam as a problem. Of course Muslim societies have many problems, so do many non-Muslim societies. What Armando's paper offers us in this discussion is that opposing modernity at the time of the hegemony of modernity becomes itself part of modernity in Muslim societies and non-Muslim societies alike. This statement includes all rims of thoughts and creation which could include architectural anti-modernity as a part of modernity in architecture, or in literature, or in poetry, or in painting. Here we have a very important and strong opponent; the tangible element of modernity is also anti-modernity. We cannot avoid looking at the experiences of modernity without understanding those who radically oppose it. These radical opponents of modernity are part of modernity independent of their own understanding and will.

This question can be formulated as, How shall we evaluate a discourse, primarily through semantic composition of it or the way that it emerges in the field and interacts with other discourses acting in the same field? Do those who radically oppose modernity understand necessarily the impact of their position? These anti-modernists, by opposing modernity, don't they in fact take modernity into their central references? The opposition to modernity seems to have strengthened its hegemonic place both as a reference and as a world outlook. Through a paradoxical mechanism the radicality of this denial and opposition of anti-modernists make them an integral part of modernity.

Charles Jencks

Are you talking about religions?

Modjtaba Sadria

The more religious arguments are used in legitimizing an antimodernity stance, in fact, the more religious arguments themselves need to use modern world outlook in order to become able to remain part of the debate and to present an attractive position within it.

Masoud Kamali

I think we have to make it clear that many of the notions and discourses that you call anti-modernity, were not actually anti-modern; they were rather different understandings of modernity. For example, the Turk's notion of modernity, the Ottoman Empire, started by the Sultan. In 1838, by *khatt-e-sharif-e gol-khane*, the discussion about modernity, the rights of all religions and citizens, and so on, started. Since then many Muslims have argued that Islam and modernity are compatible. To take another example, the Soviet system was completely modern, Johann Arnason calls it "communist modernity". You might ask why we call it modernity. To answer, I would say because the state in Soviet system was using political power for changing citizens according to their ideology, which is very modern. The liberals, Fascists, and Nazists were also doing this.

Before this, as Ibn Khaldun suggests, you could change the head of empire or state but not the constitution of society, its institutional arrangements, or doing anything about citizens. On the contrary, today we can do that. For example, the Islamic republic of Iran is re-organising Iran's society according to their ideology. Shmuel N. Eisenstadt names five different elements that political systems should have [in order] to be called modern. I think we have to leave the linear understanding of history. One should not think of modernity as something that we have, and then ask why others, such as the Soviet Union, are modern? The transnational nature of religions, as Ronald Robertson points out, is another interesting fact in this regard. He shows that religions have been transnational, they start somewhere and spread to other parts of the world, so globalisation is not a recent phenomenon. Therefore, globalisation has nothing to do with modernity.

I think what we have to leave behind is the notion of singular modernity. Capitalism and market economy are not modern developments. As Bryan Turner suggests, among the factors that helped Muhammad build a global religion was capitalism, trade and individualism. So it is possible to talk about different sources of modernity. The institutional arrangements of modernity came about fairly recently, according to Wallerstein in 1478, and according to others in 16th or 17th century. We have to stop comparing things with each other and start having a definition for political modernity, economic modernity and so on. Political modernity, for instance, is not only about state, public sphere and civil society but also the arrangement of institutions.

Asef Bayat

I am afraid I do not agree with Masoud. I find it difficult to understand what he means by saying that movements and ideas against modernity are modern. Of course, a movement could be the product of modernity, but I am not sure how necessarily the consequence of that movement, such as radical Islam, contributes to modernity. After all, in Europe, we have had movements that did not like the development of the capitalist modernity, urbanisation and costs of modernity, and they wanted to go back to their romantic past. So I do not really understand it. But more generally, two questions have been raised here. One is the question of singularity or multiplicity of modernity. Masoud, quite correctly, asked, What is the significance of this question and discussion? This is a very good question. The second question that Masoud raised is, What is the use of modernity, irrespective of its singularity or multiplicity? We should address these fundamental questions.

I think we are discussing modernity because we do not have anything else. In disciplines like sociology, we are here to create a language to speak, characterise the kind of arrangements we have in the world and in some way differentiate it from the past, the non-modern, and specially show the change and sources of change. So in this sense, it is important to discuss modernity and categorise and name it as modern. If there was an alternative concept or category, we would definitely use it. Capitalism can be one of the alternatives, but I think that post-capitalist or non-capitalist can also be modern, so capitalism might not be a substitute for modern. But we have to struggle to identify the core elements of modernity.

One reason why this concept of multiple modernities or alternative modernity was introduced was that it had a normative notion. Some people say we are modern and modernity is good, but you are not. You as a response say modernity is good and we are modern too, but in a bit different way. Therefore, we try to show that we are also modern. So there is this normative element here that we like. I am not personally in favor of this kind of argument.

The reason why I am saying that perhaps modernity is singular with different forms is to prevent violent relativism and abuse of the term modern. You cannot say that, for example, we are not interested in rights but are still modern. My argument is that you cannot say this, because rights are a very important element of modernity [and] are very much related to the individual.

Stefan Weber

The differences are a part of the process of modernity itself. To be different is not against modernity, but more for it. The interaction of different elements in societies is a very important element of modernity. The corrective movements of modernity are also a part of modernity. They use the same means and audience in the public sphere to attract people to their idea of modernity. It is not that one is modern and the other one is not; they are all part of the same process. And for us, as historians, architects, planners and people who plan for the places of public sphere, it is very important to understand that these places should reflect the interaction of different kinds of modernities.

Deniz Kandiyoti

I shall continue to play the role of the devil's advocate. I start with a simple question: If the space that we live in is defined as modern, and if radical reactions to modernity and anti-modern movements are also modern, what is the space that the term modern excludes? In other word, what is left as non-modern? The whole point about deploying a term like modernity is that presumably there is something that it excludes which is not modern, pre-modern, non-modern or anti-modern. How would you go about conceptualising what the term modern actually excludes in that case? So I think that the notion of multiple modernities makes the term modern not useful unless it can be salvaged by saying what the non-modern is. And then I am turning the question around: How on earth would you define what is not modern?

My second question is my very serious difficulty with the concept of Western modernity: What is "Western modernity"? What I am going to argue here is that there is no such thing as the West, and that the West is an ideological construct deployed for ideological purposes. First I will give you an illustration of the evanescent nature of the concept of West. I will take my example again from the Russian modernisation. This used to be a complex empire similar to the Ottoman Empire. They use to ask, Are we Western or Eastern?. They had their own discourse. However, when those same Russians went to central Asia and met their Muslim subjects, they defined themselves as the West. Now they are Western and the other ones are Eastern. In other words, the terms East and West are subject to multiple displacements.

The same is true with the Turkish modernisation. When the Ottoman Empire came into contact with the West, especially when it started falling behind, it went into a deep soul searching phase, but then the republican elites which were urban used exactly the same discourse vis-à-vis their tribal compatriots. Is Japan Western or Eastern? What is happening at the moment is something extremely crude and cynical, a lot of states like Putin's Russia, Nazarbayev's Kazakhstan, to take examples from part of the world I know well, are very happy to be integrated in world capitalism and get the rent from that integration. So they will embrace all the sort of trappings of the market economy, and they turn around and say but we cannot have democracy because that is Western, so therefore we need to have forms of unaccountable authoritarian rule are a true expression of our indigenous culture. There is a discourse of Euro-asianism that is being put about, Vladimir Putin being the first. And of course you can see quite clearly how this people are playing with modernity.

Multiple modernity or alternative modernity can be translated into Frank Sinatra's, "I'll Do It My Way". This is the powerful dictating the terms of the political game. They will tell their people how modern they will be, how many 5-star hotels will be built, because modernity is not about institutions; it is about the trappings of power. They will say, We are not interested in Western women's rights, polygamy is an integral part of our very being here. Democracy? Shut up! Are you Western? What is wrong with you? As we utilise these concepts of modernity, anti-modernity and West, what do we mean by them? What is the West? Where does it begin and where does it stop?

Charles Jencks

It is positional and it works, doesn't it?

Deniz Kandiyoti

I just told you it is positional. We have to simply suspend judgments.

Jeremy Melvin

I think you are absolutely right in saying that if we go back a thousand years, the notion of the modern has been transformed in all sorts of ways. For example, over the 19th century, some of the most scientific research was in Russia, a country that was socially quite backward by most measures. But also the whole institution of Czarism was a recreation of Roman Empire, and a lot more than that. You can see the role of Czarism particularly in the literature and the great writings of 19th century. It was a massive intellectual emotional challenge to get to terms with the split of Russia and its culture. One can also look at the pure rhetorical gesture of Turkmenistan, to take another example.

Homa Farjadi

I hear a very interesting set of gaps that people are opening between the functional dimension of modern and its other dimensions. There is forever a gap between the way in which buildings function as an image and what they do. And modernism and modernity was able to exploit this in a very fundamental way. In fact, Karlsruhe in Germany is a very good example. I was amazed to see it when it was reconstructed as a kind of post-modern archaeology of its own self with its slightly widened streets, so that cars could go through the original town, the effect of which is a very beautiful example of a "modern" city that is totally against what it says it is. It claims to be a representation of Princeliness but it is all to do with tourism.

Another example which comes to my mind is from Iranian cities that use the infrastructures as enabled by the system of *waqf*, the money or asset that is given by the devout for urbanisation, and they make a *ghanat,* which is a water irrigation system brought from the mountains to the city in order to enable urbanisation. All of this is produced as a result of focused Islamic devout belief in giving and sharing, and ultimately what it produces is what I consider a very primary modernity within the structure of the cities that it creates. So what I probably would say and what I hear from the presentations is that paradoxes of what we call modernity become much more palpable in architecture because of the fact that buildings do not do what they say, they do what they do and are always able to be appropriated.

I would say Abu Dhabi has nothing to do with Islam but has everything to do with capitalism and media at its most rampant. The fact is that it is in an Islamic place is a geographic accident. I wonder if we can call it Muslim at all. Abu Dhabi has nothing to do with Islamic culture. These paradoxes in modernity are part of what one has to accept. Maybe at the beginning of the 20th century when radio and telegraph and all of those beautiful machines were developing, we could be much more emphatic and positive, but we have kind of understood that it does not work as purely as it claims to.

Deniz Kandiyoti

My question remains unanswered. Is there any area we can define as the non-modern?

Masoud Kamali

Yes. According to definition of modernity the Dalai Lama is not modern, because he does not want to change people in the Tibet. The problem in Professor Kandiyoti's discussion is that she does not tell us if we can have modern states without democracy.

Deniz Kandiyoti

I do not have any problem with it myself. Yes, we can have a modern state without democracy.

Masoud Kamali

What is also missing here is the discussion of history of racism in Europe. *Europeanisation of Europe* that was published three years ago is a discussion of when Europe started to become Europe and against whom. You also wrote a book on infidels and the other-isation of history and the selection of history-telling. Islam has been a part of Europe as long as we have known Europe, Christianity and Islam. You have 500 years of Muslim rule in southern Europe, then you have the Ottoman Empire. When I was in Brussels two weeks ago, they were discussing the Ottomanisation of Europe. So I agree that the concept that West and Europe are constructions. What we did not discuss here is the concept of power. Who defines these concepts? Societies which were not a part of the West are now a part of the West. Poland for example, has now become part of the West.

I am conducting a European project called, "The European Dilemma" in which eight countries are engaged. When we started the project, Poland and Cyprus were part of the candidate states. So we are looking at what they are adopting from the West. The new waves of immigration within Europe and their impact on the guest and host societies are indeed interesting. History books and identities are changing. There is this continuous reconstruction of the identity against the others. We are not discussing the issue of colonialism either. What is the meaning of the West? How do you define the West? I think if we answer these questions, it is easier to go further. Modernity and modernisation are very clear in sociology. It might not be as clear for others. There is a core to it, and as Asef said, if we dismiss it, there is no reason for this discussion. We do not want to go back to post-modernity and de-construct everything.

Jacques Derrida and Michel Foucault famously discussed whether we are modern or not. What do we do about the apartheid in South Africa? Jacques Derrida said I cannot participate in the 1981 demonstration against apartheid in Paris, because I do not believe in this kind of construction. But in the morning he participated in the demonstration and when he was asked why, he replied, Because I cannot deny this problem. Today, the problem of Muslims in Europe is not the Muslims' problem. Muslims have always been a part of Europe. There is a new Orientalism going on. Wallerstein argues that colonial people are now part of us in our societies. The border of us/them is an internal border in the West. The "other" of England are not only countries like Iran, but also the northern part of [England].

Farid Panjwani

I would like to go back to the notion of modern and anti-modern as Professor Sadria was discussing and the responses of Professor Bayat and Professor Kandiyoti. Masoud (Kamali)... raised many questions and I will point to three of them. There was an earthquake in Pakistan and India in 2005. A debate took place after that earthquake which was very reminiscent of the debate that took place after the 1755 Lisbon earthquake, [which is] often called the first modern natural disaster, because a divide came out there. People like Voltaire argued we should understand this as a natural phenomenon and the other group said, no, this is divine punishment. The same kind of debate took place in Pakistan in 2005. Some people with an anti-modern attitude said the earthquake was because of the obscenity and westernisation. If, by Masoud's definition, I start to call this group modern, I will be left with no tools to make a distinction between these discourses. That is one question that I have.

The second issue I wanted to raise, referring to what was said about Derrida, is that I think ethics comes into this because these anti-modern movements are not simply an intellectual idea of being anti-modern but they also have social consequences. They deny some of the achievements made in modern times including equality of gender, anti-slavery and so on. If we accept them as part of [what is] modern, we lose the intellectual right to critique them. Is that something that we can live with? I think this goes back to what Masoud said about Derrida's issue with his own philosophy and practice.

The third issue I have is, who defines the anti-modern as modern? Because it is now moderns who are saying that anti-moderns are modern. The anti-moderns are not saying this and I think we are denying their own self-understanding of being anti-modern and saying, no, you are part of us. I think that goes against the very spirit of the idea of multiple modernities, the need to give others the right of self-definition. So these are the three difficulties I have with what Masoud suggests.

Charles Jencks

I understand that Deniz (Kandiyoti) wanted to be the devil's advocate but it appears that I am disagreeing with her. She argues that multiple modernities is a not a useful concept. Let me respond to that. I really think that we have to be historical here and see that the words modernity, modernism and modernisation have multiple meanings that arose in different ways. In a dictionary that was published in 1770, under the word modernism there is a quote from Shakespeare [defining] it as common, rubbish, vulgar, tat, and something you throw away. So the word "modern" [has not] not always meant what it means around this table: progressive, new, next, linear time, better than un-modern or anti-modern.

What I am saying here is that it would be silly and unhistorical to not have a historical consciousness. Take the battle of the ancients and the moderns in the 17th century or the revival, in the Renaissance, that Filarete and the architects, who used the word every 30 pages, had to say [that their] audience always forgets what they meant by modern, because what I mean by modern is the good revival of the ancient, the classical. He was actually saying that modern is ancient, it is the Italian revival of Rome. Two hundred years later the battle of the ancients and moderns [became] an internalised modernist debate. If we [were to] think of our discussion now on a meta level, we would see that we are having a modern debate about the word modern and we are having the same troubles: that it means multiple things. Sometimes anti-modern things can be very positive.

In 1980s David Harvey and others coined and managed to convince sociologists that the reactionary modernism of Hitler was real. Let us also admit that it referred to socialist, ecological, mass cultural improvements and that is why people went along with Hitler. This was anti-modern modern, regressive and certainly reactionary. But he was using and disputing the modern with "good modernism" if you like. I think we cannot not know that. I agree that it is a muddy, useless and changeable term, but I am convinced that it is going to be re-invented again and again, and we cannot deny it or get rid of it. I am convinced of that because people like Tony Blair, Sheikh Makhtoum and all politicians and people on the street [who are trying] to galvanise a global economy will use the word modern spontaneously again and again as an ideological word to mean progress and getting better. Why doesn't Blair say, "I want to anti-modernise the National Health Service"? He always says that he is going to modernise it. Modernise [in this sense] means to get better. Sixty years ago, when romantic classicism was brought into the corpus of modernity, modernism and modernisation, what were romantics? Where they modern or anti-modern? They were certainly anti-ninety percent of what was seen as modern. But then after twenty, thirty years they were seen as the true moderns. You cannot talk about modernism without talking about romanticism and anti-modernism anymore. Léon Krier, who was teaching here at the AA (Architectural Association School of Architecture), was a very good anti-modernist. We used to call him the Ayatollah. He was really intolerant and negative in many respects. He broke the dishes and destroyed many things. And at certain points his arguments were brilliantly good in a modernist way, because they showed what was wrong with the modern city as conceived by modern architects. I think, for a short time, his anti-modernism was incredibly modern and progressive, but has become reactionary.

Homa Farjadi

You brought this up brilliantly. Of course, there is a difference between modernity and modernism which has been described very well in architecture. Léon Krier might be bashing modernism while bringing an aspect of modernity. He might be arguing against modernism's styles, but not modernism's devices. I think it is worth separating them. I am not personally bunching them together.

Masoud Kamali

We talked about anti-modernity and Ayatollahs. But the problem is that Ayatollahs are not anti-modern. They are very modern. That is where the whole discussion of anti-modernity really started. Hans Joas has a book called *War and Modernity: Studies in the History of Violence in the 20th Century*. He argues that modernity and modernisation has two sides: over-side of modernity and under-side of modernity. Over-side of modernity, according to him, is individualisation, democracy, human rights and so on. But modernity has another side, and that is the collective solutions for the problems that the modernity itself creates. These collective solutions are Fascism, Nazism, etc. You have leaders of revolutions who want to solve the problems that modernity itself creates. These two sides of modernity always go hand in hand.

Today, you have racist parties in governments of twelve European countries. What do they want? It is a collective solution to human problems. If they have power, they can do whatever they want. Khomeini, as a radical clergy, has a different collective solution to human problems. Communism, Marxism, liberalism and market economy are among the other collective solutions to problems.

Deniz Kandiyoti

Let me push this debate forward by backtracking from "Why Modernity?" and bringing in other perspectives. The whole idea of modernity as progress, modernity as nationalism, and modernity as Enlightenment, not only has another side, which is colonialism, racism, etc., but represents some kind of a metaphysical break. This is the idea that was put about by critiques of modernity, that it is a particular way of apprehending the world that breaks completely with what goes before it, that it is the world as representation, the meta-physical creation of an inside and an outside.

Of course there are some institutional consequences that float from this, which is that society becomes an object of intervention. You measure it, you make maps, you take population censuses, and a sort of deployment of disciplinary power comes with it. But basically this the way of talking about modernity and modern orders, which, far from looking at it as an anticipatory or liberatory enterprise looks at it as a new form of governmentality, coercion, discipline and social engineering. The Soviet model is a good example, because it has such a clear blueprint of social engineering laid in words like progress, the forward march of history and so on. But somehow the idea is that the modernity itself is violence, and a modern project is a violent project. I am just starting this and I am not going to reveal what I think about it myself. I will keep this for later, but I would like to put this on the table. I sort of find it de-problematic in many ways.

Charles Jencks

What about the *Modernity and the Holocaust*, the book by Zygmunt Bauman? Do you accept the close relations between modernity and the Holocaust?

Deniz Kandiyoti

Well, at one level, yes. Technology made the Holocaust possible.

Charles Jencks

What about Marshal Berman's *All That Is Solid Melts Into Air*? He is saying that modernity is violent. It is actually the violence of society and economy against itself.

Masoud Kamali

We cannot discuss modernity without the discussion of war. War and modernity go hand in hand.

Asef Bayat

Maybe one part of the problem we have regarding the anti-modern being modern and so on is that we do not perceive modernity as a contradictory entity. So you are either against it or for it. For instance, regarding Ayatollahs as modern can be right in some way and wrong in another way. The fact that literacy and education have [been] enhanced during the Islamic Republic of Iran and that women are public players in today's Iran are modern aspects of the Ayatollahs' governance. But abrogating the individual rights that women already had and taking them away is not modern.

To me, this is a step backwards, because I think rights are very important. We should see modernity as a contradictory entity. So those who you consider anti-modern might not actually be anti-modern. They might be correctors because, as I said, modernity has benefits and costs, and they want to cover the costs. As Habermas suggests, modernity is an 'unfinished project'. Those who we consider anti-modern are actually finishing the project of modernity.

Fatemeh Hosseini-Shakib

You are all my masters, so if you allow me, I would like to ask a few questions instead of making comments. My first question is, What makes a country a modern country? What are the elements that have to gather in one country to make it modern? What is it that should be modern in a country? The people? The government? The society?

We know that Islam is not against modernisation and it is almost certainly not against modernisation in architecture. Although modern architecture has trespassed on Islamic values of Muslims and they have been victims of modernisation, they are still not against modernisation. Why not base our modernity on modern thought, reasoning, secularisation, logic and so on? What about modern individuals? What about an individual who, as Professor Bayat said, wants to be modern but cannot afford the costs of modernity because of the current political system? What kind of a person and country is this? Do you count the desire to become modern in your calculations about the degree of modernity in a society? What do you do with a nation which is far ahead of the government? I think it is a modern country, I am not sure if it is Western modernity or anything else, for several reasons and it is not because it fails to have democracy, which I see as a part of Western modernity. Are we just negating the whole thing?

Political Islam in Iran has unconsciously used modern mechanisms for their non-modern or anti-modern goals. Many of the modern tools and mechanisms brought by the Islamic Republic motivated the new generation to become modern. For example, when I was going to school during the Shah's era, the textbooks of our Islamic education courses comprised of stories of prophets and imams and Islamic ethics. But after the Islamic Revolution these books were packed with all these ideas of materialism, communism, nihilism, liberalism, etc, and Islam was introduced as a better discourse and refuting and rebutting all the mentioned ideologies.

As a result, we unconsciously learned that there are other ideologies and we learned to argue against those Islamic values. My grandmother nagged me, saying that this Islamic government is showing you that communism and liberalism and democracy exist. Before the revolution, we were only taught about God, no one explained religion, but after the Revolution everyone learned to question the official interpretation of Islam. The Islamic government is not saying that we are not interested in women's rights. They say that they are interested in it in the right way. How about the semi – or quasi – democracies, semi-elections and other semi-modern things in a country like Iran? How can we negate all this?

Stefan Weber

I would like to stress again that modernity is the very process of becoming modern, whether you like it or not. And this process is a connected process. For example, global warming is something that happens and we cannot deny it. This global warming has consequences, no matter what you call it, modern or anti-modern, because it exists and it exists because it is interconnected. Global warming would never have existed if this inter-connectedness was not there. The process of modernity expresses itself in different moments, different places, and in different layers.

Masoud Kamali

While Professor Bayat says that Ayatollahs are not modern because they take away the individual's rights, I say that they are modern exactly because they do that. Hitler did it; Fascism did it. 'Modern' is the collective answer to human problems. For instance, Paul Wolfowitz believes that if you have an educated leader, you do not need democracy and rights. To him, democracy costs too much. You and I may not like Nazism, Fascism and Wolfowitz, but we cannot deny that they are modern. When the Nazist party took power in Denmark, they took away the individual rights of people who had not been in Denmark for seven years to return to their homes. In Sweden we have 5,000 immigrants per week coming from Denmark because the Nazists are not in power in Sweden. Modernity is not necessarily good. There is always a challenge between the two sides of modernity. The ways the Ayatollahs are solving social problems are modern. You may say it is not the same as in England or Sweden, but you cannot deny it is modern. Even in Sweden, we have sociologists coming from the USA who say Sweden is not democratic, because the laws of the welfare system control everything...

Asef Bayat

But I do not understand what makes the abrogation of laws modern? You seem to have a peculiar definition of a modern state.

Masoud Kamali

To me the modern state is a state that changes and reorganises society. Before the modern era, states did not change and reorganise societies.

Charles Jencks

I have just finished my book about critical modernism and came to the conclusion that by the 1920s all the modernisms, which were many and were competing against each other, became what I call 'prefix modernisms'. The words modern and modernism were too messy, and therefore, they invented all these prefixes. Some of these prefix modernities, however, were invented after the fact, like 'reactionary modernism'. The argument that Hitler, Franco, Mussolini, and Stalin were reactionary modernists, and William Krier was a positive modernist, who became a reactionary modernist, is now completely traditional and conceivable and known. It is not an unknown argument; it has been around for more than 40 years. The most upsetting book is *Modernity and the Holocaust* by Zygmunt Bauman that takes Weber seriously. It says ok, instrumental reason: we have to take away your rights because there are massive problems here, and it is reasonable to do that. So you find here, the dark side of modernity. There really is a dark side to modernity and no one is disputing that anymore.

We are prefix modernists. All this reminds of the French Revolution done in anti-costume and Roman dress. It also reminds of the American Revolution, which was again done in classical costume, and the cases in which you dressed up and killed your father and mother just as the French Revolution did. That is how the Catholic Church, the French and American revolutions, and the West, in its terrible dirty, bloody, revolutionary modernisation, work. It seems to me that is very much how the new improved detergent works today. It is also why Abu Dhabi is challenging Dubai, because it is very real problem in Abu Dhabi, it has all the oil for the next 300 years but Dubai has managed to control these other things, which are growing much faster than Abu Dhabi. The people of Abu Dhabi are behind, and that is why they have commissioned all these good modern architects, celebrities and elites to catch [them] up. You might think it is an accident that it is in a Muslim land, but I do not think so. Let me go back to the issue of tea and opium. Opium was the best money that the world market could buy, because it was small and people wanted it. So it was the world's money market in 1820, the opium of the masses was really opium and really money. I think that it is still driving the system. I suppose I am becoming a vulgar Marxist.

Homa Farjadi

I hear all these different arguments and it looks as though that we can go back and say the Ayatollahs, Abu Dhabi, and Turkmenistan are doing different versions of modernity, but are we really talking about the same values here? Is the mere fact that they are all going forward supposed to mean that they are looking for the same human being or values? I agree that at the end we do want to say that there is a difference in their programmes, ideals and definitions of what humanity or dignity of the individual is all about. I would think that although they might have used the same instruments to reach their goals, they were looking for different things, and it is worth defining that and making a distinction somewhere.

Masoud Kamali

No, I do not think that they are looking for different things. They are all into organising society for solving collective problems. Of course, you have different kinds of solutions to collective problems…

Homa Farjadi

Is that a value-free way solving problems?

Masoud Kamali

No, a value-free society is a myth. Nothing is value-free, even our discussion here. What I am saying is that you may not like the kind of modernity that Iran has, but you cannot call it non-modern because women have not the same rights as in England and political rights are not like [they are] in England.

Homa Farjadi

So you think that modernity is an instrument, not a value?

Masoud Kamali

Different modernities have different values. Shmuel N. Eisenstadt, for example, argues that in the Soviet Union you are creating a socialist man. The socialist man has a value. In Germany, you are killing the disabled, because a good human being has to be handsome, beautiful and strong. Obviously humans have values, but you are implying that there are values that all humans share. This is not true. As Charles Taylor says, we always have conflict of values.

Deniz Kandiyoti

I really want to go back to Fatemeh (Hosseini-Shakib's) intervention. She was trying to tell us something and we cannot leave it there. I want to share with you an anecdote about Iran which I am still thinking about and cannot solve. I was full of these understandings that you can have different kinds of feminisms, which take different phases, and I went to Tehran for the first time. After a conference I was talking to a number of young girls who were all veiled. Iran is the only country in the world in which you can be very strictly veiled and look beautiful. They were about the age at which they must have been raised entirely under the Islamic Republic. So I thought they would not know the difference. I told them that I am very impressed by women in Iran and they started complaining and telling me that it is not like this. Suddenly, and this is where I want reflection, one of them turned to me and said, "Why can't we just be normal?" She did not say, 'Western', she said 'normal'. We have to think about this.

This young woman, subjectively, was experiencing what she was being subjected to as anomalous and abnormal. People are sitting in the West talking about 'Western feminism', while this girl in Iran, who knew nothing about 'Western feminism' and was raised under Khomeini regime, also wants the same thing and uses the word normal in referring to women's rights. She asked, Why can't we be normal? I had no answer for this. It had never occurred to [me to] think in those terms.

Her choice of the word normal was really interesting. I asked her where she was born. She said, In Iran, after the revolution. I said, Isn't this normal? She said, No, it is not normal. I am not making a value judgment. I am putting on the table word by word what I got from this young woman. What I asked was this: How is it that a young woman, who has known no other regime than Khomeini's regime, explains her state not in terms of feminism, modernity or democracy, but normality. This is what struck me, the use of the word normal.

Farrokh Derakhshani

It is very interesting that we are talking about what the individual and society thinks of these definitions. I think it is very important to note that each human being has got different layers, and at each moment some of these layers move up and down. And at certain moments in ones life or a society's life, these layers solidify and that is where people or societies can go wrong. But this is something that does not continue for good. The important question is, How do people and societies identify themselves?

There is a related anecdote which is interesting. Shirin Akiner – an expert on Central Asia, told me that one day in the 1990s she was sitting in her office in SOAS talking to some people from Kyrgyzstan. [They] told her that they were very upset, because since television had come to Kyrgyzstan, women were becoming more traditionalist and religious and were increasingly wearing *hijab*. She asked, Which television do you watch in Kyrgyzstan, is it the Iranian television? They responded, No, the Turkish television. She asked, Why? They said, Because the Turkish television has got all these shows and these are exactly the problem, because you do not understand us. When these singers with décolleté are shown on the TV shows, we consider them from Moscow; they are not us. But when they show people that are watching the singer, most of them are wearing veils, we identify ourselves with them. They do not identify themselves with the dancer who is half-naked, but with the religious audience.

It is interesting how one identifies oneself in a certain time in this world. People like Sheikh Makhtoum identify themselves as modern, there is nothing that is modern which belongs to someone else, they want to have *all* the modern. The same thing was going on in my generation in Iran. When I was going to university in Tehran in the 1970s, we never thought that we had anything less than other friends of mine who had come back form UCLA or London. Not only that, we thought we had another layer that they lacked. Therefore, we thought that we were superior to the Westerners, because we had more layers and were aware of them. So it all goes back to this different layers and how it works in one's mind in one moment.

Modernism is an evolution, and it is the speed of that evolution at different moments which matters. Who are the actors who are pushing some parts of each layer to go forward? And that is when modernity happens between normality. You always have this interplay of normal evolution and modernity. In social sciences, you can forget whatever is said about societies when it passes. What was said in the 1960s or 1970s was said and is now finished. But buildings remain and you cannot get rid of them. You may be able to get rid of many social and economic problems and theoretical discussions, but buildings remain as a part of reality. That is why the built environment from previous periods and thoughts can have a negative impact. The whole idea of going back and living in an old house is a very modern idea. Only for someone who lives in an urban area, living in old houses might be attractive.

Charles Jencks

Marx did say that alienation brings consciousness. In fact, consciousness is a form of alienation, because when you are conscious of two different states and you compare them as a modern shopper, you develop a shopping mentality, which I think is highly developed in Dubai. In the 19th century, they used things like gold and they were great traders. And today, it is said that shopping develops your brain. In any case, to jump from that to consciousness as a critical consciousness, and coming out of modernity, my feeling is that this argument is now so compressed everywhere that, on the one hand, everybody is fed up with it and bored with modernity, modernism, but on the other hand it keeps coming back like a fever every so often and [even] gets raised. This is because it occupies a semantic space so strongly that even if you want to kill it and say, let us not talk about it for ten years, you will not be successful. It will be reinvented tomorrow, like God, it keeps getting reinvented despite its death.

That is why I put forward both the critical modernism and prefix modernisms in which values come in. We all have very strong values, there is no question. And my view is that [if you] compress modernisms and you make it conscious, when modern artists are conscious of all the moves they can make, they become hyper-conscious and they may get very boring as artists, but they cannot get rid of the anxiety of the modern. This anxiety is just there, because of the market, progress, being taken over, tenure, etc. We are living in that culture of anxiety. And in that sense, modernisation is a driving force. We may be able to lessen its violence, but it is going to go on. So what matters is the prefix. If we call ourselves different kinds of modernists, then we can define the values to ourselves consciously and say, I am not a reactionary modernist, I believe in this and this. So we realise that there is this possibility of choice.

Even if the term modern is too messy and you want to get rid of it, it is going to be reinvented, and therefore prefix matters. And I would argue that the critical is deep in the tradition. In other words, the critical comes out of the condition of consciousness, alienation and the problem of modernity. That is why I say fundamentalism is a modern movement, look at Hamas, look at places where fundamentalism has a strong hold, and you will see that it is precisely what Masoud said. It is answering all these collective problems in a very real sense; it is feeding people, it is clothing...

Farrokh Derakhshani

Yesterday, I saw this photo of a young man who was an advocate of Hamas. He had a very western look, with a lot of gel in his hair and no beard, and a t-shirt on with the Hamas logo on it. This photo was very interesting for me, because it showed that being in Hamas today does not necessarily mean looking traditional.

Masoud Kamali

In the universities of Turkey, it is forbidden to wear *hijab*. Many Turkish women take away their scarf in the university and put it back on when they go out. They are actually protesting and saying we do not want to be normal as you say. The interesting thing about Turkey is that although there were seventy years of Kamalism and hard secularisation, Islamic parties have won the elections in each and every election that has been held in the country. That is a dilemma, Are they reactionary? Are they not responding to collective problems? Now everyone agrees that the current government of Turkey is the most progressive government it has ever had after the World War.

In Europe, it is perfectly normal to have two parties in power for 40 years or more, like in Germany and the UK. In Sweden political parties come and even change the religious books and say that Christianity is normal, but Islam is nothing. Do you call this modern or not? The thing is how we look at the normality. As Pierre Bourdieu says, we make the normal; he talks about the habituation of normality. I think it is very dangerous to go into this discussion of normal and abnormal.

Deniz Kandiyoti

You have to understand that the word normality was not used by me. I was expressing my surprise at the young woman's choice of words. What is happening in Turkey is something quite different, because in Turkey what you have, unlike Iran, is a government where women have choice. I have this famous story of a Turkish colleague who decided to do a conference… He invited a bunch of Iranian colleagues. The Iranian invitees decided to come by bus. So they got in the bus and all the women were veiled, but when they passed the Turkish frontier, all the women unveiled. However, there was a woman sitting there who was not unveiled. They told her, Hey! We are over the Turkish border. And she responded: I know, I am Turkish.

This is an important story, because here was a woman who was actually exercising choice. She was a woman who had decided that she wanted to veil for whatever reasons. The Turkish state makes it impossible for these women to exercise their choices in the universities, and they militantly protest again exercising their choice. This is a very interesting case, because Islamist parties win elections by default. When you look at the statistics, the vote that Islamist parties take has never exceeded the maximum of 34%. There has been a big nationwide survey in Turkey where people were asked, "How would you rate yourself in terms of religiosity?" 65 – 68% of people said they are very religious and devout. Next question: how many of you would favour a state based on the Sharia? Only less than 2% responded positively. We are talking about a very complex sociological phenomenon.

In Turkey you have a society where people would like to practice their religion and beliefs freely including veiling, but they are at the same time very clear about not wanting a state that will tell them what to do.

Masoud Kamali

I do not agree with that. This is against what is said in the books that we use.

Deniz Kandiyoti

This is empirically established that Turkish society is totally clear that it does not want a state based on the Sharia. Turkey has been misrepresented hugely. One of the things that I find very depressing is how stereotyped everything is that is being put about. You have this completely simplistic and distorted picture of Turkey in which there is military secularist top-downers, bureaucrats, Islamists, democracy and the people. Nothing could be further from the truth. This depiction is, sociologically, pure rubbish. A lot of books written about Turkey, media and television are propagating this distorted image of Turkey. So there are complexities and here we come back to what Professor Homa Farjadi was saying about the issue of values. Do we accept a form of rules where the power of the state is brought to bear on the latitude of choices that people are allowed to make? The authoritarian part of the Turkish state does use that power against the girls who want to veil inside universities, but of course it is much softer compared to societies where the police go around beating people and sending them home if they do not veil correctly. These women in Turkey still have a way of protesting and they are not thrown in jail for doing so. It is not perfect, but there is a degree of pluralism.

Masoud Kamali

No, this is not true. They hang people in the street. In 1916, 1922, 1944, 1968 among other dates, the Turkish government killed people in the street.

Deniz Kandiyoti

No, we are talking about today's Turkey. We are not talking about the military coup. We are talking about the legal disposition of the country vis-à-vis people choosing different lifestyles and, even though there is state secularism, at the moment nobody is being hanged or stoned or thrown into jail as far as I know. I think that this is part of trying to be a pluralist democracy. What the people who demonstrated on the street had against the Islamic government was the fact that they had started to encroach upon that area of latitude. They started slowly doing things, and the people went to the streets and the slogans were, 'Neither the army, nor the Sharia. This was the voice of civil society, saying we would like a society where we can freely choose what we want to do.

Charles Jencks

Exactly; people are slightly more sophisticated than the analysts.

Fatemeh Hosseini-Shakib

I would like to reflect on that issue of normality. I have been raised in Iran and [was] there until 2002. So I think I have the right to say what that girl means by saying, Why can't we be normal?. Wearing what you want or not covering your hair is the norm in almost all parts of the planet. What she meant was simply, Why we cannot be like all other women in the world? And then look at the history of what we call *Manto*, a long dress with which most women cover their body in Iran. It started from a very simple thing, you just had to cover your body with it, and there was no talk of its length, tightness and colour. But the women gradually changed this long and loose dress, and made it shorter and tighter with brighter colours. One can even make an animation of the gradual changes of *Manto*. The *Manto* causes practical problems in the cold and warm weather, and it looks ridiculous because it is simply not normal. But there is also another side to it.

Although women's clothes in Iran are not normal, other aspects of their lives are normal. After all, 64% of students in Iran are women now. This was not the case before the Islamic Revolution, because people who were religious did not trust the government and did not send their children to universities. I think this real presence of Iranian women in almost all social spheres is a tangible element of modernity.

Iranian Islamic Modernities

MASOUD KAMALI

Multiple Modernities

The resurgence of modernisation theory in post-WWII engaged many social scientists in an effort to plot the world's development on a linear axis. Modernisation theorists tried to integrate different parts of their theory into a coherent theoretical system that would serve to explain, in Weberian tradition, the *uniqueness* of Western civilisation in contrast to other civilisations, in such cases as they recognised other societies as civilisations. They were generally West-centric intellectuals who saw the West as, in the words of Paul Valery, "the pearl of the globe" (Kingston-Mann Esther, 1999:3).

Such an effort to see the contemporary West as the goal of human history put the theoretical uniqueness and constitution of "the West" on the research agenda of many universities and research centres. The major body of research conducted by modernisation theorists was not concerned about the internal differences among western countries but rather what constituted an internally coherent ideal type of "the West" and focused on the differences between this and non-Western countries. The rather heterogeneous developments of Western countries, developmental patterns called the French model, English model, German model, Swedish model, and so forth, were not the main subject of research or interest in a world where the narcissistic and capitalistic West was facing its rival, the "Socialist World". The socialist world was considered the Eastern enemy and, as such, non-modern. The fact that the "communist enemies" were as modern as the "Western capitalist friends" and that there hardly existed "a West" but rather several Western patterns of socioeconomic and cultural developments was neglected in the comparative research based on the modernisation theory model.

These theorists promoted the universalism of the Western experiment and saw it as a blueprint for non-Western countries to follow. This formed part of the post-colonial world's, and the former "colonialists", attitudes towards "the rest". Many evolutionist social theorists, and in particular sociologists, tried to present it as the only way towards a lasting system for all human societies and thus the ultimate goal of history. It is not only classical modernist theorists such as Hegel, Spencer, Marx, and Weber, who believed in the triumph of modern "reason in History", but contemporary sociologists, such as Francis Fukuyama and *his* ideas about "The End of History", Anthony Giddens "Modernity as our destiny", and others, such as Habermas and Beck who believed, and still believe, that this modernity is the final solution to human problems. The only variety that some of these scholars, such as Habermas and Beck, could accept as part of the global modernity project were capitalist or socialist modernities. This is still the problem of biased assumption regarding the "uniqueness" of the "West" and the West-centric understanding of modern(isation's) history.

The newly established concept of multiple modernities indicates that the features and forces of modernity can potentially be received and developed in different ways in different countries. Furthermore, the assumption that modernity has an entirely European origin is not reconcilable with historical developments. For instance conscription, which was developed in Europe both by French and English governments, is an Ottoman invention which existed long before Europe in the Ottoman Empire (Kamali 2006). Or the so well-admired freedom of religion, also an Islamic phenomenon. Freedom of religion has been a part of Islamic models of governance both in the Ottoman and Persian empires. Bazaars in Muslim countries have been at the heart of pre-modern and in many cases of the modern cities. Many features of the modern capitalist economy were part of Muslim cities and framed the life of Muslim individuals. In addition, the businessmen of the bazaar have not been exclusively Muslims, Jews have also been and still are, in countries such as Iran, a part of the bazaar. Contrary to the classics of social sciences modernity was not been an exclusively western invention, but has had non-western features and forces.

A theoretical perspective of multiple modernities should play up divergence and heterogeneity rather than homogeneity, and therefore must be a challenge to any simple dualistic, and (in relation to each other) paradoxical, models, such as Occident/Orient, modern/traditional, gemenschaft/geselschaft, Christian/Muslim, and universal/particular. Alongside this, it must also challenge the generalising concepts of Otherisation, such as the holistic imagination of the existence of a simple and homogeneous "Muslim World" or the claimed lack of civil society in the "Muslim World". This conjectural method of Otherising Muslims and Muslim societies seems to be experiencing a revival in the post-September 11th 2001 political arena, in the form of the "new Orientalism".

Iranian Modernities

Iran has gone through several modernisations periods with different modernising actors. During the reign of Qajar dynasty (1795–1925) several statesmen introduced modernisation programmes, such as the establishment of new industries, reformation of the army and the bureaucratic system, the establishment of modern school system, the reformation and modernisation of the financial system, and many attempts to reform the corrupted monarchy. One of the most important movements during the reign of the Qajars was the constitutional movement and revolution (1905–1909) by which a democratic constitutional regime replaced the monarchy dictatorship and introduced many modern reforms. However, one can not see the modernisation programmes during the Qajars as one homogeneous modernity, but as different understandings of modernity and consequently different programmes. Meanwhile some of the Qajar statesmen, such as Abbas Mirza (d. 1833) in early nineteenth century, wanted to copy some of the modern institutions of England, France or/and Belgium, others, such as Amir Kabir, who was Prime Minister in 1848-1851, had the intention to modernise the country from within by providing governmental support to national manufactures.

The constitutional modernity started in 1905 was mainly political. Constitutionalism, establishment of new parties, the conflicts and cooperation between political rivals, such as the monarch, the parliament, socialists mainly gathered in the Social Democratic party (Hezb-e ejtemaiyon va amiyon), and Muslim leaders, who played a central role in the Constitutional Revolution, militant secularists, and the armed force of the Cossack Brigade). These groups disputed over which model of modernity should be established in Iran. While some advocated a completely liberal and secular regime, socialists intended to establish a socialist regime, and some other liberals claimed an Islamic modernity in which Islam and Muslim leaders play a role. The situation was worsened by the interventions of the English and Russians, which led to the military coup of 1922 led by the commander of the Cossack Brigade, Reza Khan Pahlavi, which turned down the Qajar dynasty and established the monarchy of Pahlavis (1924–1979).

The Pahlavis' modernisation programmes are among the most lasting and thoroughgoing changes in the modern history of Iran. The first Pahlavi, Reza Shah (1924–1941) introduced several modernisation programmes such as the creation of new industries, a modern and permanent army, a modern educational system, emancipation of women for participation in educational system, labor market and social life, the establishment of a modern health care system, the construction of a modern infrastructure for communication and trade, and security for citizens. He changed the traditional relations with "Old colonial Europe" of England, Russia and France and approached the "New Europe" of Germany. England and Russia took this as an excuse for military intervention in Iran, leading to the replacement of Reza Shah with his son Muhammad Reza Shah (1941–1979). His first decade in Power was marked by the weakness of the central government and the establishment of democratic governments. The coinciding period of modernisation (1941–1953) was mainly political. Many political parities and groups could mobilise new classes which were mainly created by Reza Shah's reforms and struggled for seizure of the political power. The Premiership of the liberal nationalist leader of the National Front of Iran (NFI) Muhammad Mosaddeq in 1951 and the nationalisation of oil industries went against the imperialist interests of the USA and England who in accordance with their post-colonial programmes and intentions launched a military coup against the democratic government of Mosaddeq in 1953. This led in the arrest and execution of many political leaders and the establishment of the Shah's long standing dictatorship.

Political stability and the support of the USA for Shah's regime provided an auspicious situation for the start of many rapid modernisation programmes that can best be called the westernisation of the country. Rapid modernisation, the lack of democratic participation of people, mass movement of lower-rank people from rural areas to the cities, a growing urban population, and the creation of shanty towns in major cities led to social and political mobilisation against Shah that resulted in the Islamic Revolution of 1977-1979 (Kamali, 1998, 2001, 2006).

The political victory of the 1979 revolution brought to power a revolutionary, though provisional, government led by the liberal Prime Minister Mehdi Bazargan. The new government was strongly under the influence of the charismatic leader of the revolution, Ayatollah Khomeini. However, many of the members of the new government belonged to different political parties and organisations and had their own models for the establishment of a new system. On the other hand, there were other influential groups who were not directly members of the new government, but part of the new revolutionary leadership, with their own paramilitary groups gathered in Revolutionary Committees (*Komite-haye enghelab*) and Revolutionary Guards (*Sepahe pasdarane enghelabe eslami*). These groups' plans and models for replacement of the *anciene regime* will be discussed later. In order to provide a comprehensive presentation of modernisation projects that the Islamic Republic of Iran introduced and the challenges to different modernisation programmes that form today's Iran, we have to start by a short historical overview of post-World War II modernities in Iran.

Iranian Islamic Modernities

Islam and Islamic groups with different worldviews and interpretations of Islam have always been part of modernisation discourse in Iran. I have elsewhere discussed that the established colonial understanding of an incompatibility between Islam and democracy and "modernity" is a false theory generated by west-centric social scientists. The belief in the *uniqueness* of the West is nothing but an illusion. This "great illusion" has dominated social sciences for a long time and misled many researchers who were investigating the differences between "west and the rest", in particular between the imagined "unique West" and the imagined "Muslim World" (Kamali, 1998, 2001, 2006).

The modern history of Iran including the Constitutional Revolution (1905–1909), Liberal nationalist movement of 1940s, and the Islamic Revolution (1907–1909) witnessed the active participation of groups with Islamic beliefs in modernisation movements and developments in Iran (Algar, 1969; Arjomand 1984, 1988; Kamali, 1998, 2006).

One of the most important properties of modern sociopolitical movements in Iran has been the centrality of the relationship between the Ulama (religious scholars and leaders) and bazaris (merchants and guilds who gathered in bazaars of Iranian cities). Historically, bazaris needed the ulama for legitimisation of their businesses and activities and the ulama needed bazaris' economic support for their religious activities (Arjomand, 1984; Kamali 1998). However, the economic interests of bazaris have not always been in line with the interests of the ulama. The capitalist modern changes that included the engagement of bazaars (the traditional economic centre of each Islamic city) with the world capitalist system created a situation for bazaris that needed new orientations and strategies. Paradoxically this brought the bazaris and the ulama closer in some cases and increased the gap between them in others. As the modern political scene became more complicated, the relationship between the bazaris and the ulama became even more differentiated.

The political events during the reign of the liberal government of Muhammad Mosaddeq (1951–1953) witnessed such changes in the position of the bazaar in relation to the ulama. Although the most influential member of the ulama, Ayatollah Kashani, participated in the modern political struggles during the democratic period of 1941–1953, he opposed Mosaddeq in 1952. The bazaris did not support Kashani in his opposition. When Mosaddeq presented a bill to the Majlis concerning the increase of the legal authority of the prime minister and the opposition in Majlis managed to stop him, the bazaar of Tehran arranged large demonstrations supporting Mosaddeq (Azimi, 1989: 189). In the face of the more complicated society of modern Iran, the indigenous civil society of Iran, based on the close relationship between the bazaars and the ulama, started to lose ground. The ulama faced new challenges from both the more liberal Muslim leaders such as Mosaddeq and more radical young groups, such as *Fadaiyan-e islam* (Islamic warriors).

The democratic period of 1941–1953 challenged the traditional Shia doctrine of divided authority between the indigenous civil society and the state. Even those from the ulama who had decided to participate in modern civil society had to consider the multiplicity of the structure of authority in contemporary Iran. The authority was divided among three main actors, namely the government, the Shah, and the Majlis. Hence, the complexity of the new socio-political reality, and the absence of a new theological justification for the role of the ulama in the new society, left the political sphere to the new political groups such as liberals, nationalists, religious radical fanatics, and communists. It did not, however, mean that the clergy left the political arena. Some of the ulama participated in the democratic challenges to restore the Constitution. Some more radical religious groups, such as *Fadaiyan-e Islam*, used violence against the political and cultural elites as a political means for influencing the course of politics. Other religious radicals, meanwhile, such as Mahmoud Taleqani and the Society of Muslim Warriors, enjoined the NFI. This meant that the new socio-political mosaic of Iran could not be simplified by the traditional categories used by the ulama to justify their authority in modern society.

Although clergy had participated in modern movements and modern ideological and theological challenges since seventeenth century, two periods of Iranian modern history were more crucial for clergy's theological modernisation. The first period was the years of civil war on constitutionalism between 1906 and 1909. The military coup of Muhammad Ali Shah, supported by foreign powers, and the overthrow of the constitutional government led to a bloody civil war in young constitutional Iran. During this period some of the prominent ulama, such as Ayatollah Hai'ri, Ayatollah Tabatabai and Ayatollah Behbahani, participated in the struggle against anti-constitutionalists led by Muhammad Ali Shah by providing theological justification for constitutionalism. On the other hand, there were some of the ulama, such as Ayatollah Nouri, who opposed constitutionalism. The prominence of the constitutionalist ulama and their popularity, and theological justification of constitutionalism, isolated the anti-constitutional and conservative ulama. Ayatollah Nouri was arrested by the victorious constitutionalists and executed after the victory of constitutionalist forces in 1909. The second period was the years of the re-establishment of democracy between 1941 and 1953. The main actors of this period were Jenhe-ye azadi-ye iran (National Front of Iran, NFI), under the leadership of Muhammad Mosaddeq, and the communist, pro-Soviet Tudeh Party.

Some of the leading Ulama, such as Shari'at Sangilaji (1890–1943) criticised some clergy for being backward, conservative, and harming Islam. He believed that Islam and modernity are compatible and that the established ulama opposed to this are a danger for Islam. The internal conflicts of the ulama and the rapid development of the country and the appearance of new social groups, such as urban middle and the working classes and new leftist ideologies, together with new alliances between the bazaars and the nationalist and democratic groups, gathered in the NFI, marginalised the ulama in the political scene of the 1940s and early 1950s. This was also due to prominent ulama, such as Ayatollah Boroujerdi, prohibiting the ulama from participation in the "dirty matter of politics". This set the stage for radical changes among religious groups in Iranian society. The ulama faced a new powerful non-clerical group of young and radical groups with Islamic worldviews which propagated radical revolutionary changes in society.

The democratic period of 1941–1953 witnessed the rapid differentiation of the Iranian polity. Many new groups and parties claimed legitimacy based on new political ideas and ideologies. Liberals, nationalists, republicans, conservatives, royalists, communists, radical youth religious groups, and the ulama were among the most active groups of the time. The increasing conflicts in the opposition to the Shah, in particular the conflict between Liberal nationalists gathered in the NFI under the leadership of Prime Minister Mosaddeq on the one side, and some religious groups by the leadership of ayatollah Kashani and the pro-Soviet communist Tudeh party on the other side, paved the way for the Military coup of the summer of 1953. Shah succeeded to regain the political control by the American-supported military coup of 1953. Mosaddeq was imprisoned and many other political activists were arrested and executed.

The period after the coup of 1953 until the victory of the Islamic revolution of 1979 was mainly devoted to many socioeconomic modernisation reforms which in its main structure followed the reforms of Reza Shah (1924–1941). The new Shah, Muhammad Reza, continued his father's economic policy in "destroying the social power of the ulama", namely the traditional sectors of society. Many of the ulama's sources of income, such as vaqf properties, came under state control. The traditional allies of the ulama, such as the bazaris, also remained subject to state pressure, the state wishing to destroy their socioeconomic power. The Shah explicitly spelt out his intentions for reducing the position of bazaars in the society through economic development. He believed that the bazaris were a fanatic lot, highly resistant to change because their locations afford a lucrative monopoly (Milani, 1994:63).

Not only the bazaris, but also the ulama faced a decrease in both number and importance. During the period 1960 to 1968, the number of madrasahs dwindled from 252 to 138; the

number of *tullab* (religious students) was reduced, from 14419 to 7482 (Akhavi, 1980:187)
The clergy felt that they were slowly losing their influence in one of the only spheres of public
life in which the regime had permitted them to continue to be active: religious education.
The Shah's reforms and political attacks succeeded in undermining both their position and
influence in Iranian society. The Shah accomplished the conversion of the ulama into a
déclassé stratum (Ibid, 132).

Some of the ulama did not remain silent. The death in 1962 of ayatollah Brujerdi, the most
prominent ulama in the country, inspired many radical ulama, such as his student, ayatollah
Khomeini, to break their silence and engage in open political activities. The defeat of the
revolt of 1963, led by Khomeini, made it more obvious to the ulama that their hegemony
in the Iranian polity was broken and that they never could win any political victory without
cooperation with other political and socioeconomic groups in society. Their traditional allies,
the bazaris, were not as significant as they were in pre-Pahlavi period. New modern middle
classes, radical non-clergy groups, nationalists, and liberals were also significant. The NFI
and later Jebhe-ye azadi-ye iran (Liberation Movement of Iran, LMI) by the leadership of
Mehdi Bazargan, who became the first Prime Minister of the Islamic Republic, were attractive
alternatives to the bazaris.

Many religious modernists, such as Ali Shariati, by criticising the conservative ulama and
formulating modern interpretations of Islam attracted many students and modern urban
groups. His critical view on the conservative ulama that was presented in his lectures in the
Islamic centre of *Huseyniyeh ershad* and his famous book *Mazhab alayhe mazhab* (Shari'ati,
1378/1999) was well accepted by young Muslim students and other modern Islamic groups.
Others, such as Ayatollah Taleqani (1910–1979) and Mehdi Bazargan (1907–1995) were
more attractive to the young generation than conservative ulama. Religious modernists
understood the spirit of the time and tried to establish new institutions to compete with
traditional religious foundations such as Hozeye Elmiye-ye Qum and other traditional religious
centres.

Establishment of a non-cleric religio-political front

The decrease in the influence of the ulama led to new groups that came to play significant
roles in the course of the modern Islamic movements, Islamic revolution and its aftermath
in Iran. Among these were the LMI, the Muslim Student Associations, Islamic associations
of engineers, physicians, and teachers, Muhammad Taqi Shariati's Mashad-based Center for
the Propagation of Islamic Truth, and several other groups, about thirteen in total (Chehabi,
1990:155). These groups arose almost simultaneously and created new non-cleric religio-
political spheres in Iranian politics.

Among the non-cleric ideologists of the Islamic modernism was Ali Shari'ati (1933–1977),
who had studied sociology at Sorbonne University in the 1960s. He was highly influenced
by the student revolts and the liberation movement in Algeria on the one hand, and the

theories and ideas of Jean-Paul Sartre and Frantz Fanon, on the other (Kamali, 1998). Shari'ati was a founder, and one of the most famous members, of the "Huseyniyeh Ershad" – a centre for modern religious propaganda away from the geographic locations of *madrasahs* and mosques.

Many prominent bazaris, such as Muhammad Humayun, a prominent wealthy merchant, were the traditional allies of the ulama and helped in establishment of the Huseyniyeh. However it was not only non-cleric religious modernists who participated in the founding and activities of the Huseynieh, but also intellectual ulama, such as Ayatollah Mutahhari, Ayatollah Beheshti, Hojjatoleslam Rafsanjani, and Hojjatoleslam Bahonar, who were in close connection with Khomeini, and were part of the people participating in Huseyniyeh's activities. This group of intellectual ulama came to play key roles and occupy major positions in the Islamic Republic. The location of the Huseyniyeh in the modern part of Northern Tehran, Qolhak, symbolised the differences between Islamic modernism, and religio-political subjects and issues discussed in this modern institute, and the conservative Islam, and the traditional religious sermons presented in the mosques situated in the traditional part of the city.

Although Shari'ati's lectures at Huseyniyeh were among the most critical of both the Shah and the ulama establishment, and many of the ulama including one of those engaging in the Huseyniyeh, Ayatollah Mutahhari, tried to convince Khomeini to issue a *fatva* against Shari'ati, he rejected this and remained neutral to the Hosseyniyeh and Shari'ati. Khomeini from his exile in Iraq was very well aware of the influence of Shari'ati among young radical religious groups and university students. Khomeini himself was formulating a new Shia doctrine and knew that many conservative ulama were critical of his so called *bed'at* (revision in religion) with new ideas. However, he reminds the exiled-link between the conservative ulama and the new radical religious groups.

Another non-cleric young religious group gathered in Sazeman-e mojahedin-e khalq (The organisation of the devotees of people), who were called by the Shah as "Islamic Marxists". This group chose the armed struggle as the only legitimate way of changing the Shah's regime and establishing an "Islamic classless society". Mojahedin-e Khalq had also tried to gain Khomeini's support for their armed struggle against the Shah, but failed. Once again, Khomeini as an experienced political leader rejected to take party for or against one political group in order to not loosing any group's support of him.

The Islamic Revolution and Islamic Modernisations

One of the main reasons behind the victory of the Islamic revolution of Iran in 1979 was the clever leadership of Khomeini who, as an experienced politician, propagated "cooperation" and "unity" among all oppositional groups, including the leftists. Many unsuccessful uprising against, and the brutality of, the Shah's regime and the intact political and military support of the "western" countries of his regime, forced both the liberals and the non-clerics as well as the leftists to gather under the leadership of Khomeini in the course of the revolution (1977–1979).

Like all other modern revolutions, the religious leadership of the Islamic Revolution believed in primacy of politics for changing the ancien régime. Primacy of politics and the seizure of the state power by the ulama were completely new in Shia religio-political doctrine (Arjomand, 1984; Kamali, 1998, 2001). Khomeini's theory of *Velayat-e faqih* (Vicegerence of the Islamic jurists) legitimated ulama's seizure of the political power and their participation in the state. The struggle over the conditions and terms of participation of the ulama in the political system of the country after the overthrow of the monarchy was a mater of controversy not only in the rank of the ulama, but also among many groups that supported the religious leadership of the Revolution.

The immediate political formation was a compromise between liberals, non-cleric religious intellectuals, nationalists and the radical ulama. The negotiations of Paris, where Khomeini resided a few months before moving to Iran in February 1979, between radical clergy and non-cleric Muslim intellectuals resulted in the appointment of the liberal leader of the LMI, Mehdi Bazargan, as the head of the provisional revolutionary government. A few weeks later, he became the first prime minister of the Islamic Republic of Iran. Liberals, nationalist and non-cleric religious modernists dominated the government of Bazargan. The liberal government of Bazargan had to face a bigger challenge than the Shah. The ulama by the leadership of Khomeini and a strong popular support, as well as armed by a revolutionary interpretation of Shiism crystallised in the theory of *Velayat-e faqih*, had no plans to get back to madrasahs or mosques. They wanted to remain the head of the post-revolutionary political system. They had a modern zeal, namely to use the political power to reorganise society according to their understanding of a good society.

The victory of the revolution of 1977–1979 was a result of the cooperation between the indigenous civil society, the westernised civil society, and the bazaar. The radical ulama with the leadership of Khomeini succeeded to seize the leadership of the movement against the Shah and launch a radical alternative in the movement against the Shah. Although many decades of rapid modernisation and socioeconomic reforms that were aimed at eliminating the power of the ulama, the radical ulama showed that they are still a power factor in Iranian society. This was partly due to the Shah's rapid modernisation that created a relatively large group of marginalised people who had left their traditional rural milieus and moved to large cities after a better life. The disadvantaged groups could be mobilised by Khomeini and other radical clergy and became the main "army" of the revolution.

This unconditional support for the religious leadership of the revolution was, however, an exception. During the course of the revolution many other groups, such as liberals, bazaris, and urban middle classes, who actively participated in the protests against the Shah, were in a permanent negotiation with Khomeini and other radical ulama. This resulted for instance in the establishment of the Islamic Republic instead of Khomeini's demand for an "Islamic state", as well as the establishment of the liberal government of Bazargan. The ulama who always were one of the most powerful group against the idea of republicanism in Iranian modern history, accepted this liberal demand as a matter of *Real Politic.*

Elimination of the dualism between civil society and state

The victory of the revolution in February 1979 and the widespread popular support for the leadership of the Revolution gave the radical ulama and other clergies an opportunity to establish an alternative *Islamic* modernisation to contrast with "westernisation". The famous slogan of the revolution, "no eastern, no western, Islamic republic" is a good illustration of the tension between radical clergy and other groups participating in the revolution. They declared an *Islamic* modernisation alternative to both the western liberal and conservative ones on the one side, and the socialist and communist ones, on the other. Many Islamic groups and scholars, such as Shariati, Taleqani, Bazargan and Khomeini discussed and presented Islamic political and economic alternatives to other modernisation programmes.

However, like all other revolutions, the political groups, parties and organisations participating had no a single homogenous understanding of the new society. From the day after the victory of the revolution, a struggle began over the definition of the new regime. Liberals with the leadership of the Prime Minister Bazargan claimed a symbolic change in the notion of "Islamic Republic". Before the referendum for the change of the old regime and the establishment of the new one, Bazargan demanded that the name of the Republic should be "The Islamic Democratic Republic of Iran". This was challenged by Khomeini and other radical clergy who did not allowed the notion of "democratic" associated with both leftist socialists and the westernised liberals to be added to the "independent" name of the "Islamic Republic". Khomeini and radical clergy did not want to make more compromises with the liberals and had other plans for the country. They had in mind a society where there was no duality of civil society and state, in line with the political model of the "socialist people's republic".[1]

The provisional government of Bazargan tried to preserve and restore many of the old regime's socioeconomic institutions and change and reform its political system. In other words, and in contrast to the radical clergy's will, he had no intention to introduce revolutionary changes. As he said in an interview with the Iranian TV a few weeks after the victory of the Revolution, "we wanted rain, got inundation". He and his liberal allies wanted to establish a liberal political and economic system combined with "Islamic values", which in this case meant a kind of governmental support for internal production (soft nationalism) and redistribution of resources for establishing a welfare system. This first Islamic Bazarganian modernisation which had a long theoretical tradition in Iran with its roots in the national movements of 1941–1953 was not long-standing. This modernisation collided with a new and revolutionary group's revolutionary modernisation ideas inspired by radical socialist and nationalist revolutions.

---

[1] The fascination of many leaders of the Islamic Republic of Iran in the political and economic model of China today is a continuation of such understanding of governance.

The conflict between radical clergy's zeal for the revolutionary change of Iranian society and the soft Islamic nationalism of the liberal government of Bazargan resulted in many confrontations between him and the leader of the Revolution, Khomeini. Bazargan had repeatedly and publicly complained about the intervention of clergy in general and of Khomeini in particular in the "affairs of government". In November 1979 a group of students who supported what was called "the line of Imam" in Iranian politics, which meant the radical clergy and their revolutionary zeal, occupied the US embassy on Takht-e jamshid avenue in Tehran. This forced Bazargan to resign. The occupation of US embassy and the resignation of the liberal government of Bazargan put an end to a revolutionary period marked by the instability of government and the division of political power between the liberal government and radical clergy. The period of radical Islamic modernisation and reorganisation of society started.

Governmentalisation of society and socialisation of government

The second period of Islamic modernisation started by monopolisation and homogenisation of state power. Radical clergy excluded liberals and later other groups such as the first president of the Republic, Abulhassan Banisadr from the political power. One of the major actions of radical clergy was to reinforce their authorities as the only legitimised political group which exclusive right to reign in an Islamic Republic, in accordance with Khomeini's theory of *Velayat-e faqih*. One of the most attractive Islamic modern political doctrines in Iran, namely, Shariatism (followers of Shariati), was considered as competitor to the doctrine of *Velayat-e faqih* and should be excluded. Many radical clergy had a long-standing opposition to Shariati and his sever critics of the ulama.

The first group of Shariati followers to be determinate was a group called Forghan, with strong aspiration for Shariati that started an armed struggle against "polluted ulama" by assassinating the commander in chief of the Islamic Republic. This gave the radical clergy the best reason to present Shariatism as a dangerous doctrine. Radical clergy, who controlled revolutionary courts and armed forces, such as revolutionary committees and revolutionary guards, succeeded to eliminate the group by arresting and executing almost all of them. Another rival Islamic revolutionary organisation was Mojahedin-e khalq-e Iran (The devotees of the Iranian people). The confrontation between the radical clergy and Mojahedin resulted in tens of thousands of death and jailed. The brutal attack on Mojahedin and other leftist organisations almost eliminated any form of internal opposition to the regime. Many were arrested, executed or imprisoned. Others left the country and choose a life in exile. In this period Para-military groups were effectively used by radical clergy to eliminate both the "liberal" Mojahedin-e khalq and the leftist "threat".

The radical clergy created their own civil political organisations and parties in order to play a part even in civil society. One of the interesting modern institutions created by radical clergy was the establishment of a modern political party. Clerics led by Ayatollah Mohammad Beheshti established the Islamic Republican Party (IRP). The party emerged as the organ of the clerics around Khomeini and the major political organisation in the country. The bloody confrontations which followed, resulting from radical clergy's endeavors to homogenise and establish their monopoly over the political power, led to many deaths and executions. The political dictatorship and brutality was legitimised as necessary in a time of war with Iraq and other foreign threats.

Establishment of "The Foundation for the Dispossessed"

The seizure of power by the radical clergy created a unique situation in Iran's modern history. The ulama and other clergy, who traditionally participated in social movements and revolutions but never claimed any direct participation in the organisation of country and its political system, were, for the first time, alone at the top of the political system and controlling state power. The revolutionary regime was ideologically committed to assist its major supporter, the "army of the revolution", namely the dispossessed, who were addressed as *Mostazafin* (Kamali, 1998, 2001). The positive experience of the mobilisation of *Mostazaf* in by the radical clergy encouraged them to continue keep the Mostazafin in "the scene" for many reasons. Since the victory of the revolution the Mostazafin were used against many groups of Iranian westernised civil society. *Mostazafin*, as the radical clergy's informal army, were organised by the radical clergy in new armed and formal organisations. *Komitehaye enghelabe eslami* (The Committees of the Islamic Revolution) were formed the days after the victory of the revolution and another more important armed force, namely *Sepahe pasdarane enghelabe eslami* (Revolutionary guards of the Islamic Revolution) was established in May 1979. Both Bazargan and the Republic's first semi-liberal president, Abulhasan-e Banisadr, failed to put these uncontrolled armed forces under the control of the judiciary and government.

In addition, in March 1979, by the direct order of Khomeini, *Bonyad-e mostazafan* (Foundation for the Dispossessed) was established. Among the Foundation's first actions were the construction of elementary schools, bathhouses, and health clinics in villages and low-income urban areas and the emphasis on religious charitable giving to the poor. The new foundation in time came to be one of the largest conglomerates in the country, controlling hundreds of expropriated and nationalised factories, trading firms, farms, and apartment and office buildings, as well as two large newspaper chains. Another similar organisation named *Jahad-e Sazandegi* (The Crusade for Reconstruction) was also established in June 1979. These organisations were to serve as the new regime's platform, with economic capacity, for launching reforms.

The semi-formal *Bonyad-e mostazafan*, with its enormous economic power, played a crucial role in the economic reform programmes of Ali Akbar Hashemi Rafsanjani (the president of the republic 1989–1997). Rafsanjani's reform programmes were aimed at revitalising industries and the private sector. The fact that the presidency of Rafsanjani was limited in time and his reform programmes more lasting was one reasons for Rafsanjani's more strategic cooperation with *Bonyad-e mostazafan*. This made the formation of one of the most important political organisation in the Islamic Republic, namely Sazandegan (Constructors) by Rafsanjani accurate. Rafsanjani used his influential position in the Islamic Republic to move

Iran from the state-controlled economy of the years of war with Iraq (1981–1989) to a more market-based system.

Bonyad-e mostazafan became one of the most powerful economic actors to come out of the state with very good connections in and support from the government. It is a semi-formal organisation with many shares in different governmental and private economic projects and industries. For instance, it is one of the major owners of the Iranian telephone network Irancell.

Colonising civil society

The radical clergy was not only interested in homogenising and monopolising political power, but also in colonising civil society. The slogans such as creating "a twenty million army" of people by Khomeini, establishment of different *Bonyads* (Foundations), such as *Bonyad-e mostazafan*, *Bonyad-e shahid* (Foundation of the martyrs), *Bonyad-e janbazan-e enghlab-e eslami* (Foundation of the veterans and disables of the Islamic revolution), *Jahad-e sazandegi* (The Crusade for reconstruction), *Dafater-e imame jom'eh* (The offices of the Friday prayers) and charity organisations and founds were among the attempts of the radical clergy to be a part of civil society and its organisations. During the first decade of the reign of the radical clergy the main characteristics of governance was based on mobilisation and participation of masses in politics (Bashiriyeh, 2002).

The Iraqi invasion provided the new regime another effective possibility to control its citizens. The war and the economic boycott of Iran by the USA and its allies forced the Iranian government to ration many basic foods and other commodities. Local mosques, *Shovraha-ye mahalli eslami* (local Islamic associations), and small shops were entitled to distribute the rationed foods and basic commodities. These centres and shops became the governments extended arms for controlling citizens and in many cases were used by security forces for localising and arresting dissidents.

The radical clergy increased their political influence in society not only by direct participation in government, but also by organising themselves in civil religo-political organisations. One of the most important of these organisations was *Jame'e-ye rohaniyat-e mobarez-e tehran* (The association of struggling clergy of Tehran) which had been one of the most important religious organ in civil society that legitimised the Islamic government until 1987 when they started criticising some of the leaders of the Republic (Bashiriyeh, 2002: 115).

The Islamic regime's endeavors to eliminate the duality between civil society and state by colonising civil society resulted simultaneously in increasing competitions within the groups who controlled the government. The diversity of organisations supporting different persons in the leadership of the Republic and the alliances and compromises between different rival groups created many power centres as well as conflicts. One of the first and major internal conflicts emerged after the death of the charismatic leader of the revolution, ayatollah

Khomeini. Institutionalisation of "charismatic leadership" (see Weber, 1984) of Khomeini created competitions and disputes between two powerful men of the republic, Seyyed Ali Khamenei and Ali Akbar Rafsanjani. The conflict resulted in many compromises that led to the division of power between Khamenei, as the new righteous *Rahbare Faqih* (spiritual leader), and Rafsanjani, as the new president with extended power. The establishment of different power centres encouraged many other groups, both governmental and civil society groups, to form new political oppositional organisations. This led to creation of the most influential oppositional front, *Jebhe-ye 2 khordad* (The second *khordad* front) that brought the moderate Muhammad Khatami to power in 1997.

One of the revolutionary values that are established in Iran is the tradition of modern political legitimacy. Although the Shia tradition of *Velayat* (vicegerency of the Hidden Imam), the new leader, the *faqihs* (Experts on Islamic jurisprudence) had to legitimise their leadership by the election. As Najafabadi puts it: "In the theory of *Velayat-e faqih* as the government of the righteous, the governance is a result of a contract between people and the religious leaders. It is only the *faqihs* who are entitled to govern, but they must be elected by the people" (Najafabadi, 1984). The institution of election and people's support for the Islamic regime is crucial for the political legitimacy of the leaders. This is a problem for the spiritual leader, the *faqih*, Khamenei, when the election brings to power oppositional groups that want to limit his power in favor of other power centres, such as the parliament.

The victory of Khatami increased the gap between different radical clergy groups and created three political parties in the state apparatus of the Islamic Republic. The first group is conservative clergy called *Enhesartalaban* (monopolists) led by the spiritual leader, Khamenei. The second group is led by Rafsanjani and is known as *Sazandegan* (constructors) with more pragmatic worldview and highly market-oriented policies. The third group is reformist and moderate, led by Khatami who became the president of the Islamic Republic 1997–2005. These three groups make the main fronts of the polity of the Islamic Republic.

Sazandegan, with the leadership of the former president, Rafsanjani, has had the major role in privatisations, reinforcement of market economy and, as a result, the increasing gap between rich and poor. There were two responses to the situation, the radical conservative reaction crystallised in the election of Ahmadinejad as the president of the Republic in 2005 on the one hand, and the demands of the reformist groups for welfare programmes as a part of their electoral campaigns, on the other.

Decolonisation of civil society

Revitalisation of civil society groups, both Islamic, secular, and westernised groups since 1997 was a sign of the failure of colonisation of civil society. Many Islamic groups that have

---

2   See Majmoe-ye bayaniyeha-ye rohaniyon-e mobarez-e tehran (1990/1369). Tehran: Ofset publication.

been directly or indirectly part of the Islamic regime started distance themselves from the government and organise themselves as oppositional groups. For instance, "Jame'e-ye rohaniyat-e mobareze teham" acts as a political oppositional party which claims the intervention of the state in the market, respect for the constitution, enforcement of citizens civil rights, progressive leadership, and participation of people in collective decision makings.[2] Even some organisations which have been very close to the government and in many cases participated in the government and disappeared practically from the political scene of the Republic, such as *Sazeman-e mojahedin-e enghelab-e eslami* (Organisation of the devotees to the Islamic revolution), started acting as an oppositional group since its resurgence in 1992 (Bashiriyeh, 2002: 147). Although many limitations, the revitalised civil society increased its sphere since the 1990s. The most important groups in today's civil society of Iran are the following associations and parties:

Associations

Majma'e rohanion-e mobarez (The association of struggling clergy of Tehran).
Majma'e niroha-ye khat-e imam (Association of the movements in Imam-line).
Majma'e nemayandegan-e hezbullah (Association of the representatives of the party of God).
Majma'e nemayandegan-e advar-e majles (Association of former MPs).
Majma'e nemayandegan-e khat-e imam (Association of MPs in Imam-line).
Majma'e eslami-ye banevan (Islamic association of women).
Daftar-e tahkim-e vahdat (The office of the reinforcement of unity).
Anjoman-e eslami-ye moddaresin-e daneshgaha (Islamic association of university teachers).
Anjoman-e eslami-ye mohandesan (Islamic association of engineers).
Anjoman-e eslami-ye mo'alleman (Islamic association of teachers).
Anjoman-e eslami-ye jame'e-ye pezeshki (Islamic associations of physicians).

Parties

Sazeman-e mojahedin-e enghelab-e eslami (Organisation of the devotees to the Islamic revolution).
Hezb-e hambastegi-ye iran-e eslami (The party of the unity of Islamic Iran).
Hezb-e jebhe-ye mosharekat-e iran-e eslami (The party of cooperation of Islamic Iran).
Hezb-e kargozaran-e sazandegi-ye iran-e eslami (The party of constructions of Islamic Iran).
Hezb-e eslami-ye kar (The Islamic party of labor).

In addition there are several other associations, parties, and groups that are not officially a member of the reformist front, but are participating in demonstrations, protests, and other democratic actions.

Rethinking modernities

The social science method of comparison between different countries has been a matter of controversy from very beginning of the establishment of modern social sciences. Herbert Spencer in his classical work *The Study of Sociology* in 1878 warned for methodological nationalism that could create biases and unreliable results in sociological studies. I have elsewhere discussed the problem of Eurocentrism in social sciences when studying other societies in general and Muslim societies in particular (Kamali, 1998, 2001, 2006). The Weberian theoretical view of the "uniqueness" of the "West" have created many problems for studies of Muslim societies. The methodological nationalism that transfers the particular institutional arrangements and history of a society to be a "universal truth" has been dominating in sociological field of research for many years.

The tradition of theoretical "meta-narratives" or "master narratives" (Heller, 1994, 2004) resulted in imaginary creation of ideatypical homogenised "Western" societies and developments. This was then used as an unchangeable "touch stone" to evaluate non-western countries place on an imagined axis of development. Other societies were seen through the leans of those theoretical meta-narratives. The strong belief in a linear form of development in which all societies transfer from a lower stand to a higher one, from primitive to modern, and from undeveloped to developed created a tradition of research according to which some "western" countries became the model of development for all other countries. Modernisation was considered mostly "westernisation". The variety of modernities and the multiplicity of modern institutions were not recognised. This made the comparison of "western" and "non-western" countries on equal terms impossible. If any comparison was made, its main intension was to compare two different socioeconomic and cultural systems, namely the "modern west" against the "non-modern and traditional rest".

The theory of multiple modernities opens up the possibility for a more accurate comparison between different countries and free social sciences from its "singular modernity" bias. Modern changes in non-western countries could be studied and understood on their specific historical and social contexts without framing them as something other than the "pure western" modernity. The theory of the "uniqueness" of the "West" is not only a myth and a "scientific" imagination but also an obstacle to fruitful sociological studies of other forms of modernisations programmes and processes. The theoretical approach of multiple modernities creates the possibility for comparison between "western" and non-western societies on equal terms and conditions without falling in the trap of "linearity of development". For instance, one of these comparisons can be conducted between Iran and Sweden.

In terms of development, Iranian Islamic civil society after the victory of the Islamic revolution can be compared with Swedish civil society. The colonisation of civil society which took place in Iran after the revolution and the governmentalisation of civil society and vice versa have also happened in Sweden following the seizure of power by the Social democratic party in 1932 with long-standing consequences for the Swedish political system. Social democrats created strong alliances with major unions, such as workers central organisation,

Land Organisationen (LO). The cooperation between Social Democrats and LO and other unions as well as one of the most influential economic foundation, namely Löntagarfonderna (Workers Foundations) was so closely intertwined that some scholars rejected the existence of civil society in Sweden (see for instance, Micheletti, 1995). However, Micheletti is trapped in the tradition of singular modernity and cannot see the existence of other civil societies than the American or liberal ones. The close alliance between the unions and some other civil society organisations with the Social Democratic party resulted in a relative stable reign of Social democrats under the last seventy years in Sweden.

The relationship between civil society and state is a matter of controversy everywhere. The close relations between political parities and some major media in the USA, between the rightwing government in Sweden and almost all liberal newspapers, and between Social democratic governments and unions in Sweden, Denmark, and Norway are a few examples. In other modernities, such as the socialist ones, the colonisation of civil society by the state went much further than in Iran.[3] In Iran many civil society organisations and foundations are supporting the Islamic regime. Many others are struggling for political reforms. The 28 years old of the reign of the radical clergy in Iran has created a new situation and new oppositional groups that must be studied in its own context. The theory of Multiple modernity is helpful in this concern.

References

Algar Hamid (1980) Religion and the state in Iran 1785-1906: the role of the Ulama in the Qajar period, Berkeley: University of California Press.

Arjomand Said A. (1988) Authority and Political Culture in Shi'ism, New York: State University of New York Press.

Arjomand Said A. ed. (1984) From Nationalism to Revolutionary Islam, London: Macmillan Press.

Amason Johann P. (1993) The Future that Failed: Origins and Destinies of the Soviet Model, London: Routledge.

Azimi Fakhreddin (1989) Iran, the Crisis of Democracy, London: I. B. Tauris.

Bashiriyeh Hossein (2002/1381) Dibache-i bar jame'e shenasiye siyasi-ye Iran (A discussion on the political sociology of Iran). Tehran: Negahe ma'aser publications.

Chehabi Houshang E. (1990) Iranian Politics and Religious Modernism, London: I. B. Tauris & Co.

Heller Agnes. (1994) A Theory of History, Oxford: Blackwell.

Heller Agnes (2004) "A Theory of Modernity", paper presented in Conference: "Beyond East and West" in Elmau, Germany, 4-7 April.

Masoud Kamali (2006) Multiple Modernities, Civil Society and Islam: The Case of Iran and Turkey, Liverpool: Liverpool University Press.

---

[3]   For a discussion on communist modernities see Amason, (1993).

Kamali Masoud (2001) "Civil society and Islam: A Sociological Perspective" in *European Journal of Sociology*, XLII (3), pp. 457-482.

Kamali Masoud (1998) *Revolutionary Iran, Civil Society and State in the Modernisation Process*, Aldershot: Ashgate.

Micheletti Michele (1995) *Civil society and state relations in Sweden*, Aldershot: Avebury.

Milani Mohsen M. (1994) *The Making of Iran's Islamic Revolution*, Boulder: Westview Press.

Najafabadi Salehi (1984/1363) Velayat-e faqih: The reign of the righteous, Tehran: Rasa publications.

Shariati Ali (1378/1999) *Mazhab alayhe mazhab*, Tehran: Chapakhsh Publishing.

Spencer Herbert (1878) *The Study of Sociology*, London: C. Kegan Paul & Co.

Discussion

Deniz Kandiyoti

First of all, I have to thank Masoud for a truly fascinating and rich presentation, and say that I feel rather ill-equipped to comment on Iranian history, which is not my field of expertise. I [will] very much count on Professor Asef Bayat to fill in any gaps. I think what I might do is to start at the beginning of the presentation with modernisation theory, and maybe give a slightly different reading of the same data that we have been presented, showing which bits I agree with and where I have serious problems and questions.

I start with modernisation theory. I think that it may be helpful to make a distinction between two modernisations. The first one is modernisation as an occurring phenomenon, as a historical event, and as a great transformation. Where this modernisation occurs, it is self-contested. Some people have argued that it is not necessarily in Europe that modernisation has occurred. Some even go far as saying that the most clear experiments were in the colonies like the West Indies or India. The second side of modernity is modernity as a discursive formation, that is to say, how it is constructed as a discourse with various values like progress, Enlightenment, etc.

I am afraid there was a certain confusion between these two levels in your presentation in the sense that I think it should be still possible to talk about modernisation as a process, as distinct from modernity as a discourse, as a discursive formation with implications of racial hierarchy, assumptions of technological superiority, etc.

This is crucial because my reading of the Iranian situation is precisely that, under the Islamic Republic, a process of societal modernisation has been under way, which the state has not been able to contain. In other words, I am going to argue that the paradox of revolutions is that [the regime] mobilises citizenry that the same regime then finds difficult to contain, and has to resort to cruder and cruder ideological devices in order to do so, and this will be bring me to Ahmadinejad. I think we have to first make this crucial distinction between these two levels of looking at modernity, because otherwise it becomes totally impossible to recognise societal changes and sociological modernisation, which Iran has in common with many countries.

We may discuss why under the Islamic Republic these processes of modernisation, which happened much earlier in many other countries of the Middle East, occurred. Of course, that has to do with the political economy of Iran and the fact that it is an oil rentier state where the rulers hardly had to mobilise their citizenry. This was not the case in Turkey where the Republic had to really mobilise its citizenry and had to tax them, educate them, etc. So there are fundamental differences.

The part at which I am in full agreement in your paper is your interpretation of the modernity and novelty of the Shia doctrine of *Velayat-e faqih*. In fact, this interpretation is also found in the works of scholars like Sami Zubeida and Abbas Vali. But what I would like to take a little bit of time reflecting on is, why Islamic modernity? Because when you look at the mobilising frame utilised by the Islamic Republic and you take it apart in the manner that Ervand Abrahamian did looking at populism, you see that what is crucial there is the coming together of very different factors. One of them, very importantly, is nationalism. It is a form of Shiism as Iranian nationalism, in other words it is mobilising the religious idiom to stake a place in the Iranianness which is no longer Persepolisism, it is Shiism.

That becomes very clear in the war with Iraq. What Abrahamian and others seem to say is that there is a coming together of Shia idiom and imagery, anti-colonial Third World-ism, the great enemy outside, the Great Satan, and a recuperation of Iran in a national sense through this discourse. This discourse, for its continuation, is as reliant and dependent on an outsider that threatens the Iranian polity. This is why you have to continue having an outsider. The Great Satan is very important: it has to be there to draw the boundaries. These are not simply the boundaries of the *Ummah*, but very specific Iranian boundaries. But this is not my argument, because I am not an Iranian expert, so I will not pursue it.

What I had a real difficulty with in this paper is the way in which you utilise the concept of civil society. I will tell you why. It is because you make a distinction between so-called 'indigenous civil society', which presumably consists of what you consider to be traditional classes, *bazaaris*, *ulema*, etc., and 'westernised civil society'. However, I find that I agree with the part that you want to have a more precise usage of the concept of civil society; you do not call anything civil society. Before this we used the word socioeconomic classes and strata groups, but now we seem to have changed terminology and to have substituted civil society with the older sociological terminologies that we used to deploy. I will explain why I have problem with this distinction. In particular, I have problems with the concept of 'westernised civil society'. What is westernised about it? Taking the case of Turkey, I argue that what you call 'westernised civil society' is as indigenous as the other form.

For example, in Turkey you have very strong professional associations. With becoming part of a modern economy, you have had the creation of numerous professions, and these professions have organised themselves into organised groups, some of which are very strong. For example, the women's lawyers association in Turkey is extremely powerful. So much so that when the Islamic Government came into power and the EU said you now have to regularise your legal system and you must comply with gender equality, the Islamic government was totally unprepared, but the women's lawyers association had re-written the constitution and labour laws already. So they told the government, do not worry, here is a prepared written law. The package was passed in the parliament in one session and it is the most progressive set of laws since Mustafa Kemal Atatürk's reforms in the 1920s. This was an absolutely revolutionary and phenomenal achievement aiming at the elimination of all discrimination between genders. Why is this women's lawyers association westernised? There is nothing westernised about it.

This association consists of women in the legal profession in Turkey who have organised themselves into a lobbying association. They would certainly not consider themselves any more westernised than the ladies association of the Islamist party. Doing this has, automatically, an underlying essentialist nativistic discourse whereby only Islamically-organised civil society formations are indigenous and the rest are somehow western or westernised. So much so that these women's associations, including some women's NGOs who recently took two million people on the streets in Istanbul, had against the figure of the Islamist candidate for presidency, an American flag. In other words, it was the other way around. The secularist on the streets were claiming indigeneity for themselves and accusing the Islamist Government of being stooges of the Americans, which in some senses they could be, because they are the darlings of the investment funds. Capitalists want this government in power because they have been fantastic, they have complied with everything the World Bank and the IMF wanted and are running a brilliant neoliberal economy.

This is what Rafsanjani is saying in Iran. He is saying, Give me power and I will be good, but what I [Rafsanjani] do inside my country is my business. And that is exactly the position in Turkey. They are saying, Give us the power; we will run a great capitalist economy but what we do inside with school books, little girls, etc. is our business. But civil society in Turkey is saying, No, it is our business. I think this is why there were so many flags in the streets; it was the iconic side of it. In other words, the Quran is so powerful that you have to take an equally powerful symbol. So you have the clash of indigeneities there. It is not a fight between the westernised secularists and the indigenous Islamists. When you take that perspective, you can ask, What is westernised? Where does the West stop? Where does the indigenous start? What I am saying is that we should find another way of talking about these formations because otherwise we run the risk of becoming ideological hand maidens to those who want to politically marginalise people who do not fall in with any Islamist agenda. In other words, AKP would be delighted to call these people demonstrating 'the westernised civil society'. The foreigners are among us! What these people are saying is that we are not the foreigners, we are the owners of this country, we care and furthermore, we are more nationalistic than you because we will, if need be, protect the national interest against foreign capitalist powers better than you do. That is why there were American flags in their hand. It is very important to understand these symbols and iconographies.

Coming back to Iran, I think that there are two things that one must distinguish. One is the sociology of revolutions. What is clear is that revolutions have things in common… whatever their agenda may be, progressive, reactionary, fascist, socialist, etc., they do rely on a more mobilised citizenry. They have to mobilise their citizenry. So whether or not the Islamist government had an Islamic agenda, they had an interest in having women on the streets. The Islamic Revolution was a modern revolution, and unlike the Taliban they were happy to have veiled women marching on streets as militants of that revolution. The trouble, though, is that mobilised citizenries develop expectations of the system. Gradually, the original fervour of the revolution gets forgotten and scrutinised, and you have generations of young people who [have] grown up only under the Islamic Republic. So you have an extremely young population, around 70% under 30, that has now benefited from the mobilisational aspects of the revolution [and are] more educated, more mobile, more urban, etc.

What you have had under the Iranian Revolution is a genuine modernisation of society with speed, to an extent that did not occur under either the Reza Shah or Mohammad Reza. This modernisation was not because of the institutions of the Iranian Revolution, which were revolutionary in the sense that they did what all revolutionary regimes do: they took over society and co-opted it and created their own apparatchiks. All revolutionary systems go through a radical phase and then a phase of consolidation and corrupt routinisation. Now the real problem is the problem of corrupt routinisation, which means that the spoils are shared by various groups in society, and usually the revolutionaries themselves do not get their fair share. What happens then is that this mobilised citizenry starts making expectations and demands. Women, who are on the streets, say they want equal rights and they start pushing the Islamic regime. And of course these were the forces that were behind Khatami.

The great popularity of Khatami was because there was a young generation that was modernised wanting the government to match. But as we all know, that did not work out and Khatami could not pull it off. Actually, I do not think he could, because unless you change the constitution you cannot have a democratic government in Iran. After all, this is a system in which MPs do not have parliamentary immunity. I think as long as you have a democratic system under a constitution of that type, there is no way you can have any kind of reform. So what happens is that you have a phenomenon like Ahmadinejad who tries to revive the radical goals of the revolution.

Once you start thinking of society as having its own momentum, the modernisation that society undergoes does not have to be multiple at all, because it is a phenomenon that you have in all modernising societies. You have literate, mobile, urban populations with expectations, needs and demands. This phenomenon occurred much earlier in Turkey which is why now we are able to talk about what Masoud calls, 'westernised civil society' and I call, 'Turkish civil society' in Turkey. I think the plague of Iran precisely was that it was a rentier state and oil economy, and therefore it is only a revolution that mobilised citizenry and made it a modern society. At least that is my reading of it but, as I said, I am not an Iranian expert and I will stop here.

Abdou Filali-Ansary

Thank you very much for your most interesting comments. We will open the floor to discussion after listening to the remarks of Professor Charles Jencks and Professor Stefan Weber. After the discussions, we will give our speaker the opportunity to respond to or reflect on these comments.

Why Critical Modernism?*

CHARLES JENCKS

Critical Modernism is an idea whose time has come. The temperature of daily life is going up, and it isn't just global warming. Problems of an advanced civilisation are now understood to be chronic, a byproduct of success: pollution, congestion and the lack of wilderness, clean water and solitude. Many such problems are caused by overpopulation, but the more a country is modernised the more endemic they are because they spring from the same Pandora's Box: a growing economy and the complexity of its interconnections. It is usually called by one, or all, of the three M-words, Modernity, Modernisation and Modernism. These come as a cohesive bundle. Once a country has a modernising economy and technology, they acquire a style and ideology of progressive modernity, and a culture of modernism. That has been true in the west since, surprisingly, the fourth century. Then the Christians tried to modernise the pagan world of Rome and uttered the hopeful injunction *modernus*. With the "good" *maniera moderna* recommended by Filarete and Vasari in the Renaissance and the rise of global capitalism at the same time, the 3-M's have tightly coupled ever since.

Irrespective of labels, with the evolution of society problems multiply until they reach a critical mass or critical bifurcation point. This truth has been illuminated by the science of "self-organising criticality" and become widely known in several examples – the Perfect Storm, the stock-market crash, and the nuclear chain reaction. It also helps explain why, when modernism is so ubiquitous today, and in such previously undeveloped places as Dubai, it is likely to become self-consciously critical, a Modernism^2 or Modernism^3. Reflecting on the problems caused by oneself is an introspection likely to make one more mature, ironic and sceptical – in a word critical. Consider those who have a well-developed culture of fixing their own self-inflicted problems, that is, architects and builders. Wisely they have internalised a set of nostrums that deal with Pandora's Troubles. "Murphy's Law", or the customary fact that "anything that can go wrong will go wrong," is not only true of the building trade, but finds its counterpart in military and political equivalents (SNAFU is the most famous, "situation normal, all f... up"). That is the usual condition of the modern world, and that message is around.

---

* The essay "Why Critical Modernism?" has been reprinted here by the kind permission of the author. It replaces a presentation of the same title made at the Workshop by Charles Jencks.

Scepticism

In the 1960s the young generation became sceptical because of the lies politicians told about Vietnam. In the 2000s there was no draft and hence no generational disenchantment, but today because Iraq young and old know their politicians are lying. According to YouGov and other polls of February 2007, 16% of the British believed Prime Minister Blair was telling the truth, 50% that Britain had gotten worse over the last year and that the country will be a still worse place to live in five years. The verdict? Widespread disenchantment, private wealth and public squalor, give them bread and circuses. By 2007 most had accepted their leader was "Tony Bliar", that Blying was common, that Cash for Honours was the norm. The choice was clear: either be cynical or critical.

In architecture and planning, the sceptical Jeremy Paxman of BBC *Newsnight* cross-examined the man who put in the winning bid for the London Olympics. Was it not strange, Paxman asked, that this bid was economical with the truth, that the estimate sprawled from £3 to £6 to £9 and then some billions? "Well, it won didn't it?" That was the brazen answer of a government committed to Blying, and in this case making the arts community pay for the bread, circus and expensive architecture. John Tulsa and those dependent on art grants were not amused. Lies about Iraq are only the most public form of general disenchantment.

Bush portrait from US war dead, 2004, anonymous picture of the President made from photos of the first 1000 Americans killed. The "excess" Iraqi dead, continuously suppressed by governments, was estimated in 2006 by independent experts at 655,000. Where denial exists, Critical Modernism uses cool description. (Artist unknown, circulated on the Internet).

Angry serene

When 84% of a country believe its Prime Minister is only loosely connected to the truth, you can bet scepticism has become the reigning style and habit of mind. Such moods change the arts and architecture. Since *Look Back in Anger* and the Angry Young Man of the 1950s, since Francis Bacon's characters writhed in cages and Brutalism dominated the housing scene, more recently since Martin Amis and Damien Hirst augmented this tradition, the art of anger has been a primary mode. With Brit Art it is as common as, in the 19th century novel, the blush on the cheek of a virgin. The point for a Critical Modernism is that if chronic problems with modernisation and anger can be assumed, if they are widespread and *now completely conventional*, then the critical need not be the choleric. The new style is controlled, not the sullen but the Angry Serene. Damien Hirst adopts this mode in his best work, his "crucifixions of nature" (flayed sheep on the cross), a comment on Francis Bacon. The American artist Brian Tolle is ultra cool in his depictions of a country divided into the blue and red States, by the 2004 presidential election.

Brian Tolle, Die, or Join, installation ICA, Philadelphia, 2006. A two-headed snake, in blue and red segments signifying the division between liberal and conservative States, on occasion snaps together signifying war. The snake's moving shadow also maps out the shape of America's coastline - a content-driven work, critical of the political scene. (ICA, Philadelphia)

In the city where Critical Modernism has developed furthest, Berlin, the Chinese artist Cai Guo-Qiang has created an installation that is a composed response to the terrors and catastrophes of modernity. Ninety-nine wolves jump across space — the ultimate image of herd mentality — and hit the glass wall. Using gunpowder to create explosion paintings typifies the Angry Serene. Cai gathers a crowd of onlookers in a gallery courtyard, places stencils of wolves on a huge canvas, sets off a controlled explosion, then displays the blackened silhouettes as if they were art works lifted from Lascaux. Nothing is more raw and primitive than this, nothing as sophisticated. The Angry Serene depends for its charge on presenting the nastiness and horror of the modern world with an unruffled professionalism. No wonder these artists look to Renaisssance *sprezzatura*, when skill at making the difficult look easy was also admired.

Cai Guo-Qiang, Head On, a three-part installation at the German Guggenheim, Berlin, 2006. A wolf pack leaps to the attack, only coming to its downfall when it hits the glass wall. The drawing (above) Vortex, was created by detonating varieties of gunpowder (seen in the explosion) below stencils of wolves, thus giving the ghost image of a prehistoric cave painting. The 99 life-size wolves were constructed from painted sheepskins stuffed with hay and given marble eyes. (C. Jencks)

Cross-coding

Except for Hiroshima, Berlin is the city that suffered the most under modernity so it is no surprise that it has some of the best works of Critical Modernism. There are the many monuments to war and occupation, the two prominent Holocaust memorials by Daniel Libeskind and Peter Eisenman, and the paintings and sculpture of Anselm Kiefer. That a major art has emerged from catastrophe is no small feat. More important, that the Germans have faced and debated their recent past in the Bundestag and allowed these unwelcome facts to be memorialised right in the heart of parliament (with Russian graffiti) shows that denial and lying need not dominate public discourse. There is now a style of acknowledging the past, displaying the facts without rhetoric, that is typified by Eisenman's Memorial to the Murdered Jews of Europe. Abstract, descriptive and neutral it calls on the ubiquitous white cube of 1920s modernism, although here in Berlin to symbolise the dead they are grey cubes and in the form of graves. That makes the modern cliché iconic, semantic, gives it a spiritual role more than its meaning as the aesthetic of emptiness.

The critical approach stems as much from the complexities of contemporary life as it does the problems and tragedies. Hence if one were to list the canonic works of Critical Modernism they would include the buildings that have emerged through algorithmic design, specifically the complex ones. The most striking example of this is Toyo Ito and Cecil Balmond's 2002 Serpentine Pavilion a perfect answer to Mies van der Rohe's Barcelona Pavilion because it shows the new interest in the fractal geometry of nature, forms that mirror the processes of the cosmos. Generated by the algorithm of an expanding and rotating square, this simple formula is allowed to create a very complex, self-similar geometry in plan, elevation, section and detail.

Toyo Ito and Cecil Balmond, Serpentine Pavilion, London 2002. A clear use of a simple algorithm to generate a beautiful structure. This is modified in colour, size and shape to capture its natural green and blue setting in a striking way. (C.Jencks)

Just as the simple formula of the Mandelbrot Set, $Z=Z^2+C$, creates the most unified form of variety, a symbol of nature's complexity, so too does this rotating square. Computer design has now made the generation of complexity more economical and so the convention of Critical Modernism is to take several algorithms and cross-code them at once. Eisenman's City of Culture in Santiago typifies the mixed coding.

Peter Eisenman, City of Culture, Santiago de Compostela, 1999-2009. Five opposite codes are crossed, the coquille shell of the ancient city, the shape of the existing hill, Ley Lines, the medieval city plan and the Cartesian grid. These markings make their way through and over the building creating a new grammar as they interact, the critical as algorithmic difference. (C. Jencks)

What makes it more critical than the usual computer design is the way that conflicting codes with historical and cultural meaning play as much of a role as functional ones. To think critically is to set one set of ideas against another, to confront opposites, to admit difficulties, to stop denying the realities of modern life and start making a stark but sensual art from their conjunction. A building that does this creatively is Rem Koolhaas' Casa da Musica, a severe icon of minerals on the outside (it won a competition as the "diamond that fell from the sky") cross-coded with local Portuguese codes and a dramatic hollowed out space.

Rem Koolhaas, Casa da Musica, Porto, 2005. Opaque "milky quartz", a mineral icon won the competition with other metaphors. (C.Jencks)

Younger designers who stem from these three architects, FOA, UN Studio, Greg Lynn, swerve away from their exemplars exhibiting another aspect of the critical. When one examines the last two hundred years of Modernism a pattern of critical swerving can be found. Who did the Futurists criticise – the Fauves; who berated the Futurists for warlike art – the Dadaists; who passed judgement on the Dadaists – the Surrealists; and so it goes. As Harold Bloom showed in The Anxiety of Influence, the modern poet has to adopt a double stance, honouring the exemplars while modifying their message. This creates the immanent dialectic of modernism and the swerving pattern of history, it helps explain why the standard diagram of Modern Art, the one that Alfred Barr fashioned for MoMA in 1935 is philosophically flawed. He drew a map of the zeitgeist, lines of force ending in the box of MODERN ARCHITECTURE and abstract art, ruthlessly cutting that Dadaism and Surrealism which wasn't abstract. As Karl Popper argued a belief in the zeitgeist was what the Reactionary Modernists Hitler and Stalin foisted on followers, and as he further pointed out a Critical Rationalism is one answer to those who believe in a deterministic spirit of the age.

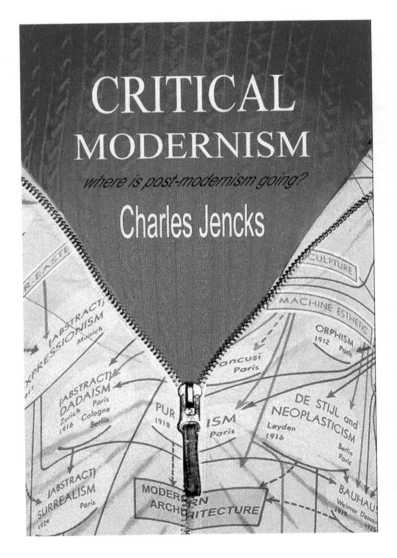

Unzipping Modernism, cover of Critical Modernism, 2007, shows the Alfred Barr diagram of 1935 parting for a more complex view of competing traditions, pink blobs restored to their semi-autonomy. (C.Jencks)

Critical Modernism unzips the zeitgeist view of history, the great white elephant theory that shows multiple bloodlines leading inexorably toward a single conclusion. Modernism, as an underground tradition, has always been critical of itself and others even if the MoMA of all views sees it all aiming in one direction. It is true Corporate Modernism and the white cube are dominant around the world, statistically. But the deeper truth is that the critical and the modern have formed a dynamic hybrid where the scepticism of the former and the transcendence of the latter make a potent cocktail, the creative tradition that lasts.

Can Modernism grow up?

Let me sum up the argument so far. The hypothesis is that nearly everyone today is one sort of Prefix-Modernist or another; that it is much harder to escape the totalising forces of the global market, electronic network and world civilisation than thirty years ago. Even so-called anti-modernists are drawn into this global logic and its assumptions. Or, as with al-Qaeda as John Gray has shown, the assumptions actually stem from modernity.[1] That is why, today, difference has to be played out in the prefix not the suffix of the definition.

Secondly, and on the question of negative motivation, there is a mounting wave of angst pushing a large part of this global civilisation into criticality – the pervasive scepticism, a simmering and serene anger, the elective dictatorships and their constant lying, the catastrophes of modernity, genocide, global warming, Celebrity Big Brother. This part of the summary could go on, the critical temperament is today, as they say, over-determined. This does not mean something positive has to come from it. Cynicism and apathy also follow from these same trends; inaction and solipsism.

Beyond this, the critical temperament is quite different from the creative, it engages other parts of the body and brain, it tends to dampen willpower and taking risks, it tends to the precautionary principle not the projective. This is why architects, who are always engaged in convincing their clients of a future-world, a fantasy where risk is essential to success, are suspicious of the critical and why there is a "post-critical" movement gaining strength. Creativity entails the momentary relaxation of the critical in order to go beyond the present impasse, the customary categories. This point was implied by Rem Koolhaas in a 1994 debate between two groups that were later to style themselves as "the critical and post-critical". As he stated the pragmatic side. The problem with the prevailing discourse of architectural criticism is (the) inability to recognise there is in the deepest motivations of architecture something that cannot be critical.[2]

---

[1]   John Gray, Al Qaeda and What is Means to Be Modern, The New Press, 2003.

[2]   These points and the quote are discussed in George Baird, "'Criticality' and its Discontents, *Harvard Design Magazine 21*, (Fall 2004/Winter 2005) pp. 16-21. The debate goes back to an article Michael Hays wrote at the same time Kenneth Frampton was writing on Critical Regionalism, "Critical Architecture: Between Culture and Form", *Yale Architecture Journal, Perspecta 21*, 1984. Those whom Baird characterises on the "critical" side of the debate beside Peter Eisenman include Manfredo Tafuri, Michael Hays, Diller and Scofidio and Michael Sorkin while those on the "post-critical" side include theorists Michael Speaks, Robert Somol, Sarah Whiting and many of the pragmatic Dutch followers of Rem Koolhaas.

This something is now called the projective side of architectural projects, but it could be generalised even further to the modernist impulse, the desire to go beyond and transcend the present situation. Indeed the romantic and post-modern aim of transcendence – getting "after", "over", "away from" customary categories – complements the "critical" quite effectively. The conjunction critical-modernism is thus a potent mixture, an oxymoron with wings, a potentially effective cocktail if one can get the mixture right.

Even then there is no guarantee of positive results; much more is needed in the cocktail. At a minimum, a self-conscious awareness of the cultural situation is called for, a maturing process that confronts the historical truths of the many modernisms; the problems they have caused, the opportunities they have opened. Timothy Ferris has described the emergence of our cosmic situation as the *Coming of Age in the Milky Way* (1988), and one might adopt the same metaphor. After two hundred years of one modernism replacing another, this might result in a more reflexive movement, one mature enough to reflect on its own dark side while celebrating creativity, a tradition come of age. What are the prospects of this?

It is hard to say. But having been recently to Berlin and looked at how this city has begun to confront its modern catastrophes, debated them at a national political level, and then having turned them into a convincing form of art, architecture and urbanism, I would say that it at least is possible. If one capital city can begin this transformation so can another. In Berlin the process grew in the 1970s as a national reflection on the Second World War gathered strength. This self-analysis was led by cultural movements and literature, the rise of the Greens, and the criticism of the recent past by architects and urbanists. In the 1980s, as underground bunkers were dug up and the debate deepened about how to recognise this past and develop the future city, a rough consensus occurred. With respect to the Nazis remains, and evidence of the Holocaust, it was soon felt that a description of the facts, with minimum rhetoric, was the best approach. Hence the fifteen or so monuments that recognise what happened under Reactionary Modernism, hence the Holocaust memorials and museums of Libeskind and Eisenman, hence the graffiti of the occupying Russians left inside the Reichstag, hence the many works of Anselm Kiefer and contemporary artists who come to Berlin to confront this past - such as the Chinese Cai Guo-Quiang. It is true there are many monuments around the world to many victims, and after sixty years there is even some grudging acknowledgement of what happened in the last world war. But there is no other city that has allowed, right at its heart, memorials and descriptions of the criminal acts perpetrated by its predecessors, and turned this into convincing cultural expression.

Contrast this with the situation, for instance, in Japan or America, countries that are still circumspect about their past. For instance, the Nanking Massacre, and what has been called for many years "the American Holocaust".[3] Before one can have some closure on these events, the governments have to admit the crimes, the populations have to acknowledge them, the lessons absorbed, and apologies (however inadequate) publicly carried through. No such historical process has happened in Japan and America, over these two events, and as a result the national populations are disclaiming knowledge. When people later find out the truth, it is a traumatic experience. There is then the double or triple guilt to deal with: the acts themselves, the cover-up by their politicians, and their own complicity in not wanting to know. Digging with the spade of denial only makes the hole deeper.

As Zygmunt Bauman has shown there is a logic at work here, the one that kept America in Vietnam or Iraq long after their policies had failed – the "law of increasing guilt". Bauman, writing on the Nazis, shows how difficult it is for politicians and ordinary people, once they have gone along with an initial decision, to change their mind and admit culpability. Much easier is to fudge and equivocate, be economical with the truth and hope other people will forget. The law of increasing guilt keeps the slaughter going well past the point when, in private, people are ready to admit they were wrong. Significantly for my argument Bauman makes these points in a book called *Modernity and the Holocaust* (1989).

There is more to growing up than confronting one's guilt. Maturity means accepting other people's values as partially legitimate and the non-lethal conflict of views as essential to the creation of meaning. As to the latter, today most people can recognise that the "others" around the globe are other prefix-modernists, and to pick a fight over a prefix is as infantile as the war on terror. A critical view accepts the reports of the CIA and other US agencies which showed that, since 2003, the war caused many of the 11,111 terrorist incidents.[4] Yet, actuarial reports showed the unlikely fact that those annually killed in terrorist incidents around the world (excluding Iraq) barely exceeded those who drown each year in USA bathtubs. Combining the two reports, critically, leads inexorably to the conclusion that either our trusted leaders better grow up fast or we will have to.

[3] David E. Stannard, *American Holocaust, Columbus and the Conquest of the New World*, Oxford University Press, 1992. The figures for the "population reduction" in North and South America are uncertain and have to be placed in a complex context, but vary from 100 million over 200 years to 50 million for the first fifty years from 1500. Germ warfare, consciously and semi-consciously used, was the great killer. The Europeans and British since 1492 kept on referring to the myths of the "New World", "discovered" by Columbus along with the "Indians", long after it was known the continent was inhabited for thousands of years. The textbooks of Japan are even worse about their massacres. The Nanking one, such as that the "official" Chinese figure of 300,000 murdered is not admitted much less the calculated genocide. The hole of denial Americans and Japanese dig is only getting deeper, a result of "the law of increasing guilt" (see text).

[4] Tom Baldwin, US admits Iraq is a terror "cause", *The Times*, April 29, 2006, p. 46; actuarial reports are in John Mueller, "A False Sense of Insecurity", Regulation, Fall, 2004, pp. 42-6, bbbb@osu.edu

Discussion

Stefan Weber

I am new to this discussion [and I] am amazed that people who have been working in these areas are still struggling with modernity, modernism and modernisation. I am happy that Masoud has brought up the notion of multiple modernities, but I still find myself uncomfortable using and applying it. I will try to figure out what is it that we are talking about in another way.

First of all, I think we have a lot of problems to distinguish, because specific things that happened in the 19ᵗʰ and 20ᵗʰ centuries have to do with a sort of modernisation that has been run by certain centres of the West. I am of course not talking about the entire West, since some local areas like the countryside in Holland, Belgium and Germany did not modernise until the very beginning of the 20ᵗʰ century and were not part of modernisation and modernity. So we have the problem that the successful model of modernisation came from the West, a model that has been very hegemonic and powerful. That is why we are always talking against the West and when we talk about how modernity expresses itself in different places we are always referring to the West and protesting against it. We are always… treating the West as a totality and missing the distinctions between it. Also, people who are looking for alternative modernities, like Khomeini, cannot totally ignore this Western model of modernity so, along with the *Velayat-e faqih*, which has nothing to do the modern nation-state, he talks about the *Majlis* and *Rahbari*, which has not been developed in the *Velayat-e faqih*.

We also have another problem with what caused this interaction in modern times, which has been developed in centres in the West, and has to do with means of communication and transportation including traffic, steam machines, steam boats, railways, airplanes, cars, photograph, telegraph, radio, television, etc... That is why we sometimes mix the machine with the process that is happening. Then we have values that are to do with modernity and being modern. Before I come back to my own solution to the problem, I will look to modernisation and the critique of modernisation theory because I think it is about what is the process [has been] in the 19ᵗʰ and 20ᵗʰ centuries, what is modernisation and the theory of modernisation and where multiple modernities may help us [to] discuss the plural expressions of modernisations, which are unequal in time and quality in different places and might be local, regional or international, as I see it from my geographical background. I think using the concept of civilisation is a kind of simplification.

If we keep mixing modernisation theories and all its critiques, like multiple modernities, we miss the definition of time and a process in time. If we say modernisation is linear because [it] has also happened there and there, we will then try to see if our linear understanding fits in different settings or not, so we then talk about the trans-regional mobilisation in the 12ᵗʰ century in a place or civil society in another or Ibn Khaldun discussing civil society, etc. and we try to fit elements of different historical contexts in this model of linear history which is really Western history. Alternatively, we might be very relative and say, No, there are plural expressions of modernity. This discussion, and being critical, is very good but does not help us with modernity, which is a concept that has to do with a process inside societies and among societies, which is then what you call the quality of modernity.

Since I am running out of time, I [will] try to very shortly give a model of how we can think of modernity. Some scholars suggest that there is a specific time, which has different expressions in different regions, but also has similarities; they are parallel processes. One of those could be modernity and another could be Enlightenment. We have problems because the notions have been developed in the West, so if we apply them to different regions, we are directly in a trap, but to think about parallel processes in different places would be very helpful. We have unspeakable inequalities between different places, but they are equal in time. Modernisation happened more or less at the same time in different places but in different ways. We might talk about differences in local, regional or global settings. For example, in the last decade, theories have been developed about local modernities in Europe. These theories distinguish between places and social strata to say this process has not happened the same way everywhere. These differences have nothing to do with Islam or the West, it is all about the fact that a process expresses itself differently in different settings.

I think modernisation is not an exclusive process. This is why one should be very critical [of] the term 'westernisation'. In a time of growing interaction of different regional settings, models are taken over and re-interpreted in regional settings, to the needs of the local society. These models are sometimes taken over and even developed further insofar as one cannot say they are copies of the West or westernisation. These are not distinguished by cultural boundaries but by different regional settings. So I think we should talk about parallel processes. And to evaluate how much societies are part of modernity, we may think about how this society was able to achieve what it needs.

The countrysides of Germany or the Mediterranean were not the ones who came up with steamboats or railways, but they made something out of them to respond to their needs. We should ask how much they have been part of this complicated cultural development and how much they have been able to take over new ideas and express them into something new for their own meaning and life. So, to think about modernity, we should think about how these different elements express themselves differently in different times and settings. For example, in Damascus houses were suddenly divided in the 19th century because of the need and desire for privacy. Our modern toilets and all the development of European houses are also to do with privacy. The same thing, the need for privacy, for example, was expressed differently in different settings. That is why I prefer to use [the term] 'alternative modernities' because 'alternative' keeps the concept and the model and regards the West as a copy of it. So to me, it is important to look at local modernities.

Farrokh Derakhshani

In reality globalisation has happened everywhere, especially in the past few decades, so nothing is private or isolated any more. Events that are happening in any part of the world are inter-connected to what is happening on the other side of the world. The way people live is under the direct influence of this globalisation. Going back to architecture, the number of houses and buildings that have been built in the developing countries, including Iran, in the past 20 years is five times the amount of buildings built during the whole [of] history. So whatever is there in Iran is very contemporary, as opposed to what we see in European countries.

I remember that once when I was invited for a conference in Isfahan in Iran. The Minister of Housing wanted to inaugurate a series of apartment houses. I went with them inside the apartments and saw this Western style of apartment with two bedrooms, a living room and an open kitchen that were built by a group of people who were extremely [doctrinaire] and Islamic. It was also interesting that they called the kitchen [an] "open *ashpazkhane!*" If you want to make Iranian cuisine, it smells so bad you need to do it in a kitchen that is private. So it was interesting that the designers of these apartments had just copied the Western model without understanding the needs and culture of their own people.

Two years later I went to Bam to contribute to its reconstruction and visited a small village 50 kilometres [away], really in the middle of nowhere. I was amazed that even in that small village the kitchens were open. Someone told me that the reason for this was that women wanted to be in the centre of the house to be able to control everything. You can see the same sort of influence in apartment houses. Before the revolution, [the] apartment house was very new in Iran. There were only a series of luxury apartment houses and those who wanted to live a Western life used to buy them. So people did not know how to live together. Living in an apartment is of course different from living in the neighbourhoods.

It is very interesting that now around 80 percent of television soap operas in Iran are about the relationships of people living in apartment houses. Is this modernity? It seems to me that people in the world are increasingly sharing the same values. They are now having more shared values than they have ever had in history. These days the whole notion of discovery, which used to be important before, has gone, because you are so much aware of wherever you go and you have more shared values. Are these shared values modernity?

Charles Jencks

In yesterdays BD there was this interesting news that Rem Koolhaas and Norman Foster, two of the world's leading architects, have clashed over claims of a "remarkable similarity" between two of their most ambitious projects. If you look at it, they are both claiming [theirs] to be the most radical design ever designed: they both claim the most ecological design ever designed. They both claim that they invented it and amazingly they both claim that it is completely traditional!

Deniz Kandiyoti

Arjun Appadurai, who is an anthropologist, coined this idea of 'modernity at large'. He is arguing that it is useless to talk about whether it is Western or not Western because now modernity is at large and it is circulating in different and unpredictable ways. So therefore, he feels that we have somehow gone beyond trying to call it local, multiple, etc., and that the circulation of objects is very important, so that television changes patterns of socialisation where everybody watches together: men, women and children. I think attacking this angle from the usage of space is actually hugely revealing, because you have concrete manifestation of change and tangibility of special use. You can see, for example, that people are no longer separated because everybody watches television. I am simply saying that this is a very productive point of entry.

Modjtaba Sadria

I think the element that allowed the universalisation a certain pattern of consumption of built environment, which one could call the ideology of bigger and more, I guess this is what Farrokh (Derakhshani) is referring to as sharing the same value, has a fundamental condition that I do not think can be continued. That condition is unlimited access to resources. If we accept that resources are limited, then the locality, including local knowledge, which would encompass notions of space, of light and shadow, intimacy and public etc., the values that are attached to that locality will re-emerge. In Japan, many involved in critical perspectives on built environments have opposed the policies of intense and rapid modernization that was requiring to let go all local references that Japanese used to have in order to become able to work in factories, on technology and live in what is symbolized in mansion buildings way of life, and now, they think that the cost of living in mansion buildings in the past and present, would be to transform the whole Japanese territory in regions threatened by atomic energy centres and their wastes. On the one hand, and on the other hand, even with this, reproducing the model of living in mansion buildings, has become quasi-impossible. The choice is certainly not as it has been argued in Japan, not to go back to the wooden and paper housing which was much of the local prior to the 1950s, but is, in trying to reinvent, recompose the local that allows well-being and generates self-esteem of the Japanese people. sold everything they had as local in order to live in mansion buildings and now they think that the cost of living in mansion buildings is transforming the whole territory of Japan into atomic energy centres, and they cannot reproduce that. And they do not want to reproduce it, they have to go back to wooden paper housing which is much more local and in much the same way that they were doing before 1950. The fundamental issue for me in this discussion about patterns of consumption, what you call globalisation, is that when we criticise global warming and this mechanism of the consumption of goods, including buildings and spaces, 1.6 billion Chinese are aspiring to the same pattern of consumption that we have. 1.3 billion Indians are also aspiring [to] the same.

Altogether, we have around 4.5 billion people are forced to want to have immediate access to the pattern of consumption that you are imposing as universal values. And there is no argument that says we have it, but you cannot get it. So we have two possibilities: either we have to 'regress' in one sense and reduce our level of consumption and say we cannot consume to the abundance that we are consuming, or we will end up in [such a] catastrophe that [we will be] looking for another planet to go and live in because [this one] will not be livable anymore. These are the two choices.

I think the diversity of local modernities is a trap because they potentially leave one universal modernity. If there is a universal modernity, it is Western. The difference between the multitude and plurality of modernity and diversity of modernity is that you can be diverse and never meet each and exist in your diversity. But the whole argument of Negri and his school about multitude is about subjectivities that are intertwined, related, and interacting with each other. Multiplicity is more than diversity and includes relation. This relation changes the objective diversity to subjective multiplicity.

So, on the one hand, these diversities are outside and, on the other hand, these diversities are meeting and we become plurality of modernities of ourselves. So if you go to a German international conference in which there are racists and neo-Nazis against Muslims, your skin will become red and you will be angry because part of your identity has been linked to a part of the world which is Muslim. But if you are here, what emerges out of you is that, Oh guys, be careful! Don't talk so much about Islam as the centrality of your identity! You are much bigger! What is fascinating in this argument of plurality of modernity which we cannot avoid, as Charles (Jencks) said, it is a coming-back fever, is that modernity has brought the capacity of criticising God and everything else, and nothing else had brought this capacity to us before. My definition of modernity is this capacity.

Modernity brought the capacity to understand, question God, to understand the mystery of creation. Before the modern age in the West it was a crime to say we have this capacity. If a human being has extended its subjectivity to the limit of understanding God, this human being can understand the universe and creation and change it. To me, this is the modernity that was achieved in the West. We did not do it in China, Japan, India, or Iran. It was the West who created the only intellectual tradition in which everything is socially expected to be criticised. This is modernity. It is not economy, industry, or consumption. Modernity is the capacity to radically criticise everything, and this can be constantly taken back and squeezed; therefore the cases that you were talking about yesterday, Fascism, Nazism, Communism, etc., are all attempts to prevent it.

Stefan Weber

How would you distinguish between the process and the qualities? What is the difference between those?

Asef Bayat

I think today's discussion is really good, because you have been trying to reach a consensus by discussing the crux of the matter and the meaning of modernity. I think we seem to have come to the conclusion that sometimes the differences that we have had in our positions seem to be semantic. I too hope that it is semantic. In terms of what is modern, what I understand so far is that at least some of us agree that there are similar things going on in the world, whether from internal changes, or through interaction, and so on, but the venues and expressions are different. In other words, there are similar processes occurring as a result of either indigenous internal developments or through flow and interaction, yet the venues of expression of this modern life could be different. However, I think we have not yet focused on what these similar processes are. What are the core elements? One of the possible elements that was mentioned here is self-reflexivity. Perhaps this is one thing we should take into account. I think this is the sphere we should focus on. I am not offering anything else but just plea for that.

Just moving quickly to the fascinating story... about the interior and open kitchen, I think we should contextualise that in the particular history of post-revolutionary Iran. The dramatic changes that have been taking place in the public spaces after the 1979 Islamic revolution is indeed amazing. This notion of *andarooni* and *birooni*, or interior and exterior, in post-revolutionary Iran has been in some ways reversed, therefore the public space becomes privatised by the ideological self of state. Leisure, for instance, became very much domesticated. Most people spent their leisure time at home, and with the changes in the architecture and apartment-isation of those traditional venues, like *sardab* and rooftops, are all gone as a result of the colonisation of public spaces that pushes any woman largely into homes. So women get creative to create spaces of sociability and freedom, like open kitchens. Of course it has the other side to it, too. And that is because we are now more and more domesticated, women come under the thumb of their father, brother and husband, which of course created a particular kind of identity in the 1980s and was expressed later on in the 1990s with the creation of the collectivities which Armando talked about in his paper.

Moncef Ben Abdeljelil

Thank you very much. To me, it was a very rich and provocative paper. I would subscribe to what Modjtaba (Sadria) had already quoted in terms of making clear where modernity happened and what kind of basic fundamentals also need to be observed. I think I have got two problems with the concept of multiple modernities and grounding it in a historical perspective, in political discourse and also in religious thinking. First of all, you remind me of an interesting student in Tunisia who said that modernity was started by Mohammed. Among other things, he talked about the *Saghifa* issue, civil society, as you said, and the *Moakhat* society that emerged in Medina. I have a simple question, How could we appropriate the whole concept and apply it to a context like Medina of 1400 years ago? Muhammad started to build a new configuration of society in Medina, dealing with a totally different shape of what we call today a civil society. In that society, what kind of [role would] religious thinking play to bind or exclude people? This is why I do not feel comfortable with this perspective of grounding the concept, which emerged in a different context, perspective and philosophy, to that period.

Now let me talk about Shiism that you talked about. In Twelver Shiism [there are] two senses for Mahdiism. Mahdi is believed to be the present Imam, who is absent while still living with us. Would you please tell us in which sense modernity could be applied to Mahdiism? There is a theory stating that Mahdiism is a whole process of modernising which changes the whole being. In the first sense of Mahdiism, Mahdi did not do well and he deserves to be absent and he needs to do better in order to come back. The second is that we [have committed] lots of sins as followers and we need to do better in order to deserve his return. History and contemporary Shiites kept the second meaning. What about the first one?

Thirdly, let me talk about Ibn Khaldun. There is a whole gap between what he said in his *Muqaddimah* and his Universal History [*Kitab al-Ibar*]. He did not apply a single theory of his *Muqaddimah* to his History. How would you combine a very brilliant mind [creating] theory and pretending that kind of civil society had been kept to *al-umran al-badavi el-hadari*? At the end you will find that the whole perception of history simply went back to this very traditional perception. This is one comment about the very careful approach that we need to look at the concept itself in its historical perspective.

I have a question for you. I will accept your discussion of the concept of civil society with all the reservations I have. Since we are talking about the tangible elements, could you please tell me what the impact is of this process of modernisation on the space of learning? I would take just one example. How are the religious seminaries in Qom now dealing with other secular spaces within the very contemporary context? What has the impact of modernity been on religious thinking within Qom and among *Marja-e taghlids*? Do not talk about Soroush and Shariati, please talk about the seminaries in Qom.

Masoud Kamali

Having commented after the presentations of yesterday, I have to admit that it was really difficult to sit here and hear all these huge reactions without having the chance to respond. But I am used to these huge reactions, because I used the concept of civil society before and I received the same reactions each time I presented it. People asked me, "how could you do that?" The fact is that I did it without any problem, although you may not like it.

First of all, I think what our discussion here lacks is colonialism. We seem to totally ignore the role of colonialism, war and imperialism in the creation of different modernities. I liked the picture of Bush that was made of 1000 portraits of American soldiers who died in Iraq. But why do the people in the West and in 'critical modernity' only react when their own soldiers are killed? The picture of Bush could be made by pictures of 500,000 Iraqis that died in four years instead of 1,000 Americans. The American lives seem to be more important than other lives. When the terrorists attacked the Pentagon and the World Trade Center, everybody talked about the attack on the World Trade Center and not the Pentagon because it made the terrorists look worse. And then the tradition of a three-minute silence was invented to respect the people who were killed in the attacks. The dean of our university forced us to go out and stay silent for three minutes, but we did not obey and played football instead. One month later, 25,000 Afghans were bombed to death including 19,000 children and women, but we did not have a single second's silence for them. What does it mean to talk about universalism that was created in the West? Only the exact statistics of the number of American soldiers killed in Iraq are available and the Westerners do not seem to care about the exact number of Iraqis killed.

War and colonialism are important tangible elements of modernities. Why do the leaders of the Islamic Republic of Iran and other revolutions in Islamic countries all try to create a powerful army? They do not want to use it against their own people, rather they want to protect their country against the West. Kamalist Turkey, the Islamic Republic of Iran and Iran under Reza Shah are good examples of this. The weakness of the army has always been the victory of the West.

Regarding the argument of Professor Sadria: first of all, who says the critique of God was first done in Europe? There have always been critics of God in societies like Iran and Greece. As I said yesterday modernity does not necessarily have anything to do with democracy. Professor Sadria said that Fascism, Nazism and Communism tried to kill their critics. This is not true. Everyone knows that the critique of God was commonplace in Fascism but not in Nazism. As I said, I cannot present everything here. I have written three books on modernity in which I wrote exactly what I mean by modernity. For instance, I gave a definition of political modernity. According to my definition of civil society, it has got nothing to do with religion. What I argued was that you can see civil society in Muslim countries. I did not talk about Mohammed's time. By giving examples, I just argued that the concept of civil society is not new. To again stress the concept of uniqueness of the West is the problem.

In my newly published paper called "Europe and Asia: Beyond East and West", I discuss the concept of critical cosmopolitanism. Beck and Jerald are the main advocates of this concept. In that article, I develop what I mean by a new way of having a global system in which racism, colonialism, and other-ism should be expelled. You cannot do that without critically changing the concepts that social scientists use for social research. I too like the philosophical discussion about modernism, modernisation and modernity. But when you come to social sciences you have to take part in the processes because the bullets are real. As I said, Derrida should make a decision about taking part in the demonstrations against apartheid. He cannot sit home and say, "according to my postmodern understanding of the world there are no such structures", so he takes part in the demonstration. When Bourdieu leaves Algeria as a soldier and goes back to his country and writes, he admits that this is against what he thinks to be right.

Michel Foucault's discussion of the connection between power and knowledge is really interesting. When I was writing my dissertation, I found an interesting book called *The Government of the Ottoman Empire in the Time of Suleiman the Magnificent* by Albert Howe Lybyer, written in 1913. He had been in Istanbul for five years to write this fantastic book. You can find the reference in my book too. At Uppsala University, researchers and professors can keep the books they borrow from the university library until someone else requests them. I kept this book for five years! At the same time, Max Weber launched his ideas about 'Sultanism'. His theory is completely different form that of Lybyer. According to Lybyer, Sultanism is nonsense. He says eight sultans were killed by civil society and expelled from power. We had other power structures other than Sultanism, not only in civil society, but also in the government. We also had bureaucrats, the army, *bazaaris* and Muslim groups. The sultan, for example, could not go to war without asking the *bazaaris* to give him economic support. Civil society had to be part of all major changes. This fact and knowledge is ignored in the 'West' and reinforces Foucault's idea about the interplay of power and knowledge. Of course, the Europe that wants to be the pearl of the world is not going to use Lybyer's book, but it loves Weber because he explains why we are different.

Moreover, all the democratic movements in the Middle East were attacked by Europe. For example, let us look at Iraq. The Ottoman Empire was defeated and the decision on the campus of Cairo was that the Ottoman Empire, the new Turkey, is not going to have oil but Iran should not be left to have access to the oil of what is now called Iraq. So they created a country called Iraq in 1923 [from] three Ottoman provinces to prevent Turkey and Iran having access to its oil. They took a King from Saudi Arabia and put [him in] Iraq. Baghdad, that had been the centre of philosophical and democratic movements in the Middle East, started a revolt against the world community because the world congress accepted Iraq as a new country after Britain introduced it to the world community. It was the aftermath of the Treaty of Versailles that made the Second World War possible. Mark Mazower's fantastic book *Dark Continent: Europe's Twentieth Century* shows all these games. The democratic movements were bombed in Iraq. They bombed democracy away from Iraq and now want to bomb democracy back into it. Do we include this part of modernisation in our analysis?

Bourdieu in his theory of 'symbolic violence' says power accepts and adopts those theories, understandings, people, politicians, theorists etc., who reproduce the power structure of society, and excludes those who are critical. For example, we know that in the USA people like Chomsky and Edward Said were excluded from many discussions and power centres. We read and write about them, but they are not discussed in the real world. When we talk about modernity and modernism, we should remember that it has [also been] a history of colonialism, genocide, holocaust, and war. These things have been modern. So this is my reaction to the notion of a single modernity. Now 'cosmopolitanism' is being discussed and many believe that we should leave this concept of modernity behind and use and support cosmopolitanism. The notion of multiple modernities helps us free ourselves from the concept of single modernity.

By indigenous civil society, I do not just mean the radical clergy or *bazaaris*. I consider Mosaddegh, liberal Muslims, etc. as part of this indigenous civil society. As a sociologist or political scientist who studies society, without categories and instruments you will be trapped in meta-narratives. That is why the whole discussion of the methodology of grounded theory emerged. We need to have new concepts and categories to understand and describe societies, otherwise we cannot tell history. The change of history during a period of time should be discussed and presented sociologically.

Professor Kandiyoti talked about the association of women lawyers in Turkey to criticise what I call western civil society. I just wanted to remind her that women lawyers never existed before in Turkey and are, themselves, Western. Westernisation and modernisation are two different things that can be the same in some parts. It is a matter of research. Regarding the discussions about Turkey and Iran, I refer you to my book on this topic, *Multiple Modernities, Civil Society and Islam: The Case of Iran and Turkey*, which discusses 200 years of interaction between civil society and state in Iran and Turkey up to 2002.

I think urbanisation is not just modernisation, although it is a consequence of it. You can have urbanisation without modernisation. Islam is very urban religion. A large body of research shows that Muslims just occupied cities when they occupied a new territory and that they were not interested in rural areas. And if there was no big city in that area they created one.

As for the discussion of globalisation, I think we need to remember colonialism and capitalism in our debate. Capitalism is part of modernity and modernisation. There have been huge discussions of the Other-isation of Muslim countries for the mere fact that they have not had capitalism, which is not true. Weber suggests that they did not have it because they did not have Protestantism. This is a myth. A number of scholars have now written about the history of capitalism in China and have shown that in the 16th century cities like Shanghai were much more developed than 17th century Europe.

Regarding the discussion about local modernities I would like to say that it is now very difficult to talk about localities. Ronald Robertson, by introducing the concept of 'glocalisation', suggests that you never have a local which is not global and a global which is not local. He argues that globalisation dates back to the 12th century and is nothing new. You had religious globalisation from hundreds of years ago. But now globalisation is speeding up. That is why anthropology is having a crisis, because you cannot anymore find indigenous communities and people that are different. I prefer glocalisation to globalisation. We now have locals that are global and globals that are local. I cannot discuss these [further] due to the shortage of time, but [I just want to] say that critical cosmopolitanism is the alternative.

Student's question

I have two questions here: How do we understand the difference between the process of modernisation and Westernisation? Can we see the process of modernisation in colonised countries as an independent process or it was connected with the Western world?

Masoud Kamali

The answer is that modernisation is a global change and westernisation is a part of it. The notion of multiple modernities takes into account and accepts the differences on an equal basis. According to this theory, you can be a Muslim in a political party and at the same time be modern. The colonial understanding of the world suggests that you can be Christian and modern at the same time, like Christian Democrats in Europe, but you cannot be both Muslim and modern, like the Islamic parties in Turkey. Westernisation is a specific kind of modernity in which Western countries want to establish the exactly the same kind of institutions in other countries and force it on them. The Shah in Iran and Atatürk in Turkey tried to westernise their countries. Modernisation can be different and at the same time have similar common institutional patterns.

Abdou Filali-Ansary

What amazes me [about this paper] is that although our discussion this morning has been very rich, it has just scratched the surface of a number of challenges that this paper offers to us. So I would suggest that people should go back to the paper. What I was hoping and sometimes fearing is that we would go into a number of concepts or terms that are proposed in the paper, each of which constitute a challenge and sometimes unsettle us in our thinking. I hope we will be able at some point to progress in this discussion in order to put order into our concept. Although we all put many cards on the table, we seem to have not been able to reach any feeling of real communication.

Aziz Esmail

When I came to this seminar I was not planning on chairing this session. It reminds of the famous line in Shakespeare, "Some are born great, some achieve greatness and some have greatness thrust upon them". By the same token, some are born chairman, some achieve chairmanship, and some have chairmanship thrust upon them. I belong to the last category. Thinking about Shakespeare makes me very wistful because my first degree happens to be in English literature and since English is my second language, before studying English I had a great deal of interest and feeling for Indian vernacular poetry. I then went in to study English at an English-style high school that was in today's Kenya. In this school, if we were caught speaking to each other in any language other than English we had to pay a ten cent fine. I actually did that many times, but I am actually very grateful in retrospect... because when I went home, I had no problem at all switching to the vernacular to talk to my parents. So I grew up as an Indian in an East African environment going to an English school and having a particular version of Islam as my faith and I never really felt that I was leaving a particular culture, language or tradition and going into another when I read Shakespeare or vernacular poetry, and so on.

We did not have the notion of the West or colonialism. Of course we knew about colonialism but saw that as a matter of rule of government. We did not relate it to Shakespeare at all and I still do not. When I went back to Kenya to teach at the university, there was a very dangerous move in the university which wanted to abolish Shakespeare and have only indigenous literature, by which they meant African authors who were writing ideologically. Anyway, and I do not think one could call them African really. That sort of consciousness is something which I feel to be a burden; I wonder if we can get away from it because [it] seems to be a peculiar problem in the humanities. If you look at the natural sciences, in biology, there has been a huge revolution and there is very little relationship between contemporary biology and biology as it was before molecular science came into being, and now neuroscience and so on. But if you go to biology conferences, they do not describe their revolution as modern. They do not have these notions of modern and pre-modern whatsoever, and it gives, I think, some kind of vitality and creativity to it.

I know that sciences are different from humanities where we are dealing with cultures and so on, but it seems to me that when Marcel Proust wrote his novel, he did not think he was writing a modern novel. It was theorists who then said that he is a modernist, and likewise with T. S. Eliot. The problem with these words is that once you get these categories in your mind, they become despotic and it is very difficult to free yourself from those concepts. I think it would be very interesting to try to put ourselves in situations where we did not have these words at all. I gave a talk some years ago in Pakistan and took a risk saying that if it were possible to have a drug which gave you amnesia for a single word [but kept] the rest of your language intact, so that you had the whole language minus this one word, then I would [have] the word Islam removed from our vocabulary. I thought that [if you were to] look away from that word you would be concentrating on the real issues, which Muslims have always done. I think that some of these words, similarly, are words for which if an amnesia [pill] could be found, it would be very welcome.

It is matter of debate, but it seems that the 'West' itself is one of these words. It is very clear that Max Weber does not know about Islam and has a very poor picture of it. But I am not sure that I would see that as representing the West as such. The Iraq war and Bush's behavior is an appalling thing, and that the lives of American and British soldiers are counted, but the lives of Iraqis are not. However, I am uneasy about having Bush, Blair, Weber, Kant, Wittgenstein, etc., in one block. I wonder if these broad, gross categories are not dangerous because one of the things it will do, for instance, is stop me from being able to appreciate Shakespeare. Many might think Shakespeare is 'the West' and if one is [to be] authentic one should stay within one's vernacular, and I think that is a very dangerous consequence. I was looking forward to comments on cosmopolitanism because this is something that we ought to take seriously, but whether the present ideological consciousness about modern, pre-modern, non-modern, West and non-West facilitates or impedes genuine cosmopolitanism, I would rather suspect that it impedes it.

From Critique in Modernity to Critique of Modernity

MODJTABA SADRIA*

If he is to live, man must possess and from time to time employ the strength to break up and dissolve a part of the past: he does this by bringing it before the tribunal, scrupulously examining it and finally condemning it; every past, however, is worthy to be condemned - for that is the nature of human things: human violence and weakness have always played a mighty role in them. It is not justice which here sits in judgment; it is even less mercy which pronounces the verdict: it is life alone, that dark, driving power that insatiably thirsts for itself.

Friedrich Nietzsche[1]

Modernity opened many new gates to the human spirit. Some of these gates have been quantitative transformations of practices existing before the emergence of modernity, while others have been qualitative ruptures. Because modernity allowed itself to be radically critical towards all pre-modern human practices, the capacity to critique all things human, (beliefs, thoughts, organisations; power, joy, or happiness) has been accepted as a legitimate and even necessary act. This critical perspective, once recognised as a legitimate act, could not be restricted to only those who proclaimed fidelity to modernity. Critique, even the most radical form of it, gained an ontological legitimacy towards modernity itself, including its aspirations for new contents, forms of beliefs, thoughts, organisations, power, joy, and happiness.

The premise of this paper is that the legitimacy of the critique of all things is one of the tangible elements of modernity; the subject of such a critique could well be modernity itself as well as the totality of its premises. The peculiarity of the critic facing modernity, even to the extent of its rejection, by explicitly recognising, or implying, the fundamental need for a dialogical relationship with modernity, becomes part of modernity itself. In one sense, it could be said that criticising modernity is part of modernity's agenda.

The variety of starting points, stances and arguments that have shaped critiques, whether soft or harsh, of modernity, both from within modernity and from outside, could have induced a consideration of the exteriority of the critique of modernity towards the modernity project. It is useful to look at the variety and the epistemic contents of the critiques of modernity in order to better grasp the possible place of the critic in modernity.

---

*   I am extremely thankful to Catherine Lee and Rebecca Williamson, for having rendered this text more readable.

[1]   Friedrich Nietzsche, "On the Use and Disadvantages of History for Life", *Untimely Meditations*, trans. R. J. Hollingdale, Cambridge: CUP, 1997, pp. 75-6.

When talking about the critics of modernity, what comes to mind first are those critics who are part of the lineage of modernity, for example, postmodernists who attack the enlightenment foundations of modernity.[2] Another case of radical critique of modernity that remains within modernity's lineage, while denouncing its implications, is the perspective of colonial modernity.[3] More interesting, and more difficult to grasp, are those who criticise modernity from outside of modernity's references, for example, the religious fundamentalists' rejection of modernity. Very often the rejection of the foundations of modernity by religious fundamentalists is a special case within the broader category of "Conservative Critics" of modernity.[4] Fundamentalism is, in fact, a radical critique of the very foundations of modernity: the enlightenment.[5]

One of the common elements of all existing religions is the existence of one or other expressions of fundamentalism among their thinkers and believers. Sooner or later these thinkers come to reject modernity.[6] One is forced to notice a common element within the broad spectrum of critics of modernity; the majority of audible critics consider themselves to be righteous for critiquing modernity, particularly in respect of their description, understanding, or rejection of modernity. Within this context, two important questions emerge concerning the degree of criticism towards the "adversary" as modernity is labelled:

- What is the inner logic of the critique, its epistemic foundations?
- What is the incidence of its radicalism?

Looking at the relationship between criticism and modernity requires a more specific reading of criticism as a specific category.

---

2   To paraphrase Jean-Francois Lyotard, "Enlightenment thoughts as mainly serving the purposes of a corrupt humanism centred around a Masterful Subject who dominates nature and everything living within it". Thus, the task becomes not to seek any revolutionary change, or even to articulate the political aspirations of a particular oppressed group, but to "wage a war on totality". See Alex Callinicos, *Against Postmodernism: A Marxist Critique*, New York: St. Martin's Press 1989, pp. 84-92

3   For some, this has three main aspects "The first is that *modernity* must not be mistaken for a thing in itself, for that slight of hand obliterates the context of political economy. The second is that once modernity is constructed to be prior to colonialism, it becomes all too easy to assume, wrongly, the existence of an origin and instrumental temporal lag separating colonialism from modernity. Thus, the third point is that the modernity of non-European colonies is as indisputable as the colonial core of European modernity", in Tani Barlow, "Introduction: On Colonial Modernity", in *Formations of Colonial Modernity in East Asia*, edited by Tani Barlow, Durham, Duke University Press, p. 1. For a brilliant presentation of the main arguments of "Colonial Modernity", see Hiroko Matsuda, *Colonial Modernity Across the Border*, unpublished Ph. D. dissertation, Australian National University, 2006. David Harvey has criticised modernity by stating that the logic that hides behind its project is one of domination and submission, see David Harvey, *The Condition of Postmodernity*, London, Blackwell, 1990.

4   Robert Kraynak, "Conservative Critics of Modernity: Can They Turn Back the Clock?" *The Intercollegiate Review*, Fall 2001, pp. 31-39. See also Martin Travers *Critics of Modernity: The Literature of Conservative Revolution in Germany, 1890-1933*, New York Peter Lang, 2001, as well as Thomas Docherty *Criticism and Modernity*, Oxford University Press 1999.

5   Pauline Westerman, "The Modernity of Fundamentalism", *The Journal of Religion*, Vol. 74, No. 1, January 1994, pp. 77-85. See also Gilles Kepel, *The Revenge of God*, Cambridge, The Polity Press, 1994.

6   For a broad panoply of religious fundamentalist argumentations against modernity see Martin Marty, and Scott Appley (Eds.) *Fundamentalisms Observed*, The University of Chicago Press, 1991.

Anatomy of the Concept of Criticism

It is difficult to define the concept of "criticism." Its commonly accepted meaning is evaluation and judgment of an object. There are, however, several explanations of the relationship between criticism and its object; how criticism perceives its object; and, what the impact of criticism is on its object or the society where the criticism occurs. The purpose of this section is to present on overview of the variety of understandings of the concept of criticism, and then offer a topological map.

The conventional explanations of the concept of criticism tend to categorise them in accordance with the approach, for example, "New Criticism," "Postcolonial Criticism," "Reader Response Criticism" and so on. These explanations are easy to understand and undeniably important. After reading these kinds of explanation, however, one feels that the definition of "criticism" becomes much more ambiguous because the boundaries between the approaches often overlap, and the focal point of each approach is often so different that it would be impossible to measure all of them with a single criterion; for example, "Feminist Criticism" has been established as one genre of criticism, but it is also considered part of "Radical Criticism". According to Scott N. Arnold, "Marxist Criticism" is also part of "Radical Criticism". For other authors, "Radical Criticism" includes so-called "Postcolonial" critics. The boundary between each approach is not clearly drawn. The focal point of "Reader Response Criticism" is the reader, opposing the assumption of a single meaning that is shared by author and reader. "Postcolonial Criticism" is focused on the power relationships that impose a "single" meaning on a society as a form of domination. Thus, the focal point of each approach is so different that it is impossible to map out the multiple understandings of the concept of criticism.

While there are many criteria which might be used to understand the concept of criticism, for example, chronological arrangements, the internal/external criterion of judgment, and so on, this paper adopts the following two axes: "Position of the critic" and "Political Orientation of Criticism". If criticism is the evaluation or judgment of something, it must include the relationships between the critics and their objects. The first axis shows how the critic positions himself in relation to his object. Some might regard critics as the representatives of universal and objective values, while others might regard them as mere addressers of their own opinions. The second criterion is the "Political Orientation of Criticism". In this sense, the term "political" does not indicate whether the critic is on the left or right, but whether the criticism itself is oriented to politics or not. Some say that criticism evaluates its object negatively, and then brings about something better. On the contrary, the function of criticism is to show the internal organic arrangement of its objects.

When these two axes are crossed, there are four quadrants, and each one shows a particular type of criticism. This paper will explain each of these types of criticism and then present a fifth approach that is beyond the boundaries of the quadrants in Figure 1.

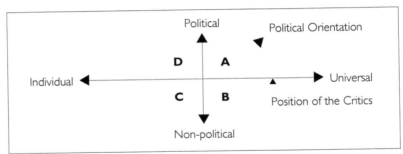

Figure 1

However, before offering the explanations, it is important to explain the reasons for and the legitimacy of adopting these two axes. It was stated previously that the basic definition of criticism is to evaluate or judge something. If this definition is accepted, it means that there are many "criticisms" because in contemporary society, thanks to technological developments and freedom of speech, there are uncountable "criticisms" from reviews, editorials, and one's impression, to professional "criticism".[7] This situation allows ordinary people to state their opinions as a kind of criticism, and the scope of the "critic" has expanded to include them.

At the same time, however, the expansion of the scope of criticism is sometimes judged negatively because it seems to bring about the depoliticisation of criticism. In 1962, Sugano pointed out that the political impact of criticism is lost in societies where the common bonds disappear. This situation has not changed. In the late 1980's, Terry Eagleton also pointed out that professional critics should have a political and precious role in contemporary society, however, he noted that in contemporary society, critics aimed only to keep their authorial position, thus depoliticising and rendering meaningless.[8]

Since the so-called cultural turn, the important focal point of discussion about criticism seems to concentrate around these two axes. The cultural turn, challenging "the generalising, decontextualising approaches of positivist analysts who attempted to formulate scientific explanations and predictions about actors' behavior, the validity of which could be assessed without considering actors' understandings of the situations that they faced",[9] has raised issues for social criticism. If the assumption that the validity of something is multiple and not pre-given is considered, what is the meaning of a "critical account" of something? In this situation the position of the addresser of criticism, and the orientation of the criticism become much more important. Thus the two axes are selected.

---

[7]   For example, Scott N. Arnold wrote about the expansion of the scope of the critics as follows, "(n)early any reflective person has grounds for dissatisfaction with the social system in which he finds himself. Most of us are social critics of some sort, though some of us are more severe than others" (Arnold 1989: 25). There are many authors who have mentioned the expansion of the scope of the critic (cf, Ruhloff 2004: 381), and the following definition by Tokio Iguchi shows the thickness of it. He stated that every discourse that includes evaluation of something, from the judgment of the art of others, to food, and personality of the others, is criticism (Iguchi 2001: 7).

[8]   Eagleton 1988: 156.

[9]   Kemp 2003: 62.

Approaches of Criticism

Adopting two axes provides four archetypal forms of criticism as follows.

1. Quadrant A: Criticism as Enlightenment

In Quadrant A, the political orientation is positive and the position of the critic is universal. This means that criticism is to be regarded as a normative activity conducted by those who bear "universal" or "ideal" standards to judge the object. In this sense, the criticism aims to show the standard which the object of criticism should have, but does not have yet, and thus expose the gap between the object and standard. Hereafter, this approach is called "Criticism as Enlightenment". In this understanding, Enlightenment means the process of making something better "by the light of reason of inconvertibly true standards, rules and maxims... the depreciation of all that failed to meet these standards, and of any pretension by "superstition", local custom, authorities, arbitrary decrees, partial representation of merely private reflection to universal and self-evident truth".[10]

The ancestors of this understanding of the concept of criticism are the ancient Greeks. According to Kauppinen, the function of Socrates' questioning was "help(ing) people already pregnant with knowledge to articulate it in explicit form, thus bringing their views and actions under rational control".[11] In Platonic Doctrine, "learning is a matter of retrieving, bringing into light, through dialogical reflection, the buried knowledge we always already have".[12] It is worth noting, however, that in Ancient Greek, the concept of critique included private subjectivity. In that period, "(c)ritique is", as Benhabib pointed out, "the subjective evaluation or decision concerning a conflictual and controversial process crisis".[13] In the period of early Enlightenment, she continues, the term lost its connection with subjective judgment, and finally, on the eve of the French revolution, "criticism" came to mean "the exercise of rational evaluation...".[14]

No brief explanation of criticism as Enlightenment can be achieved without referring to Immanual Kant's understanding of criticism. For Kant, Kompridis said, criticism is to submit something to reason's free and open examination. His explanation also shows that criticism as Enlightenment connects the term with not only "reason" but also with "public" because "(t)o submit something to critique, then, is to submit it to reason – to reason interpreted as a non-coercive medium of public justification. If something can be justified in light of reason's "free and open examination" – be it a contestable cognitive, moral, or aesthetic claim, a contestable social practice or cultural tradition – it deserves our respect (Achtung)".[15]

---

[10] Bannet 1997: 24.
[11] Kauppinen 2002: 3-4.
[12] Ibid 4.
[13] Benhabib 1986: 19.
[14] Ibid 19-20.
[15] Kompridis 2000: 24.

Then, the two characteristics of criticism as Enlightenment appear. For the first, the critic is expected to have a public role as a representative of community and to make the object better by self-correction.[16] Those who have this understanding of criticism, for instance, would "criticise the beliefs and concept informing such practices (for example slavery, apartheid, abortion, or animal exploitation) because they want to bring about their reform of abandonment".[17] Second, criticism includes political orientation: to make something better in accordance with a "universal" or "ideal" standard.

2. *Quadrant B: Criticism as Discovery*

In Quadrant B, the critics are also representative of truth, authenticity or validity, but the political implications are less direct. In this understanding, criticism is regarded as the discovery of an objects' hidden organic arrangement that decides the meaning of it. Hereafter this approach is called "Criticism as Discovery". The core element of this approach, seeking for the aesthetic meaning of the object,[18] seems to sneak into every criticism as long as it delineates the field of investigation. When one decides on an object, one is unavoidably in the process of seeking for some sort of purity.[19] Because the most popular objects for which this approach is adopted are textual, for example, literature, this explanation is based on literary theories.

This kind of criticism has been called aesthetic criticism and formalism, but the most famous version of this type of criticism is called "New Criticism".[20] This approach has political intentions and implications, but the critic does not intend to bring about political impact. According to Ochi Hiromi, New Criticism was started in the early 1930s by people who were worried about the devastation of humanity caused by developing industrial capitalism. They tried to save humanity by recovering old traditions, which seemed to have been lost.[21] However, the initial politicality of this approach soon became invisible because of the substantive method they adopted. Those who recognised the criticism as discovery advocated separating outside factors that might influence the object under investigation. Texts came to be regarded as self-contained and autonomous from other things such as social situation, human emotion or other texts. In other words, this trend required people to see the texts only in terms of intrinsic, timeless, and universal aesthetics.[22] The critics were required to find the intrinsic formations of texts.

According to O'Kane, New Criticism denied extrinsic criticism, which tried to take environmental factors into consideration to investigate the objects of criticism, because,

---

[16]   Saeki 1958: 32, Sugano 1962: 11.
[17]   Pleasant 2003: 98.
[18]   Tomiyama 1990: 14.
[19]   Ibid.
[20]   According to Tanji, Russian Formalism was highly influential on New Criticism because part of the New Criticism group in the 1930's in United States was composed of people who had fled from repression in Russia (Tanji 2003: 10).
[21]   Ochi 2006: 12-13.
[22]   McLaughlin 1994: 17.

firstly, "it was impossible to know for sure what effect any given social event had had on a text, extrinsic criticism could not say absolutely that the cause it had identified was the cause of a literary texts".[23] They preferred New Criticism's approach because "it worked with a more sophisticated interpretive sense. Unlike the simplistic hermeneutic of the extrinsic model, the approach appreciated the complex and elusive nature of poetic meaning in fact, the fundamental ambiguity of literary language was what made poetry special".[24]

When this approach was institutionalised by taking it into university curricula, the separation of texts from environmental factors resulted in two consequences. Firstly, it privileged the text as high-culture, in other words, New Criticism became part of the process of civilisation.[25] This means, it was hegemonic; "it institutionalised the "cultural and political amnesia" necessary to the uncontested expansion of imperial power".[26] By focusing only on the internal organisation of text, criticism cannot take into consideration the social situation in which text were written, published and read. Secondly, criticism became elite because "New Criticism reinforced teaching of a limited set of prescribed texts in schools and promoted a view of literature as a body of knowledge to be transmitted from teacher to students".[27]

In sum, criticism as discovery's characteristics can be summarised as follows. First, there is a single, monist and intrinsic formation in text and the critic understands it better. Second, although the results and motivation of this approach are highly politicised, criticism itself does not intend to have political implications.

3. Quadrant C: Criticism as Diversification

In the third quadrant, the critic's position is neither universal nor political. Though this understanding of criticism is popular in contemporary society where movie reviews, book reviews, editorial and personal opinions are welcomed, only a few scholars have defined criticism in this way. This understanding, according to Richardson, admits the radically indeterminate, subjective and relativistic nature of criticism, and it "would deny in theory the possibility of any model, ideal, or authorial reading. There is no autonomous textual meaning there to be recovered; the reader creates the text even as he or she reads it".[28]

This type of criticism, hereafter called "Criticism as Diversification", as Tanji pointed out, might help to diversify the possibilities of reading its objects,[29] but it does not directly

---

23 O'Kane 1998: 686.
24 Ibid.
25 Ochi 2006: 14.
26 O'Kane 1998: 691.
27 Johnston 2003: 53.
28 Richardson 1997: 32.
29 Tanji 2003: 7.

intend that the criticism should bring about political implications (this does not deny the fact that diversifying possibilities has political implications by rejecting the authoritative meaning imposed by the canonical understanding of the object, and by validating differences between readers).[30] The reason is that there is no "authority able to adjudicate between rival interpretations; any reading is always only another reading, never a better, more accurate or more comprehensive reading".[31]

4. *Quadrant D: Criticism as Transforming*

The difference between Criticism as Diversifying and the fourth type seems to be ambiguous, but the latter, hereafter called "Criticism as Transforming" has clear political intentions. In Quadrant D, "universal" validity is denied, but not the importance of possibility. In this understanding, the quasi-universality of monistic recognition of the object of criticism is denied, and it is preferred to debunk the marginalised version of reading of the object and the social situation where hegemonic understanding is possible. Bannet clearly shows this point:

"Critique is oppositional, unmasking, demythologising, subversive or deconstructive. Enlightenment thinking is always unsound: deceptively universal or partial, instrumental or normalising, ideological or logo centric, oppressive or exclusionary. Critique liberates us from such falsehoods and from the injustices they conceal; it brings down philosophies and ideologies absolutist, speculative, systematic, political, humanist, metaphysical or hegemonic to lead us to a brighter day".[32]

This trend of criticism is highly influenced by postmodern thought, where meaning is regarded as self-referential rather than fixed to an external reality, and at the same time, it is "denied that a system of interrelationships can produce a reliable system of signification". This indicates the ambivalent character of criticism: it denies universality, but at the same time, it has to transcend private evaluation because "all of evaluation is required to be correctness".[34]

What is the implication of this ambivalence for the concept of criticism? It is often said that this ambivalence of postmodern thought is fatal to criticism because it tends to end up with mere proliferation of skepticism, which leads criticism to be vulnerable and less meaningful. For example, Kompridis pointed out that though the skeptical moment of critique is, in a sense, an inherent character of critique, when the skeptical moment comes to be dominant in a critical activity, "critique becomes vulnerable to the same self-undermining skepticism it has generated in the beliefs and practices it takes as its object".

---

[30]   Willner 2002: 159-160.
[31]   Richardson 1997: 33.
[32]   Bannet 1997: 23.
[33]   Johnston 2003: 53.
[34]   Iguchi 2001: 8.

In short, he worried that "unmasking critique is consumed by the very skepticism that made its own practice possible".[35]

However, for the advocates of this approach, what this ambivalence means is not only the denial of the foundation of meaning, but also the possibility of transforming the present social apparatus, which imposes particular ways of thinking. To examine this point, this paper offers the explanation of secular criticism, which is a version of Criticism as Transforming, as presented by Edward Said.

Said criticised professionalised criticism such as academic literary criticism, literary appreciation and interpretation or literary theory because those theories were silent about political problems.[36] He suggested that criticism should be "oppositional", and that it "must think of itself as life-enhancing and constitutively opposed to every form of tyranny, domination, and abuses; its social goals are non coercive knowledge produced in the interests of human freedom".[37] In other words, criticism in a Saidian sense is, as Mufti pointed out, "a practice of unbelief; it is directed, however, not simply at the objects of religious piety but at secular "beliefs" as well, and, at its most ambitious, at all those moments at which thought and culture become frozen, congealed, thing-like, and self-enclosed hence the significance for him of Lukàcs' notion of reification".[38] This might sound like mere legitimatisation of the denial of foundations, but when the term "oppositional" comes to the centre of discussion, other possibilities will appear.

According to Arac Jonathan, the Saidian sense of the term oppositional might be equated to "contrapuntal criticism", which is also inspired by Said. The *counter* in counterpoint is, of course, a term of opposition, and Arac continues, "in the musical technique of counterpoint, such phrasings as "note against note" occur; Said argues that "in the same way" counter imperial themes may be read against the thus far predominant interpretations of many great works of Western culture". However, he insisted that "the direction of meaning here seems to me quite different from adversarial opposition".[39] In this sense, the oppositional is used to mean opening a new space, which might be called a "third space"[40] by Bhabha. In a third space, the dichotomous relation is rejected and the new articulation of knowledge is required, and in this process, human emancipation is supposed to be achieved.[41]

"Oppositional criticism is aggressive; it cuts. Contrapuntal criticism is loving; it joins. As Said says in Culture and Imperialism, "My principal aim is not to separate but to connect", his reason being precisely that "cultural forms are hybrid, mixed, impure".[42]

---

[35] Kompridis 2000: 27.
[36] Said 1983: 4.
[37] Ibid: 29.
[38] Mufti 2004: 2-3.
[39] Arac 1998: 57.
[40] Bhabha 2004: 44.
[41] Ibid.
[42] Said, Edward W. (1993) *Culture and Imperialism*, New York: Knopf, p. 51 from Arac 1998: 57.

Thus, the characteristics of the fourth approach are as follows. First, it denies any universal, ideal or monistic model, and, second, it denies depoliticisation of criticism. At first glance, this type of criticism might be seen as mere proliferation of possibilities of reading of an object, but the purpose of this type of criticism is not only to show alternative readings, but also to alter the social situation which is sustained by dichotomy.

Remarks

The section above underlined the multiple understandings of criticism by providing two axes: "position of critics" and "political orientation of criticism", which demonstrated four interpretations of criticism: Criticism as Enlightenment, Criticism as Discovery, Criticism as Diversification and Criticism as Transforming. It is obvious that each interpretation should include variations, and would need much more detailed explanations, but there is a common element. In all four quadrants of criticism, what transcends the intentionality of the criticism seems to be the following:

- The transformation of the object of criticism to the core, central, or hegemonic position.
- Implicitly, or explicitly, beyond any radicalism in construction of the argumentation, opening a way for another existence of the object of the criticism becomes possible, desirable, or unavoidable.

Are these not the very premises of modernity?

Bibliography

東浩紀，鎌田哲哉，福田和也，浅田彰，柄谷行人(1999)「（共同討議）いま批評の場所はどこにあるのか」『批評空間』II-21，pp. 6-32

イーグルトン，テリー　大橋洋一訳(1988)『批評の機能』東京：紀伊国屋書店

井口時雄(2001)『批評の誕生／批評の死』東京：講談社

磯崎新，岡崎乾二郎，山城むつみ，浅田彰，柄谷行人(2001)「（共同討議）新たな批評空間のために」『批評空間』III-1, pp. 6-26

柄谷行人(1998)「批評の『起源』—カント／マルクス」『國文学　解釈と教材の研究』第43巻10号，pp. 6-11

佐伯彰一(1958)「批評の運命」『批評』第一号，pp. 30-36

菅野昭正(1962)「批評についての断想(1)」『批評』第13号，pp. 8-15

関井光男(1998)「批評理論の消尽と再生産」『國文学　解釈と教材の研究』第43巻10号，pp. 138-141

丹治愛(2003)「読むこともまた創造である——批評理論とは何か」丹治愛編『知の教科書　批評理論』，pp. 6-30

富山太佳夫(1990)「歴史　テクスト　批評」市川浩・加藤尚武・坂部恵・坂本賢三・村上陽一郎『浮遊する意味』東京：岩波書店，pp. 1-70

バーバ，ホミ. K　本橋哲也他訳(2004)『文化の場所　ポストコロニアリズムの位相』法政大学出版局

マクローリン，トマス(1994)レントリッキア，フランク＋トマス・マクローリン編大橋洋一他訳『現代批評理論22の基本概念』平凡社　所収

Arac, Jonathan (1998) "Criticism between Opposition and Counterpoint", *boundary 2*, Vol. 25, No. 2, pp. 55-69.

Arnold, Scott N (1989) "Radical Social Criticism", *Reason Paper*, No. 14, pp. 25-31.

Bannet, Eve Tavor (1997) "Criticism and Intranslation: The End of Critique in a Democratic Society", *Argumentation*, Vol. 11, No. 1, pp. 23-33.

Barry, Brian (1990) "Social Criticism and Political Philosophy", *Philosophy and Social Criticism*, Vol. 19, No. 4, pp. 360-373.

Benhabib, Seyla (1986) *Critique, Norm, and Utopia: A Study of the Foundation of Critical Theory*, New York: Columbia University Press.

Bhabha, Homi (2004) *The Location of Culture*, London: Routledge.

Bogues, Anthony (2005) "Working Outside Criticism: Thinking Beyond Limits", *boundary 2*, Vol. 32, No. 1, pp. 71-93.

Cotkin, George (2004) "Democratisation of Cultural Criticism", *The Chronicle of Higher Education*, Vol. 50, No. 43, pp. B.8.

Eagleton, Terry (1998) *Literary Theory: An Introduction*, Minneapolis, Minn.: University of Minnesota Press.

Gans, Eric (1998) "Aesthetics and Cultural Criticism", *boundary 2*, Vol. 25, No. 1, pp. 67-85.

Iguchi, Tokio (2001) *Op. Cit.*

Johnston, Ingrid (2003) *Re-mapping Literary World Postcolonial Pedagogy in Practice*, New York: Peter Lang.

Kaupponen, Antti (2002) "Reason, Recognition, and Internal Critique", www.helsinki.fi/~amkauppi/phi/Reason_Recogntion_and_Internal_Critique (accessed 23 March 2006).

Kemp, Stephen (2003) "Rethinking Social Criticism: Rules, Logic and Internal Critique", *History of the Human Sciences*, Vol. 16, No. 4, pp. 61-84.

Kompridis, Nikolas (2000) "Reorienting Critique From Ironist theory to Transformative Practice", *Philosophy and Social Criticism*, Vol. 26, No. 4, pp. 23-47, pp. 85-89.

Mufti, Aamir R. (2004) "Critical Secularism: A Reintroduction for Perilous Times", *boundary 2*, Vol. 31, No. 2, pp. 1-9.

Mummery, Jane (2000) "Review Article, Re-Orienting Literary Criticism: Philosophy and Literary Theory", *Social Semiotics*, Vol. 10, No. 3, pp. 355-358.

O'Kane, Karen (1998) "Before the New Criticism: Modernism and the Nashville Group", *The Mississippi Quarterly* Vol. 51, No. 4, pp. 683-697.

Ochi, Hiromi (2006) "Father of New Criticism. Community of Latin American Agri-Culturalists", *Annual Bulletin of Education Department of Hitotsubashi University*, Institute of Research on humanities, Vol. 43.

Pleasant, Negal (2003) "Social Criticism for Critical Critics"? *History and the Human Sciences*, Vol. 16, No. 4, pp. 95-100.

Posner, Richard A (2003) *Public Intellectual: A Study of Decline*, First Harvard University Press.

Richardson, Brian (1997) "The Other Reader's Response: On Multiple, Divided, and Oppositional Audiences", *Criticism*, Vol. 39, No. 1, pp. 31-53. (2004) "Problematising Critique in Pedagogy", *Journal of Philosophy of Education*, Vol. 38, No. 3, pp. 379-393.

Saeki, (1958) *Op. Cit.*

Said, Edward W. (1983), *The World, the Text and the Critic*, Cambridge: Harvard University Press.

Sugano (1962) *Op. Cit.*

Tanji (2003) *Op. Cit.*

Tomiyama, Takao (1997), *Deconstruction. Practices of Modern Criticism*, Kenkyusha Shuppan, Tokyo.

Vande Berg, Leah R. Wenner, Lawrence A and Gronbeck, Bruce E (2004) "Media Literacy and Television Criticism: Enabling an Informed and Engaged Citizenry", *The American Behavioral Scientist,* Vol. 48, No. 2, pp. 219-228.

Willner, Evan (2002) "Literature as Communication: The Foundations of Mediating Criticism (Book Review)", *Essays in Criticism,* Vol. 52, pp. 155-161.

Zou, Lin (2000) "Radical Criticism and the Myth of the Split Self", *Criticism,* Vol. 42, No. 1, pp. 7-30.

Discussion

Aziz Esmail

Professor Sadria spoke with such passion that I think we should allow some passionate thoughts and questions to be put on the table.

Asef Bayat

What happens if this anti-modern that you are talking about becomes hegemonic?

Modjtaba Sadria

I think this is impossible. Anti-moderns when they produce arguments in order to refute modernity as their radical other, need their arguments to be acceptable societally in competition with those of moderns, without which they can't have any impact. They are reproducing modernity beyond their will because they do not have the instruments to be in a cluster and within the cluster totally ignore, deny, criticise, forget, neglect the mechanism of recognition of autonomy of human beings that modernity advocates and generates as the basics for social existence, and thus represents the modernity as central, hegemonic, and dangerous in order to be able to denounce it and reject it. In this way, representing modernity and its presence becomes a *sine qua non* condition for the existence of antimodernity discourse. In this way, everything anti-moderns are saying becomes purely reactive to modernity. They have not yet produced an autonomous element for building an independent frame of thought which is not reactive to modernity but proactive in itself.

Aziz Esmail

Are you saying that there is no space outside modernity, and that even the critics of modernity are themselves within the modern system? Or are you saying that it is, in principle, impossible?

Modjtaba Sadria

No, I am saying that all the anti-modern discourses that have come to the scene are reproducing modernity; I am not talking about postmoderns. By anti-modern I mean pre-modern radical discourses like fundamentalist Protestantism.

Masoud Kamali

As I said yesterday, I have a huge problem with this notion of anti-modern. None of the religious and non-religious fundamentalists say that they are anti-modern. Neither their theory nor their practices suggest that they are anti-modern. What you call anti-moderns [must] by definition be against modernity and therefore have some relation to it and [must even be] products of modernity. If modernity is gone, they are gone too. They do not have any independent existence. I have serious problems with calling them anti-moderns. As I said yesterday, modernity is two sided. You defined modernity as the social conditions in which the autonomy of individuals is accepted. I would say this is not a good definition because the Fascists, who were modern, did not believe in the autonomy of individuals...

Modjtaba Sadria

Sorry, I need to intervene because you have repeated this argument a few times. My modernity does not include Fascism. According to my definition of modernity, Fascism and Nazism are not modern. Using my terminology, you are talking about modernisation, not modernity.

Masoud Kamali

So you are only talking about good modernity.

Modjtaba Sadria

I am talking about a modernity which respects the autonomy of individuals as a foundation for societal existence.

Masoud Kamali

Ok, we seem to have different definitions. I will stop here.

Jeremy Melvin

I found Professor Sadria's definition of modernity intuitively attractive. I am not sure if fundamentalist Protestants are the best example of anti-moderns, but I do agree that the capacity for self-criticism draws the boundary between modern thought and any other kind of thought. This is central to the way architecture has interacted with modernism and modernity. At the more intellectual level, modern architecture allows itself to be critical of itself in a way that no other architectural tradition has been able to do. The presentation of Professor Charles Jencks was a good brief exposition of this. I am not familiar with the work of Taylor, but I wonder if it has any relation to Mikhail Bakhtin because I see similar elements in their theories.

Modjtaba Sadria

You are right, Mikhail Bakhtin and Charles Taylor interact very dynamically.

Deniz Kandiyoti

First I want to say how much I appreciate the opening comments of Professor Aziz Esmail... I want to examine Professor Sadria's fundamental starting premise, that we live in a uni-referential world. You take this for granted, but I want to dispute it. For all the claims that are being made about modernity and Weber's famous disenchantment of the world, I personally do not believe this to be the case. I believe, for instance, that a view of the world which is theo-centric rather than human-centric is at the very heart of world capitalism. In the US the people in power have had a Middle East policy in which Armageddon has a part to play. I believe that they genuinely believe that, and this is the frightening bit. We are in a world in which there are Jewish settlers in Israel who are living in biblical times. As far as they are concerned, their claim to the land of Israel has everything to do with what is written in the Bible.

I no more feel an affinity to East and West. In other words, wherever one positions oneself in this world, one has to simply take on board the incommensurability and simultaneity of ideologies, I am not sure if I call them pre-modern. In a sense, the relationship of these ideologies to modernity becomes irrelevant for political purposes. I think Asef (Bayat) was also trying to formulate this question. In other words, what happens when worldly power falls into the hands of people whose vision of the world is still theo-centric and who claim status or land on the basis of religion? The same applies to Hindu fundamentalism. It may be argued that these are modern ideologies. Many people do that vis-à-vis Islamism. When you talk about Nazism, somehow nobody has any problem with considering it as essentially modern, but when you talk about Islam, people think that their analytical and political task is done once they have proven that a particular view or ideology belongs to the realm of the modern. I would say that this is quite irrelevant.

In terms of the outcomes, it is totally irrelevant whether we classify a particular Muslim, Jewish or whatever fundamentalist group as pre-modern, post-modern or modern. Whatever suffix or prefix we put in, there are certain inescapable conclusions. I would say that these world views and ideologies are very much part of this world and this is not a uni-referential world. In other words, the ideologies which, according to Weber, have supposedly disenchanted the world and displaced theo-centric views… is the greatest fallacy. In fact they have not. They are with us and they are contemporaneous, very much alive and never with more worldly power. So, why then do we spend so much time trying to define what is outside and [what is] inside modernity? Should we not concentrate instead on the characteristics of these different discourses? Professor Esmail talked about amnesia and said let us forget about Islam. I could not agree with you more. We should suspend judgment. Forget about post-modern, pre-modern, etc! Look at what is in front of you and then the world stops being uni-referential, and then it becomes a question of politics and not semantics.

Aziz Esmail

I would like to add one remark to that. I entirely agree with most of what you said. You mentioned theo-centric views. I would like to add that there are also other absolutes which have nothing to do with God or religion. Human beings seem to have an inability to relinquish the absolute all together. It could well be that God was conceived as [a way to leave] more space for people to have a measure of autonomy than the absolutes that can be found in this disenchanted world.

Modjtaba Sadria

I am so happy because [this past] day-and-a-half has] allowed two positions to become very clear and converge in this last session. Most of the arguments of Professor Kandiyoti are similar to what Professor Kamali was saying about the centrality of colonialism, imperialism, and political meaning of the world. I think Professor Kandiyoti was right to bring up the political lecture of the word modern. This is very fascinating because, since yesterday, theirs was a stance that wanted a political reading of the word and my feeling was that Professor Kandiyoti was broadening it. Now some of us are converging on the importance of a political reading of the modern, which is not my stance.

Abdou Filali-Ansary

Continuing this discussion, I would like to go back to some of your premises. At the end of disputing about modernity, each one of us could say modernity for me is this, the other would say modernity which reflects the autonomy of individuals and the open future. Maybe the best way to discuss these things would be to say that the most significant 'x' for me is the autonomy of individuals or… And then we may be able to discuss how we can settle our disputes. Maybe here it would be useful to take some distance from the word in order to try to see what is at stake.

Modjtaba Sadria

What you are saying is very important. Masoud (Kamali) and Deniz (Kandiyoti) were talking about the multi-referentiality of our frame of thought, which I do not agree with. It seems to me that there is a continuum in the hegemonic discourse in the world today that is instrumental rationality. Even those who go for a theo-centric view, when they want to press their view, what they do is instrumental rational-based decision making, modelling, and simulation. When they attack Iraq or a village in Palestine, for example, their operation is based on simulation studies all of which have an instrumental rational base. But I would agree with Masoud and Deniz that, in this regard, we also have a degree of multi-referentiality, but it is not to the extent that makes me consider the world of knowledge as multi-referential. What is fundamental in understanding of human autonomy is the capacity that it creates in criticism and self-criticism as patterns of open social interactions and relations.

What Abdou (Filali-Ansary) says is more demanding epistemologically because what is at the stake is that the West, the European experience, part of Europe, a specific moment in Europe, as Asef (Bayat) was saying, or layers of Europe, as Farrokh (Derakhshani) was suggesting, came to fight, to produce knowledge, and to organise, in order to reach a societal being which is based on the foundation of autonomy of the human being. I think in Europe instrumental rationality is squeezing or reducing or amputating human autonomy and its consequence in practicing criticism and self-criticism. Meanwhile, in many parts of the world, different societies are trying to see how they can adjust themselves with the mental setting and social relations that could allow them to recognize what human autonomy and practices of criticsm and self-criticism that it allows, this autonomy of the human being. I think this is the core issue. The anecdote that Farrokh told us about the description of Iranian open kitchens shows that social actors are more and more acting, looking, searching for, and reaching that level of autonomy. They do it in the private sphere and, when they can, they bring it to the public sphere, and when the public sphere is too oppressive they take it back to the private or semi-private or semi-public realms.

In all societies that I know, one can see this search for autonomy and negotiation, often very subtlety, for allowing and generating public criticism and self-criticism as a possibility and as a practice.

To me, the critique of everything that denies the autonomy of human beings in different societies is modern. Both in a radical or very nuanced way, this criticism and the autonomy of mind that it requires has become one of the most powerful engines in the emergence of a multitude of modernities. If there is a globalisation from bottom up, this autonomy is an element of it. In different contexts people are negotiating their modernity to gain more autonomy and this is why modernity has become so important, because what they are negotiating for is being and living together societally and searching for autonomy. It is the recognition of being together societally and not extracting from society as private beings.

Aziz Esmail

I think the task of Professor Homa Farjadi is to synthesise all this. I personally think that it is an impossible task, but we look forward to hearing it.

Homa Farjadi

Thank you for the invitation. I also have to totally disclaim any effort or even attempt to synthesise something in which, as an architect, I am a tourist. What I have heard yesterday and today has certainly been very intriguing and exciting and has taught me a lot. Perhaps what I did try was to maintain an outside position as an architect, and this is what I am going to offer rather than a synthesis of the depth of arguments and discussions that were presented in their specific disciplines. I will look at it from the outside, from my discipline as an architect, to see if it offers anything that might help.

Perhaps what I found most catchy was this business of where the tangible, and I would bring here material, aspects of modernity are that we can get hold of. What are its objects and values? How does it affect lives? And how does it become an aspect of the world that is presented to us as modern? We were given all sorts of qualifications about the way modernity, modernisation and modernism were interchangeable, qualified concepts that we had to distinguish or collapse, and interact with. For my part, I too would like to make a distinction between them. It is just a try.

Maybe as an effect of architecture I see modernisation as something that has to do with a concept of time that is linear. When talking about modernisation, you are talking about science and technology, accepting what is the effect of science and technology and therefore being current and contemporary. So it is something that has no possibility of being rejected unless of course you go and live in the mountains and caves, and even in this case it might become a self-referential act situated in modernisation. Therefore, modernisation is about linear time and the effect of it in urbanisation, the use of technology, internet, and all that we are subjected to by definition as a result of the material cultures that modernisation produces. I think this is something that has to be separated from modernity which, in my view that is, would exist alongside dialogically with this linear concept of material culture that is produced.

Since yesterday, we were told, in a very exciting kind of exposition, that modernisation can be violent and politically multi-layered. It can also be killed and revived, as Charles (Jencks) suggested. And today we appreciated Aziz (Esmail's) point about a plea for its amnesia of itself. Therefore, this notion was discussed that we have to deal with [modernity] in ways that accept it but, at the same time, forget it.

On the other hand there is a sense of time that does not follow this linear arrow and it is one that wants to accentuate its heterogeneity and multiplicity. An example of it is what is created, for instance, in urbanisation, as networks, flux and concepts which are quite ancient (they are not new no matter that our computer technologies and so on might have given us new tools to deal with them) but now these notions of chaos, etc. become applied in a radical way and this radicality is a potential for the stopping of time or going within time in a certain way.

In architecture we are forever faced with two categories. On the one hand we have urban or architectural objects and buildings and on the other hand we have the world of representations of them. I think one can use this distinction to define the notions of modernity and modernisation. In this sense, when we talk about the effects of modernisation, we are actually talking about technology, material advances etc., and when we are talking about modernity, we are talking about representations of it which have nothing to do with linear time. Therefore, all that is conflictual, contradictory and paradoxical about what modernity has produced is within the realm of the representational. Architecture or urbanity... finds itself very much in this domain. On the one hand, in this kind of technological advance, urbanities in Dubai, China, Iran, everywhere, want to achieve what is at the top. We want computers, buildings, sophisticated infrastructure, and all that has an effect on us being current of the time. On the other hand how we represent it, in terms of the modern states of China, Iran or Dubai, might differ. One set of people might like what looks like the West and another may want to create alternatives. So... we are caught in this dilemma of what we do [with] our myths, which, when we are not talking about time in a linear way, the possibility of this is much more intriguing and productive.

In architecture, we have been discussing the ambiguities and paradoxes of this. One argument that I prefer is that perhaps quantitative material accumulations in urbanisation, density, infrastructure and machines are possible to shift towards the qualitative achievement of representational modernity. So for example, in the 1970s, Rem Koolhaas, who is an architect and provocative thinker, analysed the development of Manhattan as a result of sheer, violent capitalist accumulation. Of course Manhattan had produced infrastructure etc., but, nevertheless, because of the possibility of having this openness and non-centralised regulatory planning of it, it actually produces a modality, and here I would call it modernity, which is a certain notion of the metropolis that went beyond its intentionality.

When we talk about China or even Tehran, Dubai, or Abu Dhabi, we are talking about a world which is a matrix of these two aspects of modernisation and representations of modernity. How is it that one is going to make the other possible? Is it possible for one to transform from quantitative accumulation to become a quality and to become a good or bad society? Therefore the question remains for me to see how much of this is possible to be planned, how much of it is an effect, and what makes us think that in Iran people are asking for the effects of modernisation in open-planned kitchens or sewerage or whatever is in the infrastructure of the cities or metropolises and high-rise buildings. Are we here to look for centralising and planning organisational controls? Or are we here to find alternative models within these kinds of effects in a sort of hopeful way of finding a good that might be inconceivable from the good that we might have had as good planners, historically-minded and conscious of what has been the development?

Perhaps... in architecture this has been the problematic that we have had to face, and we are trying to see whether there are alternative ways against this kind of wild de-regulated urbanisation, which is an effect of modernisation and the chance accumulation of modernity, not modernity at the centre. There is certain sense in which Sheikh Makhtoum in Dubai might want the building to look like what is there in London and the West. I do not want this to sound as if there is no argument to be had between representational aspects of modernity and modernisation of technology. This to me is the criticism that is posed: Where it is that these effects of technology, advance, and linear history can be re-seen from this centre as a person in time does not have to make a choice between the linear and the centralising effects of history, what Deniz (Kandiyoti) was suggesting in terms of these already being part of the construct of how we deal with it.

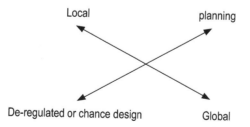

I produced a diagram that in some way might be useful for our discussion. In this diagram we have the local versus global on one axis and the linear time versus non-linear time on the other. In our discussions we were given 'glocalisation' as the context. I think this axis, local vs. global, is one that in architecture works against another axis that we can call 'planning' vs.

'de-regulated or chance design'. While 'planning' is linear, the 'de-regulated design' remains a conflictual modernity which, in Masoud's terms, is where the indigenous would be located, where we could be as far away and as near to that which is outside of linear time in modernisation. It is a construct that would have these modalities of intersection and perhaps, if we see it in a kind of three-dimensional way, it would be like a pyramid where man/woman is sitting at the top and outside of them but dominating these distances rather than being subjected to them. Here, the nature of time determines those distances and linearities just as much inside of it as is in it. That is where I will stop.

Aziz Esmail

I think we had a lot of mental stimulation. It seems to me very interesting that all architects that I know seem to be [so] theoretically concerned and sophisticated. It is very interesting for me to ask why because one does not see this in biomedicine or law, but it is more likely to hear this issue of representation from an architectural historian than from any of the other professions that one can think of.

We have had a fairly wide-ranging, open-ended and abstract discussion, but I think that in this abstract discussion, there are a few nuggets of concrete direction. It would be great if we could steal those out and see where the whole question of modernity can prove suggestive. I think being suggestive is the most it can do. I do not think it is a concept that we must profitably spend too much time trying to define, but it is a suggestive concept which is pregnant in a vague sort of way. And that vagueness of certain concepts are best kept alive because you otherwise you end up with dogma. So if we take it as a suggestive concept and then ask ourselves where it can probably bear fruit in a number of ways rather than one way, I think this discussion may prove helpful.

Farrokh Derakhshani

I would like to repeat what Professor Sadria said yesterday. In these workshops, although we are talking about the 'construction of knowledge' in a broad sense, at the end of the day we want to relate it to architecture. We at the Aga Khan Award for Architecture want to know how we can have a better impact on the built environment. Architects are one of the major agents of modernity; so it is interesting for us to discuss what the tangible elements of this modernity are, and especially where it has implications for the built environment and the construction of knowledge. It would be better if we could channel our discussion more towards the interests of the Aga Khan Award.

Aziz Esmail

The architects might have some ideas about that, because as I said it was very interesting to see the architects engage in theory, as at the same time they are trained in very strong professional ways which gives them the ability to struggle with these two domains of the abstract and the concrete in a manner that philosophers, for example, do not.

Masoud Kamali

When I was invited to this conference, Professor Sadria told me that we want to have a very concrete discussion about the tangible elements of modernity in Iran for example. So in my paper, I tried to talk about all these tangible elements like foundations, political parties, how civil society functions and so on. I also presented a comparison between Iranian civil society and Swedish civil society. As Hegel says, nothing has a meaning before it becomes concrete. This includes knowledge construction. In abstraction you can discuss whatever you want, but in order to have a meaning, you need to bring in the concrete, or at least show that in a historical or social way something functions.

To go further, I think we have to leave the discussion about modernity aside and try to see what is really happening in the world today and what the important questions that we can address are. We should also try to construct some kind of theory to understand the world today. In doing so, [we] should have concrete examples and case studies to make it understandable. I think it is very important to realise that the challenge to sociological theories is to show that it is workable by methods and that it gives you knowledge about a society, community or country. So there are many things that can be done in the next steps. One thing that I am particularly interested in is the comparative study of civil societies in different countries. By doing so, you can find elements, groups, leaders and theories, globally, locally, or glocally, as tangible elements of modernity. Doing it in this way, I think is much easier and fruitful than starting by discussing the meaning of modernity and so on.

Aziz Esmail

One of the things that strikes me... as just one element in a larger aggregate of things, is an anthropological study of how people see architecture, because it seems to me from the remark that Masoud (Kamali) just made that architecture is in this very peculiar position where architects have a professional and technical body of knowledge but demands are made on them by ordinary people who think that they know what they want. That is something that does not happen in so many other professions. For example, in medicine, it is unlikely that somebody says that I want Erythromycin and not Penicillin. People usually leave those sorts of judgments to the expert, but architects, while they are experts, have demands made on them by people who assume to know what they want. Now, if that is so, then I think some kind of comparative study of popular notions of architecture and desires in various societies and how people in different contexts place building in relationship to their own lives would be very interesting and helpful. I am sure what I am saying is not new, but it seems to me that it is one of the areas that could benefit from research.

Jeremy Melvin

I think what you said [expresses] an interesting point, but to get there it might be good to look at the demands that are made on buildings. You have a triple relationship, or a triple demand, that is put on any work of architecture that would include public spaces as well as individual buildings that are being designed. Firstly, any work of architecture has to work, has to offer opportunities, and has to have a sort of physical being to it. Secondly, it inevitably represents ideas. These two main aspects can be at times in conflict in a work of architecture and making a relationship between them is a challenge. And sometimes the fact there is not a direct relationship between them can be quite interesting. Thirdly, there are also financial demands that are put on buildings, particularly in somewhere like London where values are extremely high. An architect has to balance these, often incompatible, relationships and demands into some sort of compromise.

I think the architectural discussion has failed largely to recognise the inter-relationships of those three demands. If you read good architectural criticisms, they concentrate on only one of these demands and very rarely more than one. It would be an aesthetic criticism or a functional criticism or possibly an economic criticism. It is extremely difficult to try to look at them together and in relation to each other. This is what I have been trying to do in my work, and I have found it really difficult. I think against the background of what we have heard today and yesterday, it would come as a major intellectual task.

Homa Farjadi

Let me continue what Jeremy was saying about the way architects are often asked to respond, legitimise, and present the ideas of architecture. Jeremy was absolutely right that these three demands are part of how architects perform, but I also offer a construct which puts modernity as a kind of 'other' of the modernisation programme. We propose what we do, in an under-hand way, position what is representational content in what is otherwise a legitimisation that is totally rationalised or presented as rational. So you will see that what Charles (Jencks) was saying about how Rem Koolhaas and Norman Foster try to do exactly the same thing and argue the same position coming from very oppositional directions exposes the fallacy of the rational argument.

I am very interested in what Jeremy says about knowing architecture in its dimensions other than as a modernising effect. So the idea that what you do in order to have modernised conditions, high buildings, high technology, access to machinery, infrastructure, etc. and, on the other hand, how to be seen to be doing the right thing, becomes such a primary issue. And therefore this construct of what is seen as proto-, good, appropriate, ecological, etc. becomes the whole matrix of values that is not linear any more or self-evident. So, because of how architecture works, I am afraid to say that locality at this moment is far from geographic or anthropological, it has a lot more to do with positions of power, like the Dubai model, and it would be very difficult to promote it otherwise. Maybe it would be a very good question for the Aga Khan Award for Architecture to see how is it possible to promote locality otherwise because, as it is at the moment, the matrices of production of architecture are homogenising the representation.

Jeremy Melvin

Exactly, and the media covers up the problem.

Homa Farjadi

Exactly!

Aziz Esmail

I think the way that media and popular education is representing architecture is another area for investigation in its own right. There are too many channels through which architecture is already being constructed in the minds of people.

Homa Farjadi

If we believe that architecture is more than a machine that performs well, we get over that in modernism. I want to give one example: When you look at designs in the new cities of Kazakhstan, in architectural representation terms they are either Disneyland or representations of despotic orders like symmetrically, linearity, and representations of… power, which are totally out of date.

I think it is really interesting to discuss the concept of 'out of date' in architecture both as a productive mechanism and as fashions of architecture, which is a totally corrupt mechanism. I would say the corrupt mechanism in the case of Kazakhstan is self-evident, but, when you look at it through an anthropological eye, it does not have to always look like it is coming out of the latest computer programmes that have been invented, it can also be less sophisticated and much more basic and primitive in terms of the machine and systems of production. In this sense, that is how I understand it.

Deniz Kandiyoti

I have my own long-standing problems with architects, so I may as well comment on this. I have worked as a non-architect with a group of architects who were doing low-cost housing. My role was to tell architects what the users wanted. I soon discovered that the architects had no use for what users wanted because they had a strong belief in the pedagogic functions of space, how space would teach people to behave in certain ways.

I think that if we are looking to summarise these discussions vis-à-vis your part of this operation looking at representations of modernity and the built environment, first I always invite architects to a position of humility, which is to realise that most of the built environment is occurring without any help from architects and most of the spaces provided by architects are generally subverted by their users and put to completely different uses. The malaise of architects comes from the fact that they come into the picture inevitably within circuits of capital. In other words, the people who are asking you to build these buildings, whether it is in Astana or Abu Dhabi, are either big corporations or various rich despots who use modernity as a mere rhetorical gesture. So the question becomes, How do we understand a possibility of translating the modern, from the grass roots, neither by the big corporations nor by the various commissionaires of projections of state power but by ordinary individuals in their day-to-day life. That is where it becomes extremely difficult and that is where we do need the ethnographic.

What we need to do is to find a way of talking about the role of material culture in articulating modern identities but this gets very complicated. I want to end with an ethnography from a friend of mine who is a Turkish ethnographer who works on material culture among Turkish migrants to Germany. She did a wonderful paper for me about a coffee table. This German family, like many migrant families, was accumulating money to build a house in Turkey. They had their place in Germany and the fight broke out in that household over the coffee table they were going to buy for their house in Turkey. The coffee table that they had in Germany was a particular coffee table that was very practical, [it had a] tile-surface so that you could eat and watch television at the same time, and it was totally inappropriate to contemplate putting such a coffee table in the guest room in Turkey.

In the guest room in Turkey you have to have a coffee table that is for display, the coffee table was not to be functional. Of course, these were standardised. All the returnee German-Turkish workers' living rooms look almost identical. And, of course, there you have to ask yourselves what is it that they are trying to project and why is it that the particular coffee table that works in Berlin does not work in Istanbul? So, then it becomes the question of being able to talk about not just modernity but modernity understood through the prism of taste, distinction, class, etc. Taste, distinction and class are always expressed in a local idiom. For example, in Turkey you had something that for some reason was called a 'vitrine'. This vitrine was a completely useless thing that nobody used. It was only used for displaying objects like crystals and plates.

Architects have absolutely no power over the processes that generate these idioms. I think, as an architect, you would radically dislike the spaces generated and the kind of kitsch that they used. But this is what is happening in real life. So the architects are constantly caught in the same dilemma of wanting to survive as a profession and be able to project a certain aesthetic but in ways they can live with that are not corrupt...

Jeremy Melvin

I think you are absolutely right, and a part of the story is actually the very insecure status, and very dynamic status, of the people we call architects in society. The idea of their being architects to exist purely on fees from designing buildings and supervising their construction, is a very recent one, 150 years old, if that, and in many parts of the world it does not happen at all. I know about this more in the context of the UK than anywhere else but I think the story is probably familiar if not exactly the same in other societies.

Architects have perpetually thought that they have had a very low status and that their fees are very low. But if you look at architects now, almost all the well-known architects here get titles and almost all of them are rich, although I know ones who are not. So these are crocodile tears. I think the more interesting point is how one could examine the issues of not just what people expect from buildings but how architects form a social group, and that is partly [due] to education, but not entirely to education. Garry Stevens, who teaches in Sydney, has looked at the Bourdieuian analysis of the architecture profession but I would not say that his work has gone very far. However, I think it would need to be on both tracks to be really useful.

Homa Farjadi

I do not know Iran that well recently, but I remember that Iranian architects had a very sound spot on the social ladder. They made good money, anyway, although their fees were lower. But what is important was their access to representation, which is the point I was trying to make earlier, that in the end denial of representation and style, which was done by modernists for a while in architecture, is something that we have thankfully got over. In what one can call postmodernist strategies and attitudes towards architecture not postmodernist architecture you cannot help but understand the power of representation and its role within what gives people access to status. In the Iranian case, I would say that since people have this need for representation as already legitimate, the social status of architects is very high, no matter [that] they have not produced the best architecture.

Jeremy Melvin

I think that is a very interesting point because if one were to look at different societies, whether it is Iran or Southeast Asia, one would see quite different balances between who has the control of representation and who has control of the education of the production of space. I think that would be a very useful project.

Farrokh Derakhshani

Going back to what Deniz (Kandiyoti) said about the workers in Germany returning to Turkey, two elements are very important. You talked about representation. We also need to talk about how one wants to identify oneself and what are the rules of symbolism. These two things are very important because there is an architecture that is symbolic of [the] attitudes of people and sometimes architects are able to make something that represents that sign.

I recently saw a photo of the Aga Khan Hospital in Karachi, designed by experts of building hospitals. Its design is well-known particularly [by] the people of Karachi, it is respectful of the environment and local architecture, with courtyards etc., and very modern. When I was there, I realised that everybody who visited the hospital was impressed by the design, but those who were not happy about the architecture of the hospital were some of the doctors, because they wanted a hospital that looked like... hospitals in New York, all contained in one block.

Coming back to the issue of symbolism, we should address the question of how one wants to be identified. One interesting element is the notion of time. One very significant change that has happened in the built environment is that before the recent decades it took a long time to build buildings, whereas today you can build a big building in less than a year. May be that is one reason we are so nostalgic about historic buildings and think that the old looks nice. An interesting thing is happening in the Persian Gulf area: since the 1970s the clients there had been hiring the best British architects to design their buildings and accepted much of what they produced, but they are now much more sophisticated than 20 years ago; they know what they want.

The ruler of Dubai has been trying to make Dubai a destination. In all the commercials about Dubai you can see the building called Burj al-Arab that has become a symbol of Dubai. If you show this building to anybody in the world, they will recognise it as a building in Dubai. But it was very interesting when I heard in a presentation that this was exactly what the ruler wanted: the client had told the architect, It does not matter how much it costs, I want something that can become a symbol of Dubai. He wanted to be identified and seen as someone modern and affluent, since architecture is the combined work of the clients and architects.

I think it is also noteworthy that not all architects have the same level of qualification, knowledge, creativity and competence. Moreover, not all architects are aware of what they are doing...

Aziz Esmail

But doesn't a lot of human creation happen in that way? You do not usually know at the beginning what is really going to come out of what you do. I think that is probably an overestimation of reason when people think that you can plan to get from A to Z, whether it is architect, medicine or war in Iraq, you can see traces of these overestimations of instrumental reason in many discussions about modernity. Once you take one step, it leads to other things; it is a kind of reproductive capacity and you can never know what the outcome will be...

Homa Farjadi

That is exactly why I drew that line between planning and non-planning which can be understood as a constructive process but it should not be understood as simply a black hole that we either know or we do not know. You can assume not knowing to become productive. A lot of contemporary architectural debates are about how to deal with being diagrammatic about architecture. In what sense can we respond to things where we do not know their result. Therefore, this kind of agility with response becomes a mechanism for design rather than me sitting in my studio saying, "you better like it, because I like it". That is not the case any more.

Aziz Esmail

Yes, in a sense, retrospective perspective increases knowledge because you look back at something that was not in consciousness at the time it happened but you can now look at what it lead to. I presented this argument on behalf of historians. There is something to be learned after the event...

Homa Farjadi

... except that at that time the history has moved and you are somewhere else. You have to be dynamic in response.

Jeremy Melvin

I think this is a very interesting point and I can deal with it only anecdotally. But there are architects who would feel restrained by being expected to be brand managers. And when a client comes and says, "Do me one of those", serious architects would quite seriously react against that, but they might not be able to achieve a reaction against it, if you see what I mean. This might be because of costs or being easier just to repeat designs. But I think anecdotally there are several possible ways out of this. Traditionally, a lot of major architects were involved in teaching and some of them engaged very actively in university communities. This happens far less now, particularly in the UK where most major architects are no longer directly involved in teaching. But there are perhaps two other ways.

One thing that some firms do is that they employ people who are there to rethink what they do and indeed to generate some form of internal self-criticism. That might be a sort of narcissistic matter because I do not really know enough about what is going on in these firms. But I think, to be fair, we have to at least consider it as an attempt to give themselves a kind of internal kicking in case of complacencies. The other thing which the architect does is that he deliberately goes out and talks to people and asks them how they would like the designs to be like. Some studies have been done in places like Bradford, but nothing yet has come into fruition, apart from [within] the realm of visual imagery. It is only a tentative step but it might be a way forward. I think there are possibilities but I think Modjtaba (Sadria) pointed his finger to one of the most important issues of architecture, particularly in the way it is part of a global capitalist system.

I think the other side of this is Norman Foster, who has been an enormously influential architect and, on many occasions in a series of key projects over 30-40 years, an innovator. One may not like everything he does but there are certainly some very significant buildings in his CV. He is now such a brand that he can sell 40% of his company for 300 million pounds, [a sale] for which there is no possible commercial justification and is pure brand value.

Homa Farjadi

Obviously, in architecture just like many other disciplines, there are all sorts of practices, a point that Farrokh (Derakhshani) was trying to make, and a brand version of it is probably not the most interesting part of architectural practice. It may be the most prevalent, in the sense that somebody like Foster does more buildings than a thousand other architects might do, but if you are looking for an alternative to what is hegemonic, there are other discourses in architecture. I think Foster is hegemonic and gets trapped by his own representations. The symbolism becomes the brand and this, if you ask many architects, including me, is really the downfall of architecture.

However, there are other discourses in architecture which are more interesting than branding, in the sense that branding is a cultural phenomenon that cannot be denied, meaning all companies are after branding therefore architects to be commercially viable and make money... sell their products accordingly. But the discourse of architecture, whether it has to be dependant on branding, is something that I would say is going [off] on a specific tangent that is not necessarily constructive or what I would consider a viable discussion or an interesting way to go about it. I do not want to call it modernity even. So branding as interesting cultural phenomenon, as it is, is like fashion, style, etc., it has its own productive and destructive aspects.

Farrokh Derakhshani

One of the reasons that this topic for this workshop was chosen was to explore where in the world we are today. As Modjtaba [Sadria] said, one of the reasons we are holding these workshops is to discuss where we are and how we want to see the Aga Khan Award for Architecture in 25 years. When the Award was created some 30 years ago, the part of the world that we were concerned with was very different. In those days, you had indigenous and traditional buildings, so what was built in Kuala Lumpur was very different from the buildings in Bangladesh, Indonesia, Karachi or London. But today we are confronted with a situation in which the same tools are used in different parts of the world and everything is local. This localness of the production is where this idea of modernity came from.

Until recently, Japan was considered as an exception to the rule of Western style. We usually talked about the West while assuming that Japan is special and an exception. Now Japan is not special anymore and somehow one can see a process of Japan-isation of the rest of the world. I think this is one of the reasons that, when looking at modernity, we should see that there are these shared values. A young architecture student who is going to school and is going to practice in Kuala Lumpur feels that he can do the same thing as over here in London. This is actually happening in practice. Today we have architects who are from other parts of the world practicing in this part of the world and vice versa. We call this modernity, not contemporaneity because we want to look forward and guess what is going to happen in the next 25 years to make sure we are on the right track and not to look back. So, because of that, modernity had an important role in this discussion. Please correct me if I am wrong.

Modjtaba Sadria

I am so happy with this part of the discussion because this has been the departing point. One might argue that the homogenisation of representation is not an issue because we have a global world and 'glocalisation' does not change anything. But exposure to your profession has enabled me to give you examples of this view. When we had a conference on the critique of architecture in Kuwait, I did a lot of interviews with young architects from India who were working in Kuwait for 300 dollars and this was a high income for them. Most of them were 25 – 27 years old and this was a fantastic job for them. Did they have anything Indian in the conceptualisation of their architecture in Kuwait? Or is it a major house in London that has done the design and these Indian architects are the subcontractors and foremen of the production that we used to have in the previous stage of industrial production? In my discussion with them, the only thing that was not present in their argument was their perception of architecture. They were there for the function of foremanship. What are our choices in this situation? Submission or argumentation about it?

Globalisation and capitalism are acting and have all their power. They are creating modernisation. The Chinese government is commissioning the most beautiful buildings in the world designed by world's best architects. The number of projects your colleagues have been getting in China is incredible. All of them are asking you to provide them with the best design, functionality and symbolic elements of power, of being modern. So this is one trend in architecture that has become so powerful as the representation of these trends. Every state and every major capital is interested in moving forward in this direction.

Besides laughing at Dubai and making a joke of them, what are our arguments as professionals about preventing this homogenisation of representation? Question number 1, Shall we resist homogenisation of representation or shall we submit ourselves to it? Question number 2, What conceptual elements allow us to resist this homogenisation of representation?

Jeremy Melvin

I think it is quite a challenge to try to give an answer to your questions, because quite a part of architectural discourse is concerned with these questions. I think to some extent, these questions have also to do with how architecture has engaged with modernity. Up until 1900 there were architectural traditions in many parts of the world that were representational languages. In the UK, what you get with modernism, in its most literal form of architecture in the 1920s, is a challenge to all those previous architectural traditions. What that meant was that the notion of representation, and particularly visual representation, became hugely problematic because very few architects could do it as well as the pioneers of modern architecture [could] and trying to construct some sort of representational language had proved extremely elusive partly because there has been a tendency within architecture to resist it in any case for either ideological reasons or financial reasons. For example, the "Brutalist" movement in the 1950s was for ideological reasons. They said that they had an architecture which was "another architecture", without aesthetic. Doing so generated an extremely strong aesthetic. In a lot of architectural writing, when you look at one thing, you realise that it actually means almost the exact reverse.

I think that is a sort of background to this. Now, how can you resist or subvert it? I think that is the interesting thing. In the work that I have done, in a very small way, I have been trying to put back on the architectural agenda the issue of how buildings communicate ideas. Charles (Jencks) has also done a lot of it and this is part of his career. I know that Farshid (Moussavi) in her practice has also been doing this. Both of them have contributed to the events that I have organised on this at the Royal Academy of Arts. I would not necessarily call it resistance or submission to this issue, it is a recognition that it is an issue, and discussing whether there are ways beyond it and ways in which architecture can recognise this quality have been elided for the last 80–90 years.

That moves us into the second part of your question about the conceptual elements. I think that they reside in a lesser-explored area of what I call "aesthetic theory", which is to consider the relationship between function and experience and how we understand what we see. There are areas here that certainly touch on musicology and the psychology of perception which are not issues on which I have expertise. But there seems to be quite a strong difference because of the different mindsets between how you would interpret or experience a building if you are going to it for different purposes, you might go to a building for reading, medical treatment, entertainment, etc. There is a shifting dynamic there, and... this is something which other areas of visual arts have much less of, and indeed the trend in the presentation of contemporary visual art has been to make spaces as homogenised and standardised as possible. I am being a bit unfair here, but I do not think it is completely inaccurate in order to try and eliminate those differences, whereas architecture broadly cannot eliminate the impact of why you are going to a building or the experience you will [have] of it and therefore how you will react to it.

Aziz Esmail

While according to Weber we are living in the disenchanted world, a miracle has happened and we have the sun shining in London. So you might want to enjoy a walk outside before the dinner. I would like to make a couple of comments. This may not be a very neat ending to the workshop, but I do believe in the unconscious incubation of ideas. I think this happens after these conferences and workshops, and you never know what one retains unconsciously which then connects with something else and at the end it may want to make it a building of some sort. Secondly, I think there is a great value in the personal contacts which happen during these kinds of gatherings and some of these personal contacts may bear fruit in the future. Now I am going to hand over to Professor Sadria, who organised this workshop, to make his final remarks.

Modjtaba Sadria

Thank you so much. You have been fantastic and gave us a lot. The reason why construction of knowledge in this field has become an issue for us is that the Aga Khan Award for Architecture, and more broadly the Aga Khan Development Network has [committed] itself to the mission of improving the living conditions of Muslims. That is the departing point. But improving the conditions of living of Muslims has become very difficult to define. When I started at the Award, I read all the literature of the Award, and believe me there is a lot of literature that this Award has created. One of the most fantastic activities of Farrokh (Derakhshani) has been this memory-keeping of the Award. The archive of the Award, which includes the publications, pictures, texts and arguments, is incredible.

Having read the literature, I realised that there had constantly been a tension between the [Award's] Steering Committee and its Master Jury. The Steering Committee has kept asking the Award to do certain things and the Master Jury has reviewed a few hundred projects and responded that they could not answer these questions because it is very complex. Muslim societies have changed so fast in the past three decades [and the task of] improving the condition of their built environment now refers to so many different things, that the answer to the question is more complex. For example, we have been discussing whether improving the built environment of a relatively poor Muslim neighbourhood in the UK can be considered as [improving] the [living] conditions of Muslims. So when you go back home, please do think about this growing diversity and complexity that has made our task more difficult. When you get out of the immediacy of the tiredness of these two days, we would indeed appreciate it if you [would] come back to us to say that if the main concern is that there is a lot of improvement to be done in the conditions of the built environment in Muslim societies, what are the conceptual elements that allow us to think about it? I am here only repeating what you have taught me at the Award during these years.

This is a very important demand to all of you. If you think that there are grounds for improvement of the built environment within Muslim societies, what are these grounds and what are the concepts that helps us to go for it? We even thought to address this issue in a more general way, independent of Muslim societies. At the beginning of the 21st century, what do you think are the mechanisms to improve people's living conditions in the built environment, and the concepts that can enlarge, deepen and improve the discussion? So your task, in relation to us, is not over and these are our expectations from you after your fantastic job in this workshop. We would like very much for those of you who did not have time to finish your papers, and those of you who during these two days of intense exchanges, have come to new arguments and dimensions and wish to develop them, to finish your papers so we can move forward with publishing our proceedings. Thank you again for these two days of lively and rich contributions, from each and all of you.

Counter Space of Islamic Modernity

HOMA FARJADI

Presentations given at the London workshop confirmed plurality inherent in the concept of modernity. They also referred to specific historic instances of modernity which developed within Islamic societies from the Ottoman, Safavid and Mogul periods to 20th century Turkey and Iran. Though we were warned of the cacophonous nature of the word, useful articulations of heterogeneous modernity came through. Avoiding summarising of these intricate presentations, I will use the categories discussed by my colleagues in other disciplines and offer a response using an architectural point of view; to bring to the conversation spatial implications of the discourses of modernity.

Some basic distinctions can be underlined. The discussion of modernity refers to motives of societal development concerned with contemporaneity. That is to ask what might be relevant to do now which differs from the past, in recognition of a positive force for change.[1] Answers to this question divide the concept into two primary directions by which modernity and modernisation gather distinct characteristics and effects of change. Material modernisation refers to the impetus for physical development and technological progress, with effect in urbanisation, and development of infrastructure, technologies of communication and production and of functional objects. These technologies offer modern buildings, modern amenities, modern communications, modern objects and modern media. We all know the effects of historic changes in daily life produced by the presence of cars, trains, air travel, radio and television and, more recently, computers, mobile phones, and the internet. These purposeful changes directly impact matrices of the lived space of societies as well as the everyday life of the individuals. Their effects are felt in both public spaces and in the private domain. With concomitant advantages and disadvantages modernisation has been both radically positive and costly at the same time. While advancing meta-narratives of development and technological progress, it has brought about revolutions and wars. Though modernisation may accumulate wealth in physical terms, it guarantees neither social justice nor cultural development.

Modernity, on the other hand, with its requisite reason and rationality, refers to social change through organisational, economic complexity and secularism, with direct implications on the

---

[1] Edward W. Soja, *Postmetropolis* (London: Blackwell, 2006)
[2] Masoud Kamali, "Iranian Islamic Modernities", in this volume, pp. 49-66.

roles, rights and representations of the individual in civil society.[2] Modernity, therefore refers to the capacity for positive self critical change generated within a society and requires the openness of that system to self renewal. Critical modernity then, could be said to be based primarily on the process of representation and communication. Its spatial effects become tangible through the potential for a society to provide for such communication through both immediate and mediated environment of exchange.

Whereas spatial modernisation provides for physical development and advances spaces and objects of use according to notions of progress, *modernity* works through representation, mediates environments and creates heterogeneous spaces according to radically different perceptions of "the good life". Looking for what is a desirable space/object in any locality, discourses of modernity resist hegemonic forces and seek the intersection of local and global forces for their own cultural renewal and redescription.[3] Spatially, *open city* describes such a territory where space is open to be re-described or re-territorialised – as it has been argued by Deleuze and others – by individual representations of heterogeneity and difference. Though originally the word referred to a condition of occupation where boundaries are eroded and gates opened while cultural monuments are preserved, in its positive framing *open city* produces an open system welcoming change within its own spatial logics.

In terms of the temporality of these two discourse, I would suggest that, where modernisation works along the linear arrow of time from the past toward the future and presents a meta-narrative discourse of planning and design by government or the market, modernity belongs to the individual and his/her own narrative, simultaneously contemporary and archaic, a time of *flux* as described by Michel Serres. This is a paradoxical time of now and another time, which continually modifies the linear time of projective design by unpredictable and contingent forces of will, expression and desire. Historically this time has intersected the space of the individual *with that of society through* un-decidable signs of a *counter-design*. Whether developed by the avant garde or in its formulation by popular culture, architecturally, counter design crosses technological progress and cultural contemporaneity with popular culture and intersects the functional with the workings of desire. Contrary to architectural faith and will to design, the two do not always have a happy conjunction. Opening an alternative to what is either the historical teleology of modernist design in *blank slate* interventions, or its opposite, the *laissez faire* of individual expression, *counter design* foregrounds visionary chance in the pragmatic, locally contingent operations and prompts a new register of the archaic in modern space.

Spatial Practices of Islamic Modernity

In the context of Islamic societies, discourses of modernisation have often been entwined with those of westernisation. In many such societies physical modernisation, whether from the west or internally generated, is more accepted and even welcomed, while cultural modernity,

---

3   Modjtaba Sadria, "From Critique in Modernity to Critique of Modernity", in this volume, pp. 91-102.

with its demand for open processes of representation and cultural liberties for the individual is often perceived to be hegemonic. Whether in palaces or religious institutions, architecture and space are often discussed in terms of their symbolic representation of meta-narratives of power or faith. The key question has to do with alternative models of modernity in Islamic societies to represent the exchange between individual and society.[4] In spatial terms we may ask whether modernity is a framework or an objective. Acknowledging the objective of material modernisation, modernity's requisite cultural renewal needs to be reframed. As a framework modernity here needs to work with operations and spatial practices of daily life in the Islamic city and frame progressive environments that provide individual freedom and common purpose in relation to movement, work, leisure and communication in its public and private spaces. As an objective, avoiding quick fixes of applied or imported formal symbols whether western or Islamic, spatial practices of an Islamic modernity faces reworking its material culture to articulate its right to renewed languages of form, materials and technologies that construct the landscape of its cultural modernity.[5]

During the workshop we were reminded to ask what "Modern" excludes.[6] An *open Islamic city* not only searches for new spatial representations for the modern Islamic society but will need to actively make room for indigenous spatial practices that are able to de-territorialise, and re-describe their own forms and uses. *Open city* would involve not only the free and equal rights for the individuals to occupy, move, and use space without hindrance but also the right to security and impunity to create architecture and representations of space in the city which can be radically transformed and renewed. As such, *open city* is as much a space for recollecting Islamic identity and social cohesion as for individual forgetfulness and amnesia (cf. Henri Lefebvre).

Open city as an environment which balances modernisation with modernity is a measure by which the modernity of an Islamic space can be gauged. Temporality of this city will at once engage the contemporaneity of technological advances and the time of *flux* of the local individual expression and its archaic identity. The Following segments recall a few instances of such spatial modernity in cities of Islamic cultures which have come about by chance as much as by design.

Spatial Justice in the City

Islamic modernity has historically foregrounded its narrative of development with that of social justice. Traditionally *Waqf* has been an important instrument of progressive urban development for social good in Islamic cities, providing charitable funds for provision of infrastructure such as access to water by construction of *Ghanats* and water reservoirs, or provision of public amenities in bazaars, trading caravanserais, mosques and schools, ensuring

---

4   Masoud Kamali, "Iranian Islamic Modernities", in this volume, pp. 49-66.
5   Cf.: Michel Serres
6   Charles Jencks, "Why Critical Modernism?", in this volume, pp. 71-82.

their maintenance in perpetuity. This urban infrastructure would in turn prompt the growth of quarters around it with the fabric of housing and commerce. Part of the wisdom of this system lies in its process of funding and patronage, which ensures provision and maintenance of infrastructure of amenities and public space as generators in the planning of an urban quarter. Social justice could be said to depend on spatial justice. While *Waqf* ensures continuity of design in the public space and the right to public services and their maintenance for a quarter, the architecture of the totality of the quarter is not dictated from above and is open to the self determinant and heterogeneous processes prompted by citizens and by individual choice.

Post revolution Iran has instituted new and independent organisations, *such as Bonyad-ee Mostazafin*, or *Bonyad-ee Imam Khomeini*, among others, which expanded the role of individual charity to a public body through affiliated independent development companies that provide housing and social amenities, some in conjunction open market. Tehran and other Iranian cities may boast of many such development projects aimed at planning physical modernisation, prioritising affordability, and social justice. Their positive intentions not withstanding, the projects' urban design and provision of public space however, often follow private interests or by now disputed and dictated models of historical Modernist planning. Modernity of these projects would need to extend the requirements for housing, health and public space design beyond minimum needs to new standards of cultural relevance, sustainability, local leisure/ pleasure and spatial empowerment of a heterogeneous citizenry. Social justice in this process would acknowledge that the desired perceptions of "the good life" by the Islamic city's diverse citizens is not a prototype object building imported and repeated, but a discursive, differentiated and unstable set of material and spatial relationships in direct charge with the public space that they produce. Such discursive design needs to intersect modern needs with the local, right to have with write to relevant design to produce an un-predetermined new *counter – design* of its spaces, to achieve social justice through spatial justice.

Counterfactual Public Spaces of a Quasi - Deregulated City

After the Iranian revolution, Tehran under the Islamic Republic has found a paradoxical character in the space of its development. On the one hand its expansion has been explosive; extensive development of super-large housing complexes and urban quarters along with highways inserted into the developments. On the other hand there is a substantially deregulated speculative built-up where the opportunistic building of a random mix of high and low rise developments cover the city and surrounding foothills. The formation of this random growth ceases to be urban sprawl at points where spaces in the interstices of the two systems happen to find local contiguities in spatial nodes and configurations of programmes that create specific localities.

Tehran is a city of many centres and none at the same time. Lacking singular design, its organic expansion has produced impossible traffic jams and impassive expanses with local pockets of urban intensity produced by chance. No clear definitions of density and urban structure or infrastructure follow the design of the city for very long. Contingencies of land speculation, market forces and local strategies intersect with the evolved structure of streets and patterns of access. One prime spatial logic remains to be the consistent slope of the city from north to south, which creates patterns of valleys, both geological and agricultural, that drain water from the foothills. Modernisation of the city here has been directed by organic quasi-unregulated

Fig. 1
© Hengameh Golestan

Fig. 2
© Hengameh Golestan

growth. Whether density and sheer contiguity of development can follow into modernity of public space in the city is an open question.

Public space in this double bind of a city happens at the interstices of planning with the freedom and liberties of "occupation as design". It is clear that public space here will not be of a predetermined kind and more gathers in spaces akin to those Inaki Abalos has called "spaces of impunity". This process has led to the development of other spatial models/practices where chance played a strong role in their formation. Freedom in these public spaces is often a precarious right, not given but gathered.

During the revolution occupying the space of Tehran's roof tops was the only means of being both in and out of the city at the same time; a found set of spaces where people could sound their protest to the regime, at agreed times of the. from the roof tops of their private apartments without fear of the police. At this time, another such site was found in the hiking trails in mountains north of the city. They were spaces were physical boundaries exceeded planning control and police surveillance. These spaces developed as sites of social exchange, sporting activities and political expression all at the same time. In post revolution Tehran these appropriated mountain trails and activity centres expanded Darband foothills area as one important public space of leisure in the city. As *areas of impunity*, this *counter-planned* spaces, grew with their own temporality generated by local interest and de-territorialised space to make active an un-prescribed and un-predetermined public space in the city.

The hazard of deregulated expansion has produced its own problems in Tehran; continuous traffic jams, unaffordable real estate, etc. yet it appears that all want to be here. Tehran is now a cosmopolis out of control and a model of a city with counterfactual processes in its planning, randomly appearing and disappearing public spaces, and both designed and found infrastructure. One may ask if this is a space of bottom-up modernity and may even be a model of an Islamic "open city" by default.

Women paragliders in the mountain foothills north of Tehran (Figures1 & 2) enforce their social right to modernity, sporting flight despite Islamic dress, an example of a "claim to space" that the city would not otherwise assign; a freedom found within the odds. The image registers a moment of a counterfactual social space that finds as much functional as symbolic and representational status in the spatial practices of Iranian women under Islamic law and instantiates the heterogeneous and impromptu geographies of public space in this Islamic city.

A Destructive Vacuum:
The Marginalisation of Local Knowledge and Reassertion of Local Identities

FARID PANJWANI

Recent decades have seen many countries undergo political and economic changes brought about by the state's ostensible retreat and the market's gradual expansion. These changes are promoted by their advocates as an overdue reduction in the power of the state and its satellite bureaucracies and consistent with assumptions about the ability of institutions and individuals to perform efficiently (Jonathan, 1997). Social sectors such as health, housing, and education which were formerly run on social development consensus, requiring public regulation and resources, have been deeply affected. In the realm of education, words such as "privatisation", "export of education", "triumph of the market" and "consumer choice" have become increasingly common. Education has been re-branded as a trade item, earning increasing amounts of revenue for the producers (Altman, 2006; Czinkota, 2006; Universities UK, 2007). In this trade, the exporters are usually the developed countries and the importers the developing countries.

Conceptualising education as a service and a trade item is underpinned by a normative understanding of the relationship between education, individual and the market. In this regard, education is mainly understood as a private good, useful to individuals for acquiring skills saleable in the market. Increasingly, this market is not local or national but global. Particularly, the management of technology, people and finances are seen as trans-cultural activities thus enabling people with specific skills to become members of a global labour force. A case in point is the rapid emergence of franchised higher education institutions in the major cities of developing countries (from Cairo to Kuala Lumpur) offering almost uniform degree programmes in information technology, human resource management, business studies, etc. This trend has created a need for uniform or at-least comparable methods of assessing educated human resources from across the world for participation, or utilisation, in a global market. It is also the motivation behind various recent endeavours to create homogenising quality control mechanisms and indicators, either at regional or global levels.

The orientation of education as a private good, and indirectly, the impact of internationally calibrated quality control standards are increasingly disassociating education, particularly at tertiary levels, from local and national contexts. At the same time we are living in an age when this same process of homogenisation is creating reactions in the form of the regeneration of local identities, as persuasively shown by Barber (1995). These linguistic, religious or ethnic movements are often rooted in the fear of obliteration of the local by the global. The participation of young people in such movements across the world has been recognised by several scholars, including (Epstein, 2001; Miller, 1994; Rucht, 2002). With the continuing intensification of globalisation, it is reasonable to assume that opposition to it as well as the participation of young people in it will continue.

What happens when the education systems prepare young people for a global economy and marginalise local forms of knowledge in an age that also recreates and revitalises local identities? How does the resulting gap between local identity and local knowledge get filled? Who or what fills this gap? These questions have not received sufficient attention.

The study of Islam in educational systems can be considered as a case study in this regard. Surprise is often expressed at the participation of well-educated young people in movements propagating Islamism or political Islam. While only a fraction of young Muslims become part of such movements, the underlying un-historical and absolutist understanding of Islam is more widespread. It is common to meet Muslim doctors, computer experts and engineers, who carry strikingly un-historical views about their religious traditions. These young professionals, equipped to participate in the global economy also reflect the gap between local identity and local knowledge.

Some light can be shed on this situation by noting that while such young persons acquire state-of-the-art knowledge in their own profession, knowledge of their religious tradition comes only from early education in *madrasas* of various shades, emotionally powerful but intellectually deficient state sponsored Islamic studies and the sound bites of the media. They often enter higher educational institutions with emotional attachment to Islam and a rudimentary knowledge of terms such as *Sharia, Jahaliya* and so on. Their higher education is often bereft of any systematic, scholarly study of their religio-cultural traditions, rather it is dominated by a technical education combined with, in some cases, a sprinkling of "easy to pass" courses on Islam. Consequently, when, propelled by a variety of factors, these youngsters search for a better understanding of their religious tradition, they often find it not in their educational institutions but in the pamphlets, booklets, websites and gatherings of Islamists. Here they find religious terms already familiar to them re-interpreted into a modern dictum.

The advocates of a return to Islam have been able to make religious values, however rigid, seem relevant to modern society. They have been able to bridge traditional and modern segments of society... They have both articulated the manner in which these symbols should serve political ends and convinced large number of citizens that "Islamisation" is a necessary and beneficial process (Nasr, 2003, p. 70).

By successfully re-interpreting traditional concepts, Islamism's discourse is able to give the people both the assurance of tradition and hope for the resolution of modern problems such as unemployment, lack of social services, police state, corruption, cultural imperialism etc. In other words, it is able to fill the gap between local knowledge and local identity. Many young men and women who are attracted to Islamism's discourse do so in the belief that they are following the essential teachings of their faith. Instead of knowing the plurality and contested nature of norms and institutions, many believe them to be eternal and monolithic from the beginning of Islam. The emotional identification with Islam is thus often conjugated with a superficial and ideological knowledge about the object of attachment. The resulting cycle feeds the *Jihad versus McWorld* battles that we see all around us.

To break this cycle at a philosophical level, Ruth Jonathan's insight can serve as a useful beginning: "The merits of the free market as a principle for the distribution of "goods" in society cannot rest on an ideological justification which seeks to legitimate a universal, all pervasive set of distributional arrangements, irrespective of contingent conditions in the society in question and regardless of the logical features of the goods at issue" (Jonathan, 1997).

This means that one needs to re-assess whether educational practice lends itself to be a wholly or mainly a private good. Education is a social practice whereby individual minds are nurtured, not individually, but through a collective process. This means that *what* an individual gets educated depends on what others are educated and how much are they willing to share it, and how much of that education the individual is able to access. All this presupposes the social, cultural and economic preconditions for learning. Hence, contrary to the current dominant understanding, education needs to be understood both as public and a private good.

Conceptualising education as a public *and* private good is a necessary step towards constructively bridging the above-noted gap between local identity and local knowledge. One of its implications is that the role of higher education institutions cannot solely or primarily be to prepare young people for selling their skills in the market. They must also help students gain academically sound acquaintance with the traditions of the societies of which they are part as well as of wider human cultural heritage. The need for a well-rounded education that prepares young people not only as producers of skills and consumers of goods but also as heir to complex and multi-facted human cultural heritage has perhaps never been greater. Armed with such a conception of education, positive roles can be played by international quality-control institutions and instruments. If the quality-control and quality-assessment of higher education will incorporate both local and global knowledge, it may lead to the rethinking of education across the globe.

References

Altman, D. (2006, February 21) Managing Globalisation: Education's value in the export column, *International Herald Tribune*, from http://www.iht.com/articles/2006/02/21/business/glob22.php.

Barber, B. (1995) *Jihad VS McWorld*, New York: Ballantine Books.

Czinkota, M. (2006) Academic freedom for all in higher education: The role of the general agreement on trade in services, *Journal of World Business, 41(2)*, pp. 149-160.

Epstein, B. (2001) Anarchism and the Anti-Globalisation Movement, *Monthly Review*, 53(4).

Jonathan, R. (1997) Illusory Freedoms: Liberalism, Education and the Market, *Journal of Philosophy of Education, 31(1)*.

Miller, J. (1994) Faces of Fundamentalism, *Foreign Affairs*, 73(6).

Nasr, V. (2003) Lessons from the Muslim World, *Daedalus* (Summer), 67-72.

Rucht, D. (2002) Social Movements Challenging Neo-Liberal Globalisation, In P. Ibarra (Ed.), *Social Movements and Democracy*, New York: Palgrave Macmillan.

Universities UK. (2007) The Economic Impact of UK Higher Education Institutions, from http://bookshop.universitiesuk.ac.uk/downloads/economicimpact3.pdf.

Modernity:
Keep Out of Reach of Children

FATEMEH HOSSEINI-SHAKIB

I was invited to the Aga Khan Award for Architecture Workshop as an Iranian animation/media studies researcher who is interested in the question of modernity in the Islamic Countries; an interest that no doubt has arisen as a result of hand-on experience of being a member of the club. It was a rare opportunity to observe what happens when such diverse group of scholars with such variation not only in terms of their professional fields and level of scholarship, but in their relationship to the subject of scrutiny as "Moslem countries" would meet. It was obvious that coming to terms with such a historically problematic term such as modernity in an even more multifarious context called the Moslem countries was a site for conflict and challenge; here I have in mind those established scholars who have theorised extensively on the field but were not themselves part of that world, and those who had the opportunity to leave that "world" and look at the question from outside (sometimes staying too far or perhaps losing real contact with the contemporary accounts of the question) and those who still felt part of that world/problem (like me).

During the Workshop I was amazed at how many different anti-modern views could exist amongst a panel of individuals who were trying to spot tangible elements of modernity. I couldn't believe that the problem of overlooking the elegant distinctions of "modernity" with "modernism" or even "modernisation" (not to mention the use of these words with capital Ms, pace Charles Jencks (1996) in What is Postmodernism?) or the blurring of the boundaries between these terms could cause such hot debates. Neither could I imagine I could be sitting in a group of so many high-calibre scholars and hear that Muslim countries might not qualify for passage on the train of modernity, and that furthermore they would better be aware of the "dangers of modernity", the Holocaust being the indisputable example.

It doesn't seem enough to inform these so-called Muslim countries that they are not eligible to be "really" modern because their women are "still" wearing hijab and not allowed to wear "normal" clothes (Prof. Deniz Kandiyot) or to warn them against the drawbacks of modernity (relying on reason, for instance Prof. Jencks's ideas) because the so-called West has decided the project is no good anymore, thus announcing its termination. Get off the train, everyone!

I do not believe that the Western modern world has ever abandoned or even afforded to leave modernity at all. If the modern thought allows interrogating itself, and recognising it flaws, it is certainly its strength and validity as a system of thought, something which has allowed for the "anti"s to arise. What the Western experience of modernity and its critique shows, considering the whole possible spectrum of positions towards it, still cannot question themselves as discourses outside modernity. Subversive perhaps, and with all dangers that threatens "reason", it is not possible to avoid it. Scientific discourses with all the Foucauldian scepticism towards it, when coming to the experience of everyday life, do not meet the expense of shying away from that. The proposition of undermining modernity in theory seems a valid argument. Coming to the harsh and violent living conditions of the millions of humans, whose basic needs are endangered by a pre-modern order of life (as much as the price they are paying for the so called Western modernity) seems bizarre to me.

Here an explanation seems necessary to me. However much we hate the simplistic view of the world as divided into the West and the East, in our minds there exist such distinctions and categorisations, sometimes unavoidable, sometimes unconscious, and in certain contexts even helpful. Hence, I won't make any apologies for using the term "the West" since it represents, in my mind, not a unified or homogeneous entity but a whole set of diverse discourses which converge at a certain point when dealing with the "other". *This* West knows a lot about itself and handles each aspect of its discourses with so much care, so much subtlety. Coming to the other, however, it behaves entirely differently. It positions itself 1) in the position of Knowledge 2) Power 3) Decision-making. This West is the Parent of the World. Sometimes I imagine that the problem is located when the *West* forgets all its costly-earned "modern" capacities and treats the "other" in a pre-modern discipline.

If it doesn't sound familiar to you, to me it does. As an Iranian woman being born in the time of Pahlavis, and seeing that world collapse, witnessing a bitter war with Iraq for 8 odd years and living my adulthood in a country tolerating the aftermath of that horrific war plus my experience of living in the Western world of academia for 5 years, it does. I think *that* West theorises for itself, sees things in that light and excludes others, decides for them, stands in the position of knowledge, power and supervision. *That* West is not interested to see the subtleties and the differences (which are not all due to its relative deficiencies) of the other world. It does not take into account the history of its own dominance and the effect that has had on that other world. It has no patience for that other world to get modern, and validates only certain ways of achieving that modernity. It holds the right, even, to abandon the project of modernity, because of the flaws and failures of the Western world (not to mention the consequence of modern history that the other world has had to put up with), and forecloses any possibility that other countries can learn from the Western way of modernity. I am surprised at the level of sophistication with which the Western mentality examines itself, which stops to understand problems of a "similar" make-up in a different context. Has that sense of involvedness been forgotten, that capacity of taking in complexity all vanished?

Perhaps the main question here is *representation*. As a researcher in the field of animation I have learned to critically evaluate representations in a modern Western school of thought.[1]

These illuminating and great theories originating almost all from the West are supposed to be applicable to all artefacts and works of representation. This has informed how I have come to see the treatment, and representation, of "others". For instance, I have been trying to answer the question of how certain fragments of a book called "Arabian Nights" in the so-called Western World became representative of a host of countries and ethnicities, religions and cultures, from India to Egypt, stories expanding from pre-Islamic history to the post-Islamist time of Haroun-al-Rashid's Baghdad? Animation representation deals with stereotypes and shortcuts. Why do people who talk about "Persian Fairy Tales" associate them with images of deserts, camels, Arabic script, Baghdad and not to forget exotic veiled women? Where is the evidence of the sophisticated, multilayered, modern system of thinking?

Recently I have been trying to publicise the emergence of the animation culture in Iran and attempt to trace the roots of this emerging semi-industry. I have been thinking of how the socio-cultural changes which came with the reformist government allowed for a much more open-minded view towards cultural and artistic productions. I brought from Iran a range of animations from student to more professional work produced for broadcasting there on state TV and as commercials to conferences in the Europe and America. I always received the most desirable response from the audience. The people marvelled at how "modern" Iran is becoming, something which satisfied my initial aims, but left me with a feeling of unease and discomfort. Who do they think we are? Musing over the problem for a long time, the question changed to how really modern are we, and whether this matters at all.

I know it sounds boring. I understand that within the realm of theory we are tired of repeating old Orientalist notions and I completely understand that it is not at all fashionable to talk about postmodernism as a way to let "others" speak for themselves these days. Even modernity seems to be one of those words best avoided these days. Yet, we all know that the problems that invoked those old-fashioned terms persist. If you would like to replace the word "modernity" with some new term... take your choice. I am sure that "the world" including Muslim countries cannot afford not to go for modernity by any name, just as one cannot afford to treat cancer with "over the counter" pills and herbal remedies.

Obviously Muslim, or non-Western, countries need their own kinds of modernity, which are localised, domesticated, and made possible. The imagined or alleged discrepancy between Islam and Democracy (while some argue that there is not an essential relationship between that debate and Modernity) is an open question, or rather a red herring. We have to question whether liberal democracy in certain Western countries is *the* democracy, or whether it has anything to do with our modernity debate. We have to ask to what extent each country is indeed a Muslim country and how do we categorise a country as such? Are we talking about forms of government or about "people" in the broadest sense? Is 2007 Iran a less modern country, in all the senses of "modern", than what it was in 1975, when women

---

[1]   To put it briefly, the Althuserian theories of ideology (re-readings of Marx)/Lacanian psychoanalysis/Metzian Semiotics/Derridan deconstruction as well as Focauldian discourse/textual analysis provide the basis for critical theories of representation, especially in the moving image, and mainly cinema.

legally did not have to wear hejab nor could they divorce their husbands? Is the so-called "new Islamism" which is believed to have mobilised intellectuals and masses in some Muslim countries against modernity? Above all questions, is being anti-Western, and rejecting the West's omni-power/omni-science equal to being anti-modernism?[2]

I am mostly talking about Iran, the place where I am most in touch with the zeitgeist. In a recent lecture Masoud Kamali tried to show that the basis of the Islamic Revolution was a modern one. Political Islam, whether we like it or not, is a modern school of thought. Asef Bayat has shown us its failures and deficiencies since it had an opportunity to be practiced as the ideological force behind the Iranian Islamic Republic. Nowhere in the history of Iran have we witnessed so much challenge put forward for ideological Islam to confront. There are several trains of thoughts based on re-readings of Islam currently being debated in Iran, discourses of Islam that are deliberately or otherwise ignored and simplified in the outer world. Even more, the secular trends are totally uncared for, as if Islam is the only way one can get to know a nation as diverse as Iran. There is so much eagerness to give certain representations of Iran which can dynamically veil that diversity. And, unfortunately, this is the case with other so-called Muslim countries.

Perhaps we really need that timeless definition of modernity that Prof. Sadria suggested: "the capacity to accept the anti; disagreement, challenge and conflict". Perhaps this is what Prof. Weber calls modernity's diverse manifestations in different moments of history. It seems that we desperately need a foundation as broad as this which cannot be challenged on the mistakes, the catastrophes, even, of Western modernity. Even if the so-called Muslim countries have taken on Modernisation more eagerly than Modernity, let's not censure them just for that. Let's believe in that "capacity" which they are struggling to attain in their own altered way.

We need to know the "individual" in these countries as much as we need to know the specific social/political/cultural milieu in which the individual dwells. We can't afford to defer to the representations of collective/individual entities. Representations do not seem to re-present; they block our understanding and our access to individuals. They have blunted our senses, made our images of the world homogenised and unproblematic. The artist/architect who represents their own spatial model of their country's identity can also lead us to their take on modernity. There should be a ripeness of locality in a modern building which is made in a non-Western context, be it in Cairo, Tehran or elsewhere; the living space being representative of the quintessence of that gene. Highlighting the specific properties of modernity, in its multiple nature, within each specific context can show the way modernisation should take place in architecture, and perhaps not vice-versa. Perhaps we need a post-modern take on modernity and modern architecture in Muslim countries, after all. Not totally abandoning "over the counter" solutions and approaches, but keeping them in a safe relationship with the prescribed medicines.

---

[2] That's the way for instance Fredrick Jameson (1991) describes Iranian Islamic Revolution as an anti-modern one in his Postmodernism; or the logic of late-capitalism.

Multiple Modernities:
A Theoretical Frame

MASOUD KAMALI

The resurgence of modernisation theory in post-WWII engaged many social scientists in an effort to plot the world's development on a linear axis. Modernisation theorists tried to integrate different parts of their theory into a coherent theoretical system that would serve to explain, in Weberian tradition, the uniqueness of Western civilisation in contrast to other civilisations, in such cases as they recognised other societies as civilisations. They were generally West-centric intellectuals who saw the West as, in the words of Paul Valery, "the pearl of the globe" (Kingston-Mann Esther, 1999: 3).

Such an effort to see the contemporary West as the goal of human history put the theoretical uniqueness and constitution of "the West" on the research agenda of many universities and research centres. The major body of research conducted by modernisation theorists was not concerned about the internal differences among western countries but rather what constituted an internally coherent ideal type of "the West" and focused on the differences between this and non-Western countries. The rather heterogeneous developments of Western countries, developmental patterns called the French model, English model, German model, Swedish model, and so forth, were not the main subject of research or interest in a world where the narcissistic and capitalistic West was facing its rival, the "Socialist World". The socialist world was considered the Eastern enemy and, as such, non-modern. The fact that the "communist enemies" were as modern as the "Western capitalist friends" and that there hardly existed "a West" but rather several Western patterns of socioeconomic and cultural developments was neglected in the comparative research based on the modernisation theory model.

These theorists promoted the universalism of the Western experiment and saw it as a blueprint for non-Western countries to follow. This formed part of the post-colonial world's, and the former colonialists', attitudes towards "the rest". Many evolutionist social theorists, and in particular sociologists, tried to present it as the only way towards a lasting system for all human societies and thus the ultimate goal of history. It is not only classical modernist theorists such as Hegel, Spencer, Marx, and Weber, who believed in the triumph of modern "reason in History", but contemporary sociologists, such as Francis Fukuyama and his ideas about "The End of History", Anthony Giddens "Modernity as our destiny", and others, such as Habermas and Beck who believed, and still believe, that this modernity is the final solution to human problems. The only variety that some of these scholars, such as Habermas and Beck, could accept as part of the global modernity project were capitalist or socialist modernities.

This is still the problem of biased assumption regarding the "uniqueness"'of the "West" and the West-centric understanding of modern(isation) history.

The newly established concept of multiple modernities indicates that the features and forces of modernity can potentially be received and developed in different ways in different countries. Furthermore, the assumption that modernity has an entirely European origin is not reconcilable with historical developments. For instance conscription, which was developed in Europe both by French and English governments, is an Ottoman invention which existed long before Europe in the Ottoman Empire (Kamali 2006). Or the so well-admired freedom of religion, also an Islamic phenomenon. Freedom of religion has been a part of Islamic models of governance both in the Ottoman and Persian empires. Bazaars in Muslim countries have been at the heart of pre-modern and in many cases of the modern cities. Many features of the modern capitalist economy were part of Muslim cities and framed the life of Muslim individuals. In addition, the businessmen of the bazaar have not been exclusively Muslims; Jews have also been and still are, in countries such as Iran, a part of the bazaar. Contrary to the classics of social sciences modernity was not been an exclusively western invention, but has had non-western features and forces.

A theoretical perspective of multiple modernities should play up divergence and heterogeneity rather than homogeneity, and therefore must be a challenge to any simple dualistic, and (in relation to each other) paradoxical, models, such as Occident/Orient, modern/traditional, gemenschaft/geselschaft, Christian/Muslim, and universal/particular. Alongside this, it must also challenge the generalising concepts of Otherisation, such as the holistic imaginisation of the existence of a simple and homogeneous "Muslim World" or the claimed lack of civil society in the "Muslim World". This conjectural method of Other-ising Muslims and Muslim societies seems to be experiencing a revival in the post-September 11th 2001 political arena, in the form of the "new Orientalism".

Homogeneity of presentation of the "Muslim world"

During the rise and growing dominance of modernisation theory at the end of the nineteenth century and until the First World War, the categories of the "difference" and "superiority" of the "West" in relation to "the rest" were dominating the social sciences in general and sociology in particular. During the revival of modernisation theory following the Second World War, many social scientists, reinforced by the resurgence of the liberal "West" tried to present the "West", which was synonymous with modernity, in a selective way. Modernity was cleaned of its "negative sides", namely Fascism, Nazism and Communism. These were considered exceptions to the "linear" development of the "modern West". The theoretical tradition of the uniqueness of the "West" was revived.

As a result of the cold war, the substantial Americanisation and westernisation of those parts of the world under the direct or indirect influence of western powers was considered by many in non-western countries, including Muslim countries, as justified actions towards the modernisation of what they considered "pre-modern" societies. This was and is still a common notion in the intellectual spheres of many non-western countries in general and Muslim countries in particular. This led the field of sociology to be dominated by homogenous theoretical perspectives and methodological tools. It was not only the liberal "West" and its legacy that influenced the establishment of bad research and intellectual works in many Muslim countries but also the influence of another (un-recognised) modernity, namely the communist modernity. In both cases, many researchers and intellectuals of Muslim societies were viewing their societies through the eyes, theories and methods of the classics of social sciences, such as Hegel, Durkheim, Weber, and Marx (cf. Turner, 1994). This is a major challenge for social scientists to overcome even today. The problems and legacy of a single western modernity is still haunting the social sciences, hindering the development of social theory in Muslim countries.

This forms the very ground for a long-standing "homogeneity of presentations" of Muslim societies and their modern developments. We have to scientifically challenge the established social and political meta-theories about a single western modernity and the existence of a, completely different, singular "Muslim world". In a global world we need new methods, scientific tools and theoretical perspectives for exploring and understanding different societies. The following are some theoretical suggestions for breaking free of the destructive legacy that hampers creative both sociological research and the development of social theory not only in Muslim countries, but in western mainstream universities and research centres, as well. We should:

- Use the theoretical tools of multiple modernities for understanding Muslim societies' modern history.
- Challenge the ideas and theories of the *uniqueness of the "West"*.
- Conduct new research in Muslim countries by using the theoretical tool of civil society/state relations, in order to better understand new developments, including the emergence and reinforcement of Islamism, in those countries.
- Conduct new research about the role of European and "extended-European" powers and interests in the destruction/improvement of democratic movements in Muslim countries.
- Conduct new research about the diversity of modern developments in Muslim countries.

These are among a few scientific actions that would help us understand many modern developments in Muslim countries, including the characterisation and categorisation of Muslim modernities. Challenging the established "meta-narratives" through which the world simplifies and dichotomised into an "us" and "them" is one of the most important and fruitful scientific developments in a post-structural theoretical paradigm. We need a change of the established paradigms and a *scientific* emancipation from "meta-narratives". In other words, social sciences need a heterogeneity of perspectives free from "methodological nationalism" and "west-centric paradigms" in order to understand the world in general and Muslim countries in particular.

Some Reflections on "Tangible Elements of Multiple Modernities"

DENIZ KANDIYOTI

One of the noteworthy features of the dialogues and conversations that took place during our deliberations on "multiple modernities" was the creative tension between the contributions of those of us involved with designing and understanding the built environment and the social scientists concerned with analysing the concept of modernity and its application within diverse societal contexts. While the former were alert to the "modern" as a genre, and the contemporary effects of the global circuits of capital on the circulation of tastes and styles, the latter grappled with issues of difference and disjuncture between the West and Islam, between the notion of a singular modernity as opposed to plural modernities.

The best points of entry for a discussion of the "tangible" elements of modernity were provided by deceptively simple observations concerning the changing use of space. For instance, the preference of Iranian families for open plan kitchens that eliminate the separation between women's cooking quarters and include them in the social space where television is watched and members of the family interact. Or the fact that this preference is not confined to affluent Tehranis but also exists among those villagers in Bam rebuilding their homes devastated by the earthquake. I suggest that these observations provide us with lines of inquiry as valuable as pondering the modernity of Khomeini's theory of rule or the novelty of *Velayat-e faqih*. To elaborate on this idea, however, I must first draw attention to some conceptual distinctions between the terms "modernisation" and "modernity" which were invoked repeatedly throughout our discussions.

The first sense of modernisation, ushered in through the work of early masters of social theory such as Marx, Weber, Tonnies and Durkheim, invoked the notion of a fundamental break with a historical past recast as "tradition". This process of change was multidimensional and exhaustive, comprehensively transforming societies from demographic patterns to belief systems. After World War II, these insights were translated into so-called "modernisation theory", which widely acknowledged as a product of the Cold War. This theory presents social change as a uni-linear, teleological, process that inevitably leads to liberal capitalism, any deviations being interpreted as "transitional" or "pathological". Soviet theorists had a counterpart in the Marxist-Leninist sequence of the stages of socio-economic formations. It was not too long before "convergence" theorists argued that modern societies had a common "core" regardless of their political systems: faith in science and technology, similar technologies of production, bureaucratic modes of governance, mass societies, etc.

Another approach treats "modernity" as a condition or an ideological trope that represents the realisation of the Enlightenment project of progress and emancipation. This sense of modernity is specifically related to the historical trajectory of the West. Critiques of modernity have abounded - from Foucault's analyses of the underside of modern institutions, to the colonial, racist and sexist discourses implicit in narratives of progress and emancipation. These critiques have turned categories such as "backwardness" on their head and reframed "tradition" as resistance, nowhere more so than in the encounters of Western colonials in Muslim lands. This has inadvertently opened the way to a reification of culture and romantic populisms that glorify national "authenticity" defined in opposition to the West. The debate as to whether these diverse forms of social/political expression constitute "alternatives to modernity" or "alternative modernities" rages on, but these discussions have almost always been reliant on an implicit notion of internally homogenous cultures, or civilisations, confronting one another, an assumption which for many has, sadly, turned into conventional wisdom.

If we are to find our way back to an appreciation of the popularity of open plan kitchens in Iran, we must first jettison this theoretical baggage and achieve a workable understanding of the processes of social change that are shaping social relations today. We must be able to understand that the Iranian state is not only as an Islamic state but a modern revolutionary state that, like all revolutionary states, relies on the mass mobilisation of its citizenry, including women. We must be able to reflect on the internal contradictions created by a youthful, now extensively literate and mobile, population with heightened expectations for betterment and self-expression and a regime that utilises fairly crude instruments of policing and social control. It is quite clear that these instruments have been inadequate, giving rise to reformist longings and feminist contestations. It is not so much a case of modernity being or not being compatible with Islamic rule but a case of societal change inevitably forcing and testing the boundaries of what is acceptable under such rule — a challenge that is of a totally *political* nature regardless of the culturalist arguments deployed about the evils of the West and the assumed authenticity of Islam.[1]

This discussion is not intended to deny the existence of a powerful and hegemonic model emanating from the capitalist West. This is in evidence, sometimes quite forcefully, in the economic and governance packages imposed by institutions of global governance, especially in the context of armed interventions. However, since our focus is on modernity we must necessarily complicate this picture. Appadurai's observations that "modernity is decisively at large, irregularly self-conscious and unevenly experienced"[2] and that modernity surely involves a general break with all sorts of pasts are quite productive. He proposes that migration and the media are two features of globalisation that are constitutive features of modern subjectivity and collective imaginaries.

---

[1]   Notice how Islamic fundamentalists and crusading imperialists are totally reliant on one another's demonologies, all one has to do is invert their terms.

[2]   Arjun Appadurai, *Modernity at Large: Cultural Dimensions of Globalization* (Minneapolis and London: University of Minnesota Press, 1996).

The local phenomena thrown up by these negotiations between diverse pasts, a globalised present and contested futures are, by necessity, dizzyingly complex. Yet placing all the diverse manifestations of emergent public spheres, social movements, and civil societies under the rubric of "modernity" does not absolve us from the task of recognising the implicit ethical choices and *politics*. Referring to "multiple modernities" should not give us an out in that respect. We must live with the uncomfortable knowledge of the existence of Evangelical Christians willing to blow up abortion clinics in California, fundamentalist Jews treating the Bible as a title deed to Palestine, Indian Hindus calling for religious unity under the saffron flag, with their Muslim co-citizens cast as aliens, and Muslims calling for the slaughter of infidels under the guise of *jihad*. Are these modern movements? Undoubtedly so. They are also both transnational and diasporic. We must be mindful not to allow some crucial differences in worldview, which incidentally cut across East and West and a multiplicity of faiths, to be occluded by our search for multiple modernities.

Multiple Modernities in Contemporary Architecture

JEREMY MELVIN

Modernity, whether in architecture or any other cultural phenomena, has multiple manifestations. While some of these manifestations share roots with manifestations of plurality in other disciplines, architecture's many modernities have their own particular characteristics, which can be divided into two categories. The first are those that spring from the contingent historical circumstances around which modernity and its related terms, modernisation and modernism, became part of the discipline's discourse. The second category includes those which arise from certain conditions inherent to architecture in circumstances beyond what we might call modern. In this short paper I hope to draw attention to some of the implications of the relationship between these two categories.

Around the year 1900 there were numerous movements that struggled with the concept of modernity in architecture. They formed under various political regimes, from the democratic USA to Tsarist Russia, from Imperial Japan to the European states of Germany, Italy and Austria-Hungary. Each would have considered themselves modern, and despite varying levels of technological capability, had some reason for doing so. Soon after World War I, however, one architectural movement seemed to claim modernity itself. This is the architectural "modernism" characterised by white walls, flat roofs and some attempt towards industrial production. Its rhetoric was extraordinarily powerful. Through the writing of Siegfried Giedion, Nikolaus Pevsner, Henry-Russell Hitchcock and Philip Johnson, it evinced a universal applicability. The last two writers just mentioned coined the term the "International Style" for a famous and hugely influential exhibition at the Museum of Modern Art in New York in 1932.

Although subsequent historians, like Giorgio Ciucci and David Watkin, demonstrated that this form of modernism was far more heterogeneous and self-contradictory than these early writers would make it seem, the legacies of their rhetoric remain and continue to appeal to many practising architects. For this reason the multiple modernities of contemporary architecture can only be understood in light of a movement which was itself based on a series of fictions originating in the western world at a particular time. An architect working today can hardly claim to be modern without acknowledging modernism, even if that acknowledgement is in the form of a rejection.

This condition sets the background for a consideration of the multiple modernities in contemporary architecture, and how their inherent characteristics interact with modernity in a traditional sense. Central among these characteristics is that architecture is both functional and communicative: it serves a particular activity or combination of activities, and simultaneously represents and conveys ideas. In a pre-modern society function and representation generally serve the same ends. When discussing the political model of cuius regio eius religio which took hold in western Europe after the Peace of Westphalia in 1648, Armando Salvatore might well refer to one concrete example: the German city of Karlsruhe, where avenues radiate from the Elector's palace through the city and into the surrounding countryside. This spatial construction is precise analogous to the political organisation in which it was formed: function and appearance reinforce each other.

Most notable architecture up to this period had been built for secular or religious authorities, or at least those who had access to power and resources through one or other of those routes. As the Westphalian settlement resolved the long-running duality in western society between Church and State in favour of the latter, so architecture followed.

This sort of setting and its associated model of patronage and building production was not likely to motivate architecture towards modernity. That happened by and large through the economic and social effects of megalopolitan cities, including Chicago, New York, Berlin and Vienna. In Europe countries which had either recently unified – appearing to resolve multiple political identities into one – like Germany and Italy, or states with an inherent heterogeneity like Tsarist Russia and the Habsburg Empire, tended to foster trends which augured modernity, and by no means coincidentally.

Even before the emergence of great 19th century metropolises there were many challenges to the relationship between architecture and power. They might be crudely grouped under three headings: Intellectual, Political and Technological. The first group of challenges includes the emergence of aesthetics as a category of thought, opening new interpretations of sensory experience; the second group obviously includes the change and mutation of regimes from the French Revolution onwards; the final group includes the technologies of the Industrial Revolution which had an immediate effect on how buildings were being built, an increasing impact on their appearance, and the purpose which the buildings serve.

All of those developments placed a new emphasis on architectural theory. With the purposes of the discipline no longer clear and the possibilities of form, function and appearance becoming more diverse, architects needed guidance. The eventual result was to unbalance conventional assumptions, such as the architectural analogue in the Westphalian political model. That created a dynamic and fluid relationship between architect and state power. Architecture's engagement with modernity did not just effect one irrevocable change, but made change an irrevocable part of its being.

One factor in this transformation is the fragmentary and ambiguous nature of much architectural theory. Despite various attempts there were no unified theories of architecture and, intriguingly, many theoreticians seemed simultaneously combine progressive and reactionary ideas in their attempts. Examples of this include AWN Pugin (1812-52) who sought to create a new society under the dual guise of revived 15th century Gothic architecture and Roman Catholic religion, or CN Ledoux (1735-1806), architect of a famous salt works which reinforced the Ancien Regime's hated monopoly, and who later re-worked his designs into radical proposals for an ideal city in the years after 1789.

Despite its falsely constructed homogeneity, or perhaps because of its inherent heterogeneity, architectural modernism also demonstrates this ambiguity. In the 1920s it could symbolise social democracy in Holland and Germany and give birth to the legendary Soviet Man in the USSR. The Italian Fascists could use it for their own purposes in both their own country and in Eritrea (still part of Ethiopia in the 1930s), where the city of Asmara is an extraordinarily conceived and partly realised modernist city. During the 1950s Jawaharlal Nehru could commission the most influential modernist architect of all, Le Corbusier, to design Chandigarh in newly independent India, even though it echoes elements of New Delhi's colonial architecture. Modernism appealed to the Brazilian communist architect Oscar Niemeyer and to multi-national businesses.

Paradoxically, the less experience a society or individual had of modernism at first hand, the more likely they were to accept its claims at face value. While in some cases it did partially fulfil its social claims, the rhetorical momentum behind modernism appealed to architects, politicians and the occasional industrialist, all of whom were interested in social change. Architectural modernism promised significant benefits both for corporate efficiency and social services such as housing, education and medicine.

Modernism made sweeping and ambitious claims for its ability to bring about a new society. But by the 1970s it was evident that modernism alone was insufficient and possibly not even necessary. Its failings spawned another generation of multiplicity which included a revival of interest in historical styles, new ways of engaging with physical context, and a growing awareness of the impact of energy use. Each brought a new emphasis on how architecture related to location and society. The future of architecture will depend on how effectively architects engage with that agenda.

New theories, themselves responses to the social, economic and political changes that underpin modernity, blew apart the belief system that had led to designs like that of Karlsruhe. Politics, form, function and architectural style were delaminated and their relationship became a matter for individual contingent negotiation, potentially in the instance of each and every building. This is how modernity became an element of architectural discourse and how it continues to act on architecture's ability to do and to represent.

Any comments I make about architecture in a non-western context must regarded as extremely tentative, but I would suggest two relevant considerations. First, that the pervasive legacy of modernism continues to affect any sense of architectural modernity wherever it occurs, and second, the relationship between form, function and appearance cannot be taken for granted. It could be that new ways of thinking about how buildings relate to their location and climate on one hand, and their particular purpose and its place within a broader social context on the other may help to retain what is valuable in modernism and to transcend what is not.

Entangled Modernity
Multiple Architectural Expressions of Global Phenomena: the Late Ottoman Example

Stefan Weber

The artistic and architectural expressions of a society are mainly received in terms of its cultural background. In order to interpret them, it is necessary to ask about the context of cultural production. But discussing the cultural setting of artistic production is quite problematic. In many cases observers apply conceptions of culture and history that a based on exclusive and essentialist models. Individuals and societies often have constructed other cultures ex negativo as a foil to their self-image. Along these lines we generally assume that different cultures have different historical experiences and that the material cultural manifestations are monuments to otherness. Sure, the Taj Mahal, the Cathedral of Cologne, Versailles and the Süleimaniye Mosque are congenial constructions of cultures of differing geographical settings and historical experiences. But in our need for the other we lose sight of joint features and parallel developments occurring in different cultures or common experiences. Even through cross-cultural interaction and identities are the reality in most urban settings, Samuel P. Huntington's self-fulfilling prophecy has developed an enormous identification power for our day's societies. While thinking of the past, of concepts of cultures and its heritages we often apply essentialist views on self and other, similar to Huntington's reading, and we are inclined to subscribe to well confined, distinctive cultural unites – a tendency which tourist industry uses successful for marketing strategies. This article follows a revisionist trend of historiography and argues for a shared but multiple heritage of an "entangled modernity".

Entangled Modernity and its theoretical background

Historiography has made its contribution to penetrate the above sketched mental boarders. Already Fernand Braudel's view of the Mediterranean had introduced new perspectives on intra-regional interactions and gave cultural exchange and hybrid cultures new importance.[1] The concept of *histoire croisée* or entangled history, of multilayered, interconnected trans-national developments, became important, and not only for economic historians,[2] and postcolonial studies allowed new views from and on peripheries.[3] Recent discussions of an

---

[1]   Cf. as well: Hodgson, Marshall, *Rethinking World History; Essays on Europe, Islam and World History*, Edited with an Introduction and Conclusion, by Edmund Burke, Cambridge (1993).

[2]   Werner, Michael/Zimmermann, Bénédicte: "Vergleich, Transfer, Verflechtung, Der Ansatz der Histoire croisée und die Herausforderung des Transnationalen", *Geschichte und Gesellschaft* 28 (2002), pp. 607-636.

[3]   See among others Nalbantoglu, G. B. and Wong, C. T. (eds.), *Postcolonial Space(s)*, New Haven 1997.

"Islamic Enlightenment" go even a step further to claim parallel historical processes on both sides of the Mediterranean.[4] Contested but not entirely rejected, R. Schulze's approach is based on phenomena that are often different in expression but close in time, motivation, and to a certain extent, character. Parallel processes can be explained by intellectual exchange or similar historical experiences, based on a configuring *zeitgeist*, a *genius saeculi*. If we neglect pure synchronism, and look for causality we encounter difficulties in the search for contact zones and we are not yet well informed about intellectual and cultural exchange in the early modern Mediterranean. How should a *zeitgeist* exist or be shared in settings of limited trans-regional interaction?

The picture becomes more complex when we account for the differential experience of modernity. Certainly the age of colonialism, the Industrial Revolution and intensifying globalisation, with the steamboat, trains and telegraph, contact zones became even denser and the flow of ideas followed in an increasing rhythm. For historians of the 19th century these contact zones are much easier to identify due to newspaper and print media which assumed an important role in the experience of the common modern time.[5] But even this, what now appears to be obvious, took a long time to find its way into scholarly debates. Still many historians of the West continue to see modernity in the non-west as derivative from "modernity proper". Modernity was subjected to the teleology of a linear concept of history. The experience that different pre-modern societies did not follow a single developmental template, i.e. western model of modernity, but many forms of it, had confused numerous development theorists. For many decades the notion – modernity as a result of technological modernisation – had been an article of faith and an essential part of a sense of western superiority and non-western alienation.[6]

Today, debates offer a number of challenges that move beyond the logic of presences and absences of markers of modernity, as industrialisation, urbanisation, secularisation, rationalisation, individualisation, etc., inherent in such thinking. They were very important phenomena but not the only and exclusive way how modernity was expressed or developed in different contexts. One line of argument is that the assumption of European uniqueness has overlooked the extra-European cultural borrowings and developments that enabled modernity or negated alternative forms and expressions. Recent economic and social developments in East Asian for example have forced modernisation traditional theorists to

---

4   Most prominent is the discussion among German scholars, Cf. as its main protagonist: Schulze, Reinhard: "Das islamische 18, Jahrhundert, Versuch einer historiographischen Kritik", *Die Welt des Islams* XXX (1990), pp. 140-159; and "Was ist die islamische Aufklärung?", *Die Welt des Islams* 36 (1996), pp. 276-325. See also more recently Rouayeb, Khaled, "Opening the Gate of Verification: The Forgotten Arab-Islamic Florescnece of the 17th Century", *LIMES* (2006), pp. 261-281.

5   Anderson, Benedict R.: Imagined communities: reflections on the origin and spread of nationalism. London 1983, 22 f. For some of its material consequences in Damascus see: Weber, Stefan, "Images of Imagined Worlds, Self-image and Worldview in Late Ottoman Wall Paintings". In: Hanssen, J./Philipp, Th./Weber, St.: The Empire in the City: Arab Provincial Capitals in the Late Ottoman Empire, BTS 88, Beirut (2002) 145-171.

6   For a common, unique and homogenised modernity cf. for example: Smith, David H., Becoming modern. Individual change in six developing countries, Cambridge/Mass. 1974.

revise previous concepts.[7] Postcolonial theorists have also opened the gate for a rethinking of the experience of modernity of the 19th and early 20th centuries outside Europe and North America. They have argued that the experience of colonialism have affected not only the peripheries but played a decisive role in shaping metropolitan modernity.[8] But much more than a horizontal reciprocal relationship, global modernity can be seen as a cultural fertilisation across multiple layers of interacting, opposing or negotiating dynamics amidst unequal power relations between the West and the non-West.[9] Even if Europe plays a dominant role, it is not necessarily normative. There are many more forces in this interdependent net of local forms of modernity.[10]

Many names, like multiple, local, or even alternative modernities were given for vernacular experiences or expressions of modernity, but it is important to bear in mind that they are not isolated but synchronic, or more precisely *interlinked*, developments and different manifestations of global phenomena. Some might be in opposition to hegemonic patterns, looking for alternative models, some might be vernacular or locally very specific – it is the communication and interaction, the dependence and simultaneous deviation from the other which makes this development an "entangled modernity". Modernity is by definition global and has affected nearly every society – it is a shared heritage with multiple but not independent manifestations.[11] We need to distinguish between the process and expression of historical developments. The expressions might look different; ways of resistance, integration, imitation, adoption, inspiration and creation of new cultural patterns *ex novo* are quite diverse as the case may be – active forces, concepts of time and space, and motivations are often similar. To understand how far these elements have influenced and changed the pre-modern organisation of a given society, the expression of cultural change, architecture and urban design, for example, need to be analysed in their specific contexts.

The Ottoman case

This study follows the epistemological critiques of autobiographical accounts of western modernity. At the same time, it will reconstruct empirically the dynamics of different local societies focussing on the example of architectural expressions of vernacular modernity in the late Ottoman Empire. For our purpose the Ottoman case is a stimulating example: it was

---

7   Shmuel Eisenstadt, for example, one of the leading scholars, revised his theories. Cf.: Eisenstadt, Shmuel N.: "The Basic Characteristics of Modernisation", in: Eisenstadt, Shmuel N., Modernisation, protest and change, Eaglewood Cliffs 1966, pp. 1-19, Eisenstadt, Shmuel N. (ed.), Multiple modernities, New Brunswick 2002.
8   Cf. among others: Chakrabarty, Dipesh, Habitations of Modernity; Essays in the Wake of Subaltern Studies, with a foreword by Homi K. Bhabha, Chicago 2002; Gaonkar, Dilip Parameshwar (ed.), Alternative modernities, Durham 2001. This directly influenced concepts of diverse experiences of modernity inside Europe and North America regarding urban and rural societies or different social strata.
9   Mitchell, Timothy, "The Stage of Modernity," in The Question of Modernity edited by Timothy Mitchell, Minneapolis/London 1999, 1-34.
10   Cf. Bayly, C.A., The Birth of the Modern World, 1780-1914. Global Connections and Comparisons, Oxford 2004.
11   Nederveen Pieterse, Jan: Globalisation and Culture, Global Mélange, Littlefield 2004.

one of the very few areas in the Muslim World not formally colonised, and its last significant world power. During the 18th Century and especially after the 1830s the Ottoman Empire became a playground of European trade. The powers, which deeply affected societies by their centralist policies and colonialism, military and economic expansions, and the revolution in transport and communication, mass production and consumption patterns, set the pace and directions of supra-regional realities. Counter – and corrective movements, sometimes as violent as the experiences which had occasioned them, were very much part of the process. This generated naturally different experiences in the peripheries (in periphery of the colonised world and of Europe) than those in production centres of discourses of modernity (European metropolises and to a certain extend Istanbul). Actors divided vertically by socio-economical strata or horizontally by cultural-geographic setting within the different centre-peripheral relationships adopted and developed phenomena according and fitting to their circumstances. Middle-class ladies or gentlemen in London, Istanbul or Cairo were living quite different daily lives in 1850, but the reasons and dynamics that led to change were very much interconnected or even the same. To do justice to a social agent or a society it is important to understand how modernity became or was already an ontological reality that was in process in the local contexts. The negotiation and redefinition of existing patterns of organisation as a search for ways to cope with the new dynamics happened from within. For a long time the research literature on this period assumed that the reforms in the Ottoman Empire were an entirely top-down affair, somewhat reluctantly imposed without any voluntary dimension. The initiatives from Istanbul were, in turn, assumed an unwelcome derivative from Europe. Only in the last three decades has academic opinion come to see that numerous high-ranking civil servants promoted internal renewal of the Empire. Any popular autochthonous dynamics in society towards a change of patterns of live along current supra-regional developments had previously been discounted – since modernity was still understood as a certain set of defining criteria which was absent in the Ottoman context (like industrialisation) or had simply taken another form and expression. Recently several studies on the provincial centres of the Empire have shown much more in detail how local societies negotiated, accommodated and redefined modernity in their contexts.[12] Some examples of urban design and architecture of late Ottoman Damascus illustrate this.

---

12 On Beirut: Hanssen, Jens, Fin de Siècle Beirut, The Making of an Ottoman Provincial Capital, Oxford 2005; Bodenstein, Ralph, Domestizierter Wandel. Wohnhaus und bürgerliche Wohnkultur in Beirut zwischen Osmanisierung, Europäisierung und sozialem Wandel, 1860-1930, unpublished dissertation thesis TU Berlin 2007; on Aleppo: Watenpaugh, Keith David, Being Modern in the Middle East; Revolution, Nationalism, Colonialism, and the Arab Middle Class, Princeton 2006 and Weber, Stefan, Damascus 1900; Urban Transformation, Architectural Innovation and Cultural Change in a Late Ottoman City (1808-1918). In: Proceedings of the Danish Institute Damascus (in preparation, 2008); for the German version see: Zeugnisse kulturellen Wandels; Stadt, Architektur und Gesellschaft des spätosmanischen Damaskus im Umbruch (1808-1918) EJOS IX (2006), No. 1, I-XI + 1-1014 (http://www2.let.uu.nl/Solis/anpt/ejos/EJOS-IX.0.htm). An interdisciplinary project of how modernity is expressed in different fields of daily life in diverse strata of an urban society is recently started in the city of Tripoli by Juren Meister, Karla Börner, Christian Sassmannshausen and myself, working on a micro historical level.

The Architecture of late Ottoman Damascus

Damascus, one of the major provincial capitals of the Ottoman Empire, experienced during the second half of the 19th and the early 20th century profound transformations. Along the establishment of a new administrative system a new public centre, the Marja-Square, with its administration buildings was founded in the 1860s. Nearly all the markets *(suqs)* were remodelled in the last decades of the 19th and the beginning of the 20th century. Many public buildings were set up, including some 70 schools, 8 hospitals and sanatoriums, 2 municipal parks, 3 railway-stations, electric lights, a tramway-system and dozens of streets. New forms of public spheres came into being: not only the venues, such as parks, coffee houses and theatres, but ways of practices as well. Election campaigns, party meetings, public welfare gatherings or manifestations with political speeches had not been known before, even though some of the pertinent spaces, praxis and institutions were exclusive and, depending on their function, highly sexually or socially regulated.

Fig. 1: Marja Square, town hall, hackney cabs and streetcar, around 1910. (courtesy of: W.-D. Lemke)

Fig. 2: Public holiday at Boulevard Jamal Basha/ Nasr Street, about 1918. (courtesy of: W.-D. Lemke)

A new urban institution, the municipality, was introduced in Damascus in the 1860s, and had a great effect on the urban developments during the last five decades of Ottoman Damascus: On the basis of a new corpus of engineering and building codes, this new municipality, a council of yearly elected city residents, had control over many private construction activities and launched an extensive programme of public building, including devlopment in infrastructure, commercial, health and education. Not everything that was planned was realised, however. Mismangement and corruption was addressed in local newspapers. The new office of engineers at the municipality conducted and overlooked public building activities, mainly new streets and street enlargements, and made sure that they were in compliance with the new building codes. Private investment in commercial or residential architecture was registered, too, and partially overssen by the municipal engineers. The private sector played an important role during this process of reshaping an Ottoman provincial capital. Apart from rebuilding thousands of residential houses following new models of design, several huge trade buildings were constructed by local individuals. Especially privately founded "modern" schools evinced a new understanding of state, city, society and the self. But private houses were by far the biggest undertaking in the period of Ottoman reform. Household organisation and established systems of social order were being transformed (expressed as well in clothing fashions such as the *fez/tarbush*). These cannot be explained by official decrees and government-sponsored building programmes. The city was not yet subject to direct colonialism and counted very few Europeans among its residents. Rather, we have here an urban society engaging in the developments of the epoch and interpreting them in its own way within the local context – even if many of these trends did not originate in the Ottoman world.

Despite the many changes in the city no European visitor or author of research literature would describe Damascus as a modern city. Quite the opposite, Damascus was often taken as a model of a *typically Oriental city*. There were no real signs of industrialisation or of an emerging labour movement, which were typical of modernity in other places. Not a single street would remind one of Haussmann's Paris and cultural production was not as innovative as fin de siècle Vienna. But the conception of Damascus as a city that had "refused" or was forgotten by modernity – based on the absence of "markers of modernity" – is wrong and caused by a misunderstanding or ignorance of the vernacular cultural expressions of modernity. Modernity developed into other forms and most of the observers were not trained, not able or not willing to read them.

Two examples for vernacular expressions of a global phenomenon

Traditional dwellings in Damascus, like many cities of the Middle East, were courtyard houses. Rooms were distributed around a central courtyard, a feature that remained stable in spite of heavy changes in interior decoration and room layout throughout the 19th century. During the last decades of Ottoman rule, however, houses became more and more reduced in size. Smaller courtyard houses, small single apartment houses (mainly in traditional techniques as an adoption of a recent development in Istanbul) and terraced courtyard houses appeared. Terraced courtyard houses were a synthetic transformation of an old building type occasioned by new planning models (municipality and building codes) and changing dwelling patterns. Based on a 1907 census we know that core families were not rare but did not always live in their own private houses. In most cases they formed house communities with other families. In 43.8 % of the houses there lived core families and extended core families even though these made up only 34.1 % of the recorded persons.[13] The numbers of core families were growing but the much faster growing amount of terraced courtyard houses, smaller courtyard houses in the old city and smaller apartment houses mainly reflect a growing wish for privacy, a typical 19th century trend. Looking for new and more private forms of dwelling the smaller apartment houses came into view as a model that was available in the region. The terraced courtyard houses, on the other hand, adapted a local building tradition to new needs.

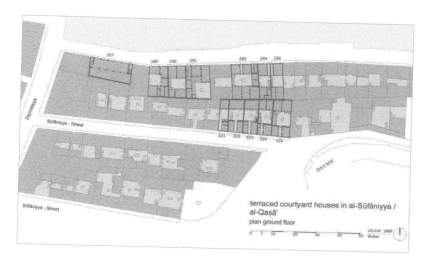

Fig. 3: Terraced courtyard houses in al-Sufaniyya (Weber 1999).

The 19th century saw the appearance of bazaars which were quite different from their predecessors. With their modern designs, regular façades à la mode on two floors, large shops with glassed showcases, stylish barrel-vaulted metal roofing and new construction materials such as steel girders, they corresponded more to modern arcades than to the old narrow and dark bazaars. The Suq al-Hamidiyya, erected between 1884 and 1894 thanks to the municipality and private investment, is the best example of this new style of commercial building. In this almost straight bazaar street, nearly 450 m long, the distance between the two rows of shops (8.70 m to 9.90 m) is much wider than in a conventional *suq*. The structure of the façades is almost regular for hundreds of meters. The shops were much more spacious than before, when they were not meant to be entered, the customer being served while standing outside. Now the window displays and showcases of glass tempted the client to come in. Several shops had a second floor storeroom while others were open on two floors. The traditional, mainly plain or gabled wooden roofing was replaced by huge barrel-vaulted wooden, and later metal, constructions.

---

[13]   Cf.: Okawara, Tomoki: *Size and Structure of Damascene Households in the Late Ottoman Period as Compared with Istanbul Households*. In: Doumani, Beshara (ed.), Family History in the Middle East; Household, Property, and Gender, New York (2003) 56 ff.

The Suq al-Hamidiyya had an enormous impact on the city and its new layout and became the model for other *suqs*. In this context it is a curiosity of cultural – and architectural history that arcades, namely the Passage du Caire, came to Europe with Napoleon as a reception of Middle Eastern market streets and then became in vogue all over Europe. However, in this context it is important to notice that the Suq al-Hamidiyya had always been received as a suq and an authentic part of the cityscape, both local and competitive with modern Europe. The celebrated journalist and intellectual Khalil Sarkis highlights this during the visit of the German Kaiser Wilhelm II to Damascus in 1898:

- "The *suqs* of Damascus are famous for their spaciousness and beauty so that even some European dignitaries said that they did not have any architecture to rival some of the *suqs* in Damascus". [14]

Fig. 4: Suq al-Hamidiyya about 1890.
(courtesy of: W.-D. Lemke)

Fig. 5: Suq al-Hamidiyya about 1905.
(courtesy of: Library of Congress)

---

14 Sarkis, Khalil, al-Sham qabl mi'at 'am, Rihlat al-Imbiratur Ghiliyum al-Thani, Imbiratur Almaniyya wa-Qarinatuhu ila Filistin wa-Suriyya, 'am 1316 h./1898m. First edition 1898, reprint published by Hasan al-Samahi Suwayran, Damascus 1997, p. 114, 122.

Possibly the longest shopping "arcade" in the world at the turn of the century, it is an impressive example of the modification of a classical urban institution to new planning modules and patterns of consumption.[15]

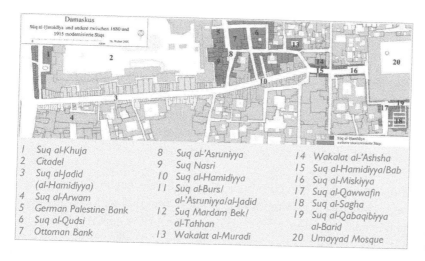

1 Suq al-Khuja
2 Citadel
3 Suq al-Jadid
   (al-Hamidiyya)
4 Suq al-Arwam
5 German Palestine Bank
6 Suq al-Qudsi
7 Ottoman Bank
8 Suq al-'Asruniyya
9 Suq Nasri
10 Suq al-Hamidiyya
11 Suq al-Burs/
    al-'Asruniyya/al-Jadid
12 Suq Mardam Bek/
    al-Tahhan
13 Wakalat al-Muradi
14 Wakalat al-'Ashsha
15 Suq al-Hamidiyya/Bab
16 Suq al-Miskiyya
17 Suq al-Qawwafin
18 Suq al-Sagha
19 Suq al-Qabaqibiyya
    al-Barid
20 Umayyad Mosque

Fig. 6: Suq al-Hamidiyya
and surroundings
(Weber 2005).

Conclusion

Both examples from Damascus, the new from of housing and the *suqs*, are the direct outcome of local experiences of modernity. They differ from residential architecture or markets in Cairo, Rome, Paris, New York or London. To understand dimensions of modernity in different geographical settings, it makes little sense to create a binding set of criteria of modernity based on a limited number of models. The degree of cultural change needs to be first understood in its proper local context. This should not result in an equalising relativism and should not obstruct, but sharpen, our view on the similarities and diversities of the experience of modernity. Analysing vernacular expressions of entangled modernity one needs to follow the strings of connection, to find the engine and to identify the agents of change – elements of a very complex and multilayer process.

In a dense net of interaction and communication, ideas originating at one point, spread fast and became common good. An interacting world was experienced in many ways, one may recall only the visual revolution of photography. Many elements became part of the intellectual horizon as soon they appear. The telegraph was not invented in Damascus, but people took and used is as a matter of course and wired their complains to Istanbul. Thoughts being transmitted internationally in word and picture became rapidly proper local reality.

---

[15] The 450m long Suq al-Hamidiyya is noticeably longer than any arcade in Europe. The famous "Galleria Vittorio Emanuelle II" in Milano (1865-1877) amounts to a total length of 301.72m (longitudinal axis 196.62m, transversal axis 105.10m) The "Passage du Caire" in Paris (1799), the largest one in the city, consists of three branches that run up to a total length of 370m. The "Passage Brady" in London (1828) had a total length of 216m. See for these arcades and others: Geist, J. F., Passagen, ein Bautyp des 19, Jahrhunderts, Munich (1969) 228 f., 261, 284.

Social agents in late Ottoman Syria often referred to European centres that they saw as a model and measured their own expressions of modernity by the model. Some models were stronger then others and as part of the experience of modernity people referred to hegemonic patterns – often parallel to power relations or inspired by innovative centres. They embraced them, or copied them, or adopted and changed them or rejected them. But even the conscious rejection of western models expressed it self in early 20th century Damascus in a political society (al-jam'iyya al-muhammadiyya), a form of societal organisation new for city. The rejection was in communication to supra-regional changes and was very much part of it. The proposed concept of entangled modernity is based on inclusive phenomena, a web of many strings: they were different, but connected and referring to each other. Actors were moving in this net, thus it is not the question *if* people were modern, but how modernity was expressed in different social strata and cultural-geographic settings.

As part of the process the local context is in communication with different sets of references and subject to larger developments. The interlocking of local, regional and supra-regional processes of cultural change makes it often difficult to understand, how certain phenomena developed in local context: why there was a trend towards privacy of dwelling in late Ottoman Damascus, similar to other places (but expressed in different architecture)? Was it caused by similar experiences of the time or by normative discussions in newspaper, stating that a modern Damascene should apply a certain set of practices? Why consumption patterns did change? Mass production and availability of discounted fabrics from Manchester does not explain the new way of shopping in Suq al-Hamidiyya. Developments in different contexts often establish elements that are typical for their time (like urbanisation, changes in the syntax of public space, rise of middle class, increasing privacy of dwelling by simultaneous upgrading of public façades etc.). Some of them are based on known forces, for other we still do not understand why they appear in quite diverse settings.

A comparison to other experiences of modernity is helpful, but to understand dynamics of a given place, it is essential to observe whether new concepts of living reformulate social and architectural spheres within a society, based on experiences of modernity in the local context, probably in connection with the relevant supra-regional developments, inspirations or hegemonic discourses. The characteristics of this process are much better observed and judged in view of the ability of societies to adopt and appropriate new meanings or new shapes adequate to their needs. It is of crucial importance that the members of a society are able to make meaning out of a changing world and to create from there *ex novo* new forms suitable for their own contexts. It is the arrangement with and of *their* modern world, being an object of it and a subject in it.[16] The Suq al-Hamidiyya is a very good example of how supra-regional trends were reformulated to something unique, being very much part of its place an society.

---

[16] On the experience of modernity: Berman, M., *All that is Solid Melts into Air, the Experience of Modernity*, London 1988.

Discussing the architectural heritage of the 19th and early 20th century in terms of entangled modernity stress a certain aspect of it by giving the phenomenon a new name, but is based on the scientific debates as discussed here. Thus it is surprising that many of these locally adopted or developed forms of 19th – and early 20th – century modernity are valued by contemporary societies only in the terms of the period's contribution to nation-building. The reasons of this are many and go beyond this paper, and the consequences are much more dramatic than just the neglect of heritage. Uneasiness with experiences of modernity, as it has been discussed now for several decades, and thus the little value which is given to the particular, "entangled" forms of 19th – and early 20th – century modernity is directly connected to the fact that, in a hegemonic discourse of modernity, cultural expressions of peripheral societies only enter the maelstrom of history as folkloristic, inauthentic (if too revolutionary) or as a soulless copies of Western models. To make matters worse, the period, and thus its symbols, are conceived of as a memory of colonialism, a memory continuously refreshed by contemporary power relations. Since the cultural production of the 19th century Ottoman realm are often overlooked or dismissed as expressions of modernity they are very much received as alienation and labelled Europeanisation or Westernisation. The consequences of this examination are of key importance for heritage management and new planning processes because only the feeling of authenticity and identification with spaces and architecture gives them value for the society in question.

Fig. 7: The Amin Mosque in Beirut (Weber 2006).

The disruption of 20th century cultural developments, the stunted feeling of self-esteem and the rejection of one's own history has led to a very complicated and disturbed relation with the past and its material heritage. Many of the responses to this have been very creative and successful, of which the archive of the Aga Khan Award for Architecture may contain the best evidence. Others tend to be less promising. In a search to redefine what can be seen as culturally authentic some paradoxically apply the orientalising concepts of the West, accepting the Otherness that the West has ascribed to the "Orient" as their mantra.[17] Monumentalising often very kitschy mosques like the Amin Mosque in Beirut, the Hassan II Mosque in Casablanca or the Shaykh Zayed Mosque in Abu Dhabi are good examples of this state of affairs, reproducing or inventing out of context patterns of the classical past. Seldom are the architectural remains of the 19th/early 20th century received as modern heritage and the period seems to be excluded of what is defined to be authentic. The same applies to modernist architecture of the first half of the 20th century. One reason why Suq al-Hamidiyya is packed with Damascenes every day, and figures as one of the main tourist attractions, is that it is received as an authentic piece of architecture: an Oriental *suq* and not a modern arcade. A much welcomed misunderstanding!

---

[17]   Cf.: Stephen Sheehi, *Foundations of Modern Arab Identity*, Gainesville 2004.

List of Participants and Contributors

Moncef Ben Abdeljelil
Professor and Head of Educational Programmes, Aga Khan University – Institute for the Study of Muslim Civilisations, London, UK

Asef Bayat
Professor of Sociology and Middle Eastern Studies, Academic Director of International Institute for the Study of Islam in the Modern World (ISIM), Leiden University, The Netherlands

Farrokh Derakhshani
Director, Aga Khan Award for Architecture, Geneva, Switzerland

Aziz Esmail
Governor and former Dean, Institute for Ismaili Studies, London, UK

Homa Farjadi
Architect and educator, USA and UK; member of Aga Khan Award Master Jury, 2007

Abdou Filali-Ansary
Director, Institute for the Study of Muslim Civilisations – Aga Khan University, London, UK; member of Aga Khan Award Steering Committee (2004) and Master Jury (2001)

Fatemeh Hosseini-Shakib
Animation and Media Researcher, University College for the Creative Arts at Farnham, UK

Charles Jencks
Architect and architectural historian, USA and UK

Masoud Kamali
Professor of Sociology, Institute of Social Work, Mid-Sweden University, Sweden

Deniz Kandiyoti
Professor in Development Studies, School of Oriental and African Studies, London, UK

Jeremy Melvin
Scholar and writer specialising in architecture; consultant, Architecture Programme, Royal Academy of Arts, London, UK

Farid Panjwani
Senior Instructor, Aga Khan University – Institute for the Study of Muslim Civilisations, London, UK

Modjtaba Sadria
Professor, Aga Khan University – Institute for the Study of Muslim Civilisations, UK; member of the Aga Khan Award Steering Committee (2007) and Master Jury (2004).

Armando Salvatore
Senior Research Fellow, Institute for Advanced Studies in the Humanities, Essen; Reader, Institute of Social Sciences, Humboldt University, Berlin; Associate Professor of Sociology of Culture and Communication, School of Arab-Islamic and Mediterranean Studies, University of Naples – L'Orientale

Stefan Weber
Assistant Professor, Aga Khan University – Institute for the Study of Muslim Civilisations, UK